RENEWALS 458-4574

DATE DUE

The Entertainment of His Most Excellent
Majestie Charles II

medieval & renaissance texts & studies

Volume 43

Renaissance Triumphs and Magnificences
New Series • Volume 3
General Editor
Margaret M. McGowan

The Entertainment of His Most Excellent Majestie Charles II

in

His Passage through the City of London to His Coronation

by

John Ogilby
London, 1662

A FACSIMILE

WITH INTRODUCTION BY

Ronald Knowles

Medieval & Renaissance Texts & Studies
Binghamton, New York
1988

The British Academy has generously assisted in meeting the publication costs of this book.

© Copyright 1988
Center for Medieval and Early Renaissance Studies
State University of New York at Binghamton
Binghamton, New York

Library of Congress Cataloging-in-Publication Data

Ogilby, John, 1600-1676.
  The entertainment of His Most Excellent Majestie Charles II in his passage through the city of London to his coronation.

  (Medieval & Renaissance Texts & Studies ; v. 43)
  Includes index.
  1. Charles II, King of England, 1630-1685 – Coronation. 2. Festivals – England – London – History – 17th century. 3. Processions – England – London – History – 17th century. 4. London (England) – History – 17th century. 5. Arches, Triumphal – England – London. 6. Kings and rulers in art. 7. Coronations – Great Britain – History – 17th century.
  I. Knowles, Ronald, 1940- . – II. Title. – III. Series.
DA446.O35   1988   941.06'6'0924   86-31164
ISBN 0-86698-026-1 (alk. paper)

Printed in the United States of America

Contents

Introduction 9
Multa dies variusque labor 11
Adventus Augusti 18
Volvenda dies 26
Neptuno Britannico 32
Pro rege exacuunt 36
Conclusions 39
Notes 42

Index of Sources 50
The Facsimile 53
Bibliographical Note 53

THE ENTERTAINMENT 57

Acknowledgments

The British Academy graciously provided a subvention to help meet costs of production. Research for this volume would not have been possible without the resources of the British Library and the Warburg Institute. We wish to acknowledge the help of the Society of Antiquaries of London, which allowed their copy of Ogilby to be microfilmed, and the Research Board of the University of Reading, which generously made an award to meet photography costs. This was used in the preparation of the Introduction. For technical reasons, this copy could not be used for the facsimile itself. We thank the Huntington Library for providing a microfilm of their copy [RB 141718] and for permission to base the facsimile on that copy. The unflagging tenacity of Margaret McGowan greatly helped bring about publication. The readers and editors at MRTS are thanked for their suggestions and patience. Michael McKeon's friendship and unrivalled knowledge of the period proved immensely valuable. As indicated in the text and notes, my greatest debt is to Sydney Anglo and Howard Erskine-Hill, whose teaching and scholarship have remained a lasting inspiration.

Augustos enim decent augusta.
Pontano, *De Splendore*, 1498.

for what preserves you Kings more than Ceremony ... the King must know at what time to play the King, and when to qualifie it, but never put it of; for in all triumphs whatsoever or publick shewing yourself, you cannot put upon you too much King.

The Earl of Newcastle's *Letter of Instructions to Prince Charles for his Studies, Conduct, and Behaviour, 1638.*

Introduction

The Royalist, Sir John Reresby, recalling the coronation of Charles II, observed that "The triomphall arches, pagiants, musick, made to receive and entertain him and the whole Court and other attendants as he passed, were fairer or richer than was ever known upon the like occasions in England ... but as to particulars it is more the business of an historian then mine to relate them."[1] Nineteenth-century historians either mention John Ogilby's *Entertainment* briefly, as an antiquarian item,[2] or refer to the triumphal arches without mentioning Ogilby at all.[3] Historians of the English coronation and English pageantry, respectively, mention and summarize Ogilby's festival.[4] The *Entertainment* is duly noted in a biographical paper, and some peripheral aspects of the spectacle have received scholarly attention.[5] The triumphal arches have provided illustrations for scholars of Dryden and of the English theatre.[6] In critical terms two essays recognize a larger cultural significance in Ogilby's work.[7] However, in more recent years two major studies to a large extent rehabilitate Ogilby as a subject of some historical importance.[8] Katherine S. Van Eerde devotes a full book to Ogilby's career, bringing together all biographical source material, and in her third chapter providing a descriptive summary of the *Entertainment*. Howard Erskine-Hill's monumental study, in its extensively perceptive critical scholarship, judiciously assesses Ogilby's contribution to English Augustanism. Hereafter, Ogilby should not be remembered solely as a butt of Dryden and Pope.[9]

As Van Eerde shows, Ogilby's career was varied and resilient. Beginning as a dancing master and teacher, Ogilby actually founded the theatre in Ireland, eventually becoming master of the revels there. In mature years he made himself a translator of Homer and Virgil. And in spite of much misfortune he became the king's cosmographer and geographic printer, a noted publisher of magnificent volumes.[10] The 1662 *Entertainment* is a vastly expanded and illustrated version of an earlier volume, *The Relation of His Majesties Entertainment* (1661). The 1661 *Relation* is very much smaller in every way. Commentary is limited to a basic account of the decorations and inscriptions of the triumphal arches with some additional speeches and entertainments. There are several variations of this edition. The 1662 *Entertainment* was first printed by Thomas Roycroft and a second issue was brought out later in the year by Mariot and Dring. The texts are the same in these two editions, but there are some variations concerning illustrations. In fact, of the several copies in the British Library no two copies are identical, and all the indications are that this is the case elsewhere. Either frontispieces are missing or portraits have been added, or some of the arch engravings have been misbound or removed; some copies do not have the same number of the double engravings of the cavalcade as others. Fortunately, Fredson Bowers has provided a summary of the complex publishing history of these volumes.[11] However, of critical importance is the addendum to the 1662 *Entertainment* by Elias Ashmole which will be discussed in terms of the highly self-conscious preparations for the coronation.

Ogilby's extensive folio is the most elaborate surviving document for any English festival. The range of more than a hundred and thirty sources almost amounts to a compendium of seventeenth-century English neoclassicism. Though Latin antiquity tends to predominate with the figures of Virgil, Ovid, and Claudian, Ogilby draws widely on Greek literature, and from the vantage point of 1660 he uses the heritage of Renaissance antiquarianism—particularly compilations of classical inscriptions and ancient coinage. Ogilby's knowledge of Virgil is of the greatest importance in the *Entertainment*. In 1649, 1654 and 1665 he published his translations of the poet and in composing the *Entertainment* he added his own illustrative translations which are used in this introduction, unless otherwise stated.

However, Ogilby's themes do not derive solely from his direct sources. Detailed examination of Restoration panegyric will show that Ogilby's festival also developed from shared *topoi* appropriated by Royalist sympathizers. The collection of tracts, amounting to twenty-three thousand items, made by the publisher George Thomason between 1641 and 1662, provides an incomparable source for study of the Restoration year, which may be broadly defined as that period between Charles's entry into London on his birthday (May 29th, 1660) and his coronation on St. George's day (April 23rd, 1661).

The following discussion of Ogilby's *Entertainment* is divided under several heads taken from the work itself. *Multa dies variusque labor* (many days and various work) begins with the historical setting, moving from the national to the metropolitan to the personal—Ogilby's use of Sir Balthazar Gerbier's knowledge of an earlier Rubens festival. Preparations from another, complementary, point of view, both divine and royal, are seen in the carefully calculated timing of Charles's entry into London on his birthday and his coronation on St. George's day, both celebrated in spontaneous popular acclaim in panegyrics of the day. Such calculation even extended to the publication of Ogilby's volume as a whole, and to Ashmole's appended account of the coronation ceremony, in particular. *Adventus Augusti* (the arrival of Augustus) offers a reconstruction and appraisal of the Virgilian themes of the first arch in the light of contemporary panegyric, continually stressing the central Augustan texts of the *Fourth Eclogue* and book six of the *Aeneid. Volvenda dies* (revolving days) expands on this by recognizing the way in which the advent of Charles was hailed as a kind of Platonic great year or phoenix period, and as a kind of messianic imperialism, as details of the arches show. Again, the evidence of contemporary panegyric is adduced to show how popular these themes were. *Neptuno Britannico* places Charles, as the British Neptune celebrated on the second arch, against the seventeenth-century controversy concerning the dominion of the sea. Here Ogilby applies Claudian in what is ostensible advocacy of commerce and empire, yet, as will be argued in part of the final section (*Conclusions*), the arch was probably seen in a more religiously sublimated way. Exploring this kind of ambivalence, *Pro rege exacuunt* (they sharpen [their stings] for the king) examines Ogilby's and his contemporaries' use of the neoclassical bee as an emblem of loyalty and industry.

Ogilby's main themes are found on the first two arches for which twice as much space is given to sources, both literary and pictorial, than to those of the third and fourth arches. The importance, richness, and variety of allusion, even where conventional, is much greater on the first and second than on the third and fourth arches which are largely given over to traditional motifs supporting Concord and Plenty, such as the cardinal virtues, Ceres, Flora, and so on. Where Ogilby does give significant details, these are included with discussion of the relevant features of the leading two structures.

Multa dies variusque labor

The Restoration came about as a result of the recognition that power, of either despot or oligarchy, could only be curtailed by the legitimate rule of the old forms, that is to say the ancient and fundamental laws of the kingdom embodied by king, lords and commons.[12] Richard Cromwell's first parliament ratified the title "Protector" but it could not ensure the inheritance of the power that invested it under Oliver Cromwell. The generals were too powerful for Richard, but it was a power without either right or executive means. Instead of allaying the dread of military rule, the army's restoration of the Rump of the Long Parliament only served to exacerbate the need for a fully restored parliament. Following the public disquiet which culminated in Royalist uprisings the army expelled Parliament, thereby forcing the wily and reticent commander of the army in Scotland, General George Monck, to show his hand and protest his parliamentary loyalty. Monck crossed the Tweed on January 2nd, 1660, and in the same month a new Common Council of London was formed, some prominent members of which promptly raised a sum of money on behalf of the exiled king. In order to discredit Monck and intimidate the antagonistic Council, the Rump members charged the general to arrest prominent members of the Council and to pull down the city gates. The reversal of their intentions followed. Guildhall was sympathetic towards the apologetic Monck and popular opinion went against the Rump in the months of February and March. Parliament was dissolved, Charles's letter *To his Peers* and *Declaration to his subjects* appeared respectively on March 20th and 30th, preceding the *Declaration from Breda*, which was drawn up in Holland between April 4th and 14th and published in London on May 31st. A favourably inclined parliament having been returned, Charles was invited to return, and was welcomed at Dover by Monck on May 25th. Charles entered his rejoicing capital on the 29th of that month.

On February 9th, 1661, the city fathers were notified of the king's intention to retread the path of his royal predecessors[13] and progress through the streets of London from the Tower to Whitehall, "... with such magnificence as was due and becoming the Majesty of so great a King."[14] The preparations for the king's entry appear to have been rather hurried.[15] Ogilby himself says that "The parts of which this Entertainment consists were carried on by several persons, who performed all to Admiration, and considering the Shortness of the Warning much beyond what could have been imagined."[16] Investigating the accounts in the Corporation of London Record Office, Halfpenny has shown that payments for construction work on the four triumphal arches date from the beginning of March, when £350 was paid to Edward Tasker to distribute among the master carpenters and tradesmen simultaneously employed on all four arches, as the warrant indicates. Although the period between February 9th and April 23rd would appear to be rather limited for the completion of such elaborate structures—involving alterations to existing buildings—it was not until February 25th that we have any documented evidence about the city's intentions. On that day one contemporary diarist noted "Greate preparations in the Citty of London, makeinge of pagion and triumphall arches againe the coronation of his Majesty on St. Georges day, the 23 of Aprill next."[17] In addition, it is probable that there was some uncertainty about whether Charles would follow the example of his father or grandfather; this possibility, coupled with a revised coronation date and relatively short notice, did in fact mean that the building work was very hurried indeed, though the designs for the triumphal arches might well have been made a little earlier.

By 1661 John Ogilby's royalist sympathies and associations were sufficiently well known to earn him the prestigious commission of organizing an appropriate spectacle for the royal entry (and procession to the eventual solemnity of the coronation). Remarking on the "Shortness of the Warning," Ogilby provides a list of artificers, naming for "*The* Architectural Part ... *Mr. Peter Mills, Surveyor of the City, and another Person, who desires to have his Name conceal'd.*"[18] The mysterious "person" was another of nature's survivors, Sir Balthazar Gerbier[19] – a man even more remarkable than his associate, John Ogilby. Colonizer, engineer, projector; secret agent, ambassador, traitor; picture collector, miniaturist, architect – apart from these accomplishments, Gerbier also held the position of master of the ceremonies, which had been granted to him by patent, succeeding to the place of Sir John Finet, on May 10th, 1641. Returning to England in the autumn of 1660, Gerbier published a pamphlet addressed to Charles on December 5th[20] which was answered by a warrant of December 16th suspending him from his office[21] (the following February an old rival, Sir Charles Cotterel, was granted the emoluments of a master of the ceremonies during Gerbier's suspension[22]). In 1662, in competition with Sir William Davenant, Ogilby was made, by patent, master of the revels in Ireland, a position which he had held, by warrant and the patronage of the Earl of Strafford, since the late thirties. Thus, in London at the same time in early December were Ogilby and Gerbier, the two officials qualified to devise a regal festival just at the time when it was believed that the coronation would be held in early February.[23] Politically Gerbier was *persona non grata*, but artistically he was invaluable to Ogilby. Gerbier not only contributed to the "Architectural Part" but also made available his knowledge of Rubens's designs for an earlier Habsburg royal entry (1635) which provided an immediate source for Ogilby's *Entertainment*.

Of considerable importance is the relationship between Ogilby's 1662 *Entertainment* and the commemorative volume of the Rubens festival, the *Pompa Introitus Honori Serenissimi Principis Ferdinandi Austriaci Hispaniarum Infantis ...* (Antwerp, 1641),[24] of Jean Gaspard Gevaerts. This beautiful folio commemorates what must have been one of the most elaborate royal entries of the seventeenth century, that of the Habsburg prince, Ferdinand, into Antwerp in 1635. Rubens had been commissioned to design the entire spectacle consisting of several triumphal arches, numerous *pegmata* (pageant facades), and a spectacular *Porticus Caesareo-Austriaca* depicting twelve Austrian 'caesars.' Gevaerts, Rubens's lifelong friend, supplied the numerous inscriptions adorning the structures, and, with publication, the explanatory commentary. The engravings were made by Theodor van Thulden.

Ogilby cites "*Gevart*" only once (p. 46) but he uses his volume throughout the *Entertainment*. The *Relation* gives little more than a general outline of the arches, mainly noting the inscriptions. Very few iconographic sources are given. However, in the 1662 volume, Ogilby concentrates on supplying details concerning the engraved face of each arch, particularly the first two. In expanding the first book he must have had the *Pompa Introitus* before him. Ogilby's largest single borrowing is found in his discussion of Bellerophon (pp. 122-25), which he lifts straight from Gevaerts (cf. *Pompa Introitus*, pp. 162-64), roughly translating the commentary and using his literary and numismatic sources, yet adding his own quotation from Virgil. Again, in providing sources for the iconography of the Harpies (pp. 28-30), Ogilby generally follows the *Pompa Introitus* (cf. pp. 119-20), yet prefers to cite Rhodiginus's commentary on Virgil rather than use Gevaerts's reference to Servius to the same passage, and inserts his own interesting note paraphrasing a marginal gloss of Nicolaus Erythraeus on Virgil.[25]

Ogilby could have come across the Gevaerts volume independently, by way of his own publishing endeavours and interests, but the facts concerning Gerbier indicate that he was most likely responsible for bringing the festival to Ogilby's attention. For fifteen years, since the first meeting in 1625 until shortly before the death of the great artist, Gerbier was in touch with

Rubens. He corresponded intermittently over the years[26] and he was the London host during Rubens's nine month stay. Gerbier's wife was a favourite model of the painter.[27] Gerbier negotiated the commission, purchase and transportation of the Whitehall ceiling paintings which were finished in 1634 and delivered in 1635. Finally, Gerbier was in Antwerp during the autumn of 1634, exactly when Rubens must have been designing the festival, since building began December.[28] Eight months later Gerbier wrote to Secretary Coke (on 10/20 April, shortly after Ferdinand's entry), noting the "many triumphant arches and other showes" in Antwerp.[29]

The four original drawings of Ogilby's triumphal arches still exist as part of the Burlington-Devonshire Collection in the Royal Institute of British Architects. The scale of the drawings is the same as that of the engravings which David Loggan made for Ogilby's *Entertainment*.[30] Though the drawings are unsigned, the hand is that of a miniaturist like Gerbier, and the design intimates a knowledge of Rubens's work for the Habsburg entry. Gerbier himself actually testified later to his part in the preparations for the king's progress. In his small book, *A Brief Discourse Concerning the Three chief Principles of Magnificent Building* ... (1662), after congratulating himself on his work near the York watergate, Gerbier claims "that divers judicious persons will not deny, that the excellency of the several Triumphal Arches Erected in the City of *London*, consists not in their Bulk ..." (p. 42). There is further evidence for Gerbier's connection with the festival from the short account of Charles's passage through London, published in 1661 at Venice and entitled *Il Trionfo D'Inghilterra*. This tract is a selected paraphrase of Ogilby's 1661 *Relation*, and the title page tells us it is translated "nella lingua Italiana, per il Capitan Giorgio, Gerbieri D'Ovvilly Della Citta di Londra Armigero; Altramente detto Giorgio, di San Giorgio." The translator would appear to be Gerbier's son, George Gerbier D'Ouvilly:[31] presumably Gerbier forwarded him a copy of the *Relation*, possibly at the suggestion of the Venetian ambassador in London, Francesco Giavarina,[32] when interest in the restored monarch of England was at its height in Europe.

Given these details concerning the relationship between Gerbier and Ogilby's work for the city spectacle, I feel convinced that Gerbier, as a friend and admirer of Rubens, had acquired a copy of the *Pompa Introitus*, had been approached by the city authorities (or offered his services) in late 1660, and had decided to use parts of the Antwerp volume in the prospective London festival—a decision which he recommended to the less experienced Ogilby who, accepting the advice, eventually incorporated much of Gevaerts in the 1662 *Entertainment*. Thus Gerbier, the former detractor of Charles I,[33] probably supervised a large part of the festivities for the coronation of the son of that monarch, though it was Ogilby who imposed the Augustan theme, formulating "the Poetical part ... consisting in Speeches, Emblemes, Mottoes, and Inscriptions."[34] However, Ogilby's preparation of the symbols was significantly complemented by Charles's own preparation for a symbolic reappearance, and both were anticipated by Royalist panegyric.

"Felicitas Brittaniae 29 Maii 1660" was the legend struck on a medal to commemorate the king's royal entry into London "which was also his birthday: for which reason he probably delayed his approach to the metropolis."[35] Details in *Mercurius Publicus* (May 24th to May 31st, 1660) suggest that the entry date was as calculated as the revised coronation date. The *Naseby*, "as clean washed and scraped as a trencher," received both the king and his name, and proceeded to Dover where Charles landed "between three and four of the clock in the afternoon" of the 25th.[36] Charles then entered a coach outside the town and travelled to Canterbury, where he remained until Monday the 28th when he moved on to Rochester, before entering London in the early afternoon of the symbolic 29th, after reviewing troops assembled on Blackheath in the morning.[37] The two day sojourn at Canterbury, in spite of Garter ceremonials and the Sabbath, would seem to be disproportionate unless accounted for as a conscious act politically calculated to fulfill what was foreshadowed at Charles's birth.

A whole myth had grown around the appearance of a star at midday on Charles's birth. To Abraham Cowley, at the Restoration:

> No *Star* amongst ye all did, I believe
> Such vigorous assistance give,
> As that which thirty years ago,
> At *Charles* his *Birth*, did, in despight
> Of the proud *Sun's* Meridian Light
> His future *Glories*, and this Year foreshow[38]

while to Edward Matthew the topic was sufficiently important to warrant a whole book which he published in 1661: χαρόλου τρισμεγίστου ἐπιφανία *The most glorious star or celestial constellation of the Pleiades, or Charles waine. Appearing ... in a miraculous manner in the face of the sun at noonday.* It was believed that Charles's return was a resurrection, or a re-birth day, and was accordingly recorded as such in the statute book, no less, as *An Act for a Perpetuall Anniversary Thanksgiving on the nine and twentyeth date of May*, where the 29th was considered "the most memorable Birth day not onely of his Majesty both as a man and Prince but likewise as an actual King, and of this and other His Majesties Kingdomes all in a great measure new borne and raised from the dead on this most joyfull day."[39] Charles's re-entry on his birthday had the semblance of something as inexorable and preordained as a completed cosmological revolution. Similarly, the revised coronation date itself, "changed for many weighty reasons"[40] from February 6th to April 23rd, St. George's day, only a few days after Charles had installed "so many of St. George's Knights (the greatest that was ever known since the first founding of the Order by King Edw.),"[41] was obviously intended for a symbolically spectacular effect. Though the Garter ceremonies were an established tradition, the choice of April 23rd for the coronation was unique. No other English monarch had been crowned on St. George's day.

Clarendon relates that Charles urged him to take care in searching out all ancient precedents for the coronation ceremony:

> the Novelties and new Inventions, with which the Kingdom had been so much intoxicated for so many Years altogether, might be discountenanced and discredited in the Eyes of the People, for the Folly and Want of State thereof; his Majesty had directed the Records and old Formularies should be examined, and thereupon all Things should be prepared, and all Forms accustomed be used, that might add Lustre and Splendour to the Solemnity.[42]

The ceremony, following not only the Garter installation but also the creation of sixty-four Knights of the Bath, was an eminently successful series of pageantry. Francesco Giavarina reported to the doge and senate of his native city that "in a few days will take place two of the most splendid functions which are performed in this country." He was not disappointed: "The ceremonies reported having been performed last week, his Majesties coronation has been accomplished this week, so desired by his subjects, with all possible splendour and decorum, no one sparing his money to make it exceptionable and memorable for ages to come, and it was certainly the most conspicuous solemnity that has ever been seen in this realm."[43]

Again, Charles's patronage of the Order of the Garter, though consciously calculated, was anticipated by the Restoration panegyrics. After the demise of the Rump, satirists inevitably seized on the name as an object of scatological vilification. As in Lutheran polemic, scatology is never very far from eschatology and the Rump became the "Scarlet Beast" attempting to reintroduce popery, and then, finally, the archetypal apostate. Consequently Monck was regarded as a St. George rescuing the maiden, *Ecclesia Anglicana*, from the jaws of the dragon, or hydra—conceived in apocalyptic terms.[44] In the post-Reformation Protestant tradition St. George was regarded variously as "an emblem designed to incite the valiant Garter Knight to war down the Dragon, the dreaded Anti-Christ of Rome," or, "an analogy of Christ vanquishing the Devil and delivering the Church."[45] The events of the interregnum gave even more credence to these views and Ogilby applied them on the first arch.

Though Ogilby gives several sources for the design of the Harpies, he does not bother to explain the Hydra-Rump figure beyond a cursory description. The centre table of the first arch is manifestly an iconographic representation of popular ideas integrated by juxtaposition into a generally Virgilian setting. If the uneducated apprentices, workmen, and housewives of London could not follow the Latin inscriptions, the identification of the visual with the verbal image of topical ballads was transparent. Ogilby, in 1661, simply transfers the role of St. George from General Monck to Charles himself, following the practice of the poets, "another George with better right / Then that suspected Cappadocian Knight / ... Our Royal Charles."[46] The equestrian representation of Charles "in calm motion" derives overtly from that of Marcus Aurelius by way of Titian's painting of Charles v, and Van Dyck's representation of Charles I,[47] but an obvious incrustation of meaning by April 1661 would be the added significance of Charles as St. George defeating the dragon. Only three days before the coronation cavalcade two tracts had been sold on the streets of London celebrating Charles as the sovereign of "the most noble order of St. George."[48] These pamphlets anticipate the culmination of Tudor-Stuart revivals of the order in Elias Ashmole's monumental *The Institution, Laws and Ceremonies of the most noble order of the Garter*, which appeared in the same year (1672) that Sir Robert Vyner dedicated the notorious equestrian statue of John Sobieskby trampling on a Turk which he had had deftly re-sculpted into Charles II trampling on Oliver Cromwell.[49]

The same concern for effective ceremonial can be seen in Charles's order to replace the traditional installation litany by a hymn[50] composed almost entirely from the Psalms of David, but also quoting a verse from 2 Samuel 23, the same chapter from which one of the above mentioned pamphleteers, imitating the official *Liber Niger*, derived a biblical example of a chivalric order in "David's mighty men." Hence, in the procession to St. George's Chapel Windsor, during which the hymn was sung, we see a symbolic unification of what may appear unrelated, King Charles as the knightly sovereign of a chivalric order, and King Charles as an anointed Davidic king. The panoply of chivalry becomes an aspect of biblical priest-kingship; St. George is one with King David.

The replacement of the litany by the hymn is one of a number of minor occurrences which, put together, suggest a conscious calculation on the part of Charles, Sir Edward Walker (the Garter king-of-arms) and the commissioners for the coronation. The earlier significant date of Charles's re-entry into London and the postponement of the coronation are the more obvious factors; in addition to these are the curious details relating to the publication of Ogilby's 1662 memorial volume.

Having received the king's patent on April 11th, Ogilby proceeded to publish the unelaborate *Relation*. Yet in May of the same year the king, aware that Ogilby was preparing an enlarged work, prohibited his "publishing the form of His Majesty's proceeding through London and of the coronation, although he has approved it, until it has been submitted to Sir Edward Walker, Garter, by whom the proceedings are chiefly drawn up."[51] Eric Halfpenny observes that "this is the first suggestion that Ogilby had even proposed to include the coronation itself within his purview."[52] Walker, as the official responsible for the ceremony, presumably wished to vet any printed account, especially in the event of any inaccuracies. Even a year later when Ogilby had finished his treatise he received the same warning that the work must be presented for the Garter's inspection.[53] What must have prompted the king's intervention, as Halfpenny suggests, was the account of the coronation ceremony written by the Windsor Herald, Elias Ashmole, one of the printed copies of which, with a number of corrections and deletions, is in the Public Record Office.[54] This copy, with the corrections made, was that published at the end of Ogilby's *Entertainment* in 1662, but with Ashmole's name withdrawn.

It is considered that the corrections in the P.R.O. copy were made by Sir Edward Walker out of personal jealousy of the newly appointed Windsor Herald.[55] C. H. Josten, agreeing that "Walker's ... criticisms may account for the fact that the second edition of Ashmole's text is shorter than the first," further speculates that Ashmole withdrew all the copies of his account in order not to arouse Walker's jealousy. The Garter himself prepared an extensive account of the coronation ceremony, which Josten also feels accounts for his punctilious censorship "fearing that ... Ogilby's book ... might prejudice the success of his own...."[56]

However, if we look at the corrections in the P.R.O. copy which Fredson Bowers agrees are in the hand of Sir Edward Walker, it becomes apparent that Ashmole is naively inept in his including an account of a most embarrassing occurrence, a brawl concerning a ceremonial canopy between the king's footmen and the barons of the Cinque Ports. The incident may be humourously relished by Pepys in the private shorthand of his *Diary*,[57] but to describe it in a volume intended for posterity was a mistake which probably chilled the Garter's loyal heart. Ashmole's indecorum is further exemplified in his excessive citation of the anthems sung, and his pedantic inclination to enumerate the particular names of the officials in attendance. Walker explains the baron's misadventure in a discreet sentence enclosed in brackets, shortens the citations, and deletes the particular names of officials, simply noting their functions at the ceremony. Ardent Royalist companion of the king in exile, jealous or not, and leaving no evidence that he even attempted to publish his own account, Walker was determined that the hieratic, sacramental nature of the coronation should accordingly be left on record as such.

On the morning of April 22nd the king "proceeded in solemn cavalcade to Whitehall attended by all the peers, grandees and officials of the realm, richly attired...."[58] "It is impossible to relate the glory of this day,"[59] exclaimed Pepys, and in examining the themes of the arches we must not forget the splendour of the setting against which they appeared. As the diarist commented from his position at "Mr. Young's, the flag-maker" in Cornhill, "so glorious was the show with gold and silver, that we were not able to look at it, our eyes at last being so much overcome with it."[60] Perhaps expecting the sacrilegious splendours of a sinful Babel, one disgruntled Puritan preacher entered in his diary for May 3rd, "Rid into London and saw the triumphal arches, stately vanity; no rich cost."[61] The cost to the city was, in fact, approximately £11,000,[62] which was criticised then and after. "Never were such Pageants, Triumphal Arches, and Sumptuous Feasts seen in the City before," recalled Roger Coke, "for which the Poor Orphans Money in the Chamber of *London* must pay the greatest Part."[63] But Sir William Petty dispassionately justified "such pageants," noting the subsequent increase in the circulation of money:

> Men repine much, if they think the money leavyed will be expended on Entertainments, magnificent Shews, triumphal Arches, &c. To which I answer, that the same is a refunding the said money to the Tradesmen who work upon those things; which Trade though they seem vain and onely of ornament, yet they refund presently to the most useful; namely, to Brewers, Bakers, Taylours, Shoemakers, &c. Moreover, the Prince hath no more pleasure in these Shews and Entertainments then 100000 others of his meanest Subjects have, whom, for all their grumbling, we see to travel many miles to be spectators of these mistaken and distasted vanities.[64]

However, the greater expense would be that involved in the ceremonial equipage of the cavalcade. Allowing for the hyperbolic activities of many-tongued Rumour, compare the figures in the following letter of a Royalist, William Smith: "For the Coronation, the Lord Wharton's furnitures for his horse (as is said), will amount to 8,000 l., the bit of his bridle being valued at 500 l. The Duke of Buckingham has written to some friends (as they say), that notwithstanding the malice of the cards and dice, he has bestowed 30,000 l. upon a suit to attend His Majesty at his coronation."[65]

The decoration of the arches, like the cost of equipage, was a matter of guesswork until shortly before the actual cavalcade, as the title of a contemporary pamphlet indicates: *The Cities Loyalty display'd or the Four famous and renowned Fabricks in the City of London Exactly described in their several representations, what they are, with their private meanings and perfect actions at the day of publick view, which is not yet discovered.*[66] A competitive journalist, the anonymous author confidently guesses at details, continually stressing the stupendous proportions of the structures. To the above mentioned Puritan the arches in general represented "Heathnisme"[67]—a view doubtlessly shared by the survivors of Venner's Fifth Monarchy Men who had planned to burn down the arches, shortly before their apprehension by the authorities on April 16th[68]—whereas the Drury Lane "cavalier" anticipated representation of Hierarchy, Monarchy, and, above all, the triumph of Episcopacy over Presbytery. As Smith's speculations probably typify Royalist gossip, it is worth quoting at length, concluding this section with surmise before turning to facts of the next:

> The chiefest affairs now in hand are His Majesty's coronation and marriage, the first of which draws near, the four stately standing Pageants being now almost finished. The first His Majesty shall encounter is in Leadenhall Street, and it presenteth Anarchy and the confusion which that government brings: the second is erected at the Royal Exchange, and it holds forth Presbytery, and with it the decay of Trade; the third, which is the most sumptuous, stands in Cheapside, relating the honours due to the Hierarchy, and showeth the restoration of Episcopacy. In this magnificent building, His Majesty is to be treated to a stately banquet, and to show the power which Episcopacy has over Presbytery, just at His Majesty's departure will arise the form of the old Crosse, which anciently stood at the same place, at whose appearance Presbytery

vanisheth. The last, which is also very glorious, stands in Fleet-Street, and represents Monarchy, whereby the former disorders are brought into their first conformities.[69]

Adventus Augusti

The first triumphal arch, "imitating therein the antient Romanes,"[70] was erected in Leadenhall Street which Charles approached eastwards from the Tower. On one pedestal in front of the arch he was faced by the live figures of Rebellion "mounted on a Hydra," boasting herself "Hells Daughter/Satan's Eldest Child," with "Her attendant Confusion, in a deformed shape." On another pedestal stood "Brittains Monarchy supported by Loyalty" who, to the accompaniment of appropriate music, rebuff their opponents, allowing the restored monarch to pass through the arch. This physical action is symbolized on the arch itself, and thus the progress of the cavalcade becomes an integral part of the *Entertainment* just as, similarly, earlier Stuarts had eagerly taken part in court masques designed to enhance their divine office of kingship.[71]

"The first painting on the South-side is a Prospect of His Majestie's landing at Dover Castle" greeted by a figure obviously intended to represent General Monck. The figures are in contemporary dress, but the inscriptions above and below derive from antiquity. *Adventus Augusti* and *In Solido Rursus Fortuna Locavit*,[72] Ogilby explains, alludes "to that of Virgil":

> Multa dies, variusque labor mutabilis aevi,
> Rettulit in melius multos; alterna revisens,
> Lusit, & in solido rursus Fortuna locavit

and which he translates:

> The various Work of Time, and many Days,
> Often Affairs from Worse to Better raise;
> Fortune, reviewing those she tumbled down,
> Sporting, restores again unto the Crown.

Against this, on the north side, is a trophy of "decollated heads," the most prominent of which resembles that of Oliver Cromwell. Above is the inscription which Ogilby claims is taken from Horace, *Sequitur Rebelles / Ultor a tergo Deus*[73] ("Gods Vengeance Rebels at the Heels pursues"), and is explained by Ogilby as "representing in a Trophy the late Example of God's justice apon the Rebels, who committed that most horrid murther apon His Majesties Royal Father of Blessed Memory. To which Rebels the Motto beneath also referreth"—*Ausi immane nefas, Ausoque Potiti*.[74] Ogilby explains the motto *Ultor a tergo Deus* as "in reference to the coyn of the Emperor Claudius which represents Martem Ultorem ... but more particularly to that History of Augustus, who, after the wars ended, which he undertook for the revenge of his Father's blood, murdered by some Common-Wealth's men in the Senate House, consecrated a Temple Marti Ultori, which he had vowed during the war."[75] The Augustan theme implicit in the phrase *Adventus Augusti* now extends to the historical emperor in the account of the motto *Ultor a tergo Deus*.

The painting above the dedicatory inscription "represents the King, mounted in calm Motion, Usurpation flying before him, a figure with many ill-favoured Heads, some bigger, some lesser, and one particularly shooting out of his Shoulder, like Cromwell's; another head apon his Rump, or Tayl." The inscription is taken from the ninth book of the *Aeneid* (line 7), *Volvenda dies en attulit ultro*, which Ogilby renders

> What none of all the Gods durst grant, implored,
> Successive Time does of its own accord.

In this central painting above the dedicatory plaque and below the symbolic figure of Charles against the royal oak—alluded to by Dryden in his *Coronation Ode*[76]—bearing not acorns but swords and sceptres, is seen a conflation of a number of motifs which will repeatedly be referred to in demonstrating the traditional and topical nature of the iconography. Meanwhile, it must be pointed out here how Ogilby has transferred Rebellion's self-identified provenance from an amorphous "Hell" to that of the classical Erebus. We see Usurpation fleeing into the jaws of Hell, but superimposed on this is, primarily, the Erebus introduced by the lower inscription *Ausi immane nefas ausoque potiti* ("All dar'd bold crimes, and thrivd in what they dar'd") which "is taken out of Virgil, who spoke it of those, who were, for the like Crimes, condemn'd to the Pains of Erebus."[77]

The painting on the left of the centre table is surmounted by the motto *En quo discordia cives*, which Ogilby describes as being on the east side, without mentioning the corresponding painting on the right, clearly surmounted by the words *perduxit miseros*, thereby completing the citation from Virgil's *First Eclogue* (lines 71–72). The physical relationship of the details of paintings and inscriptions is of great importance here, because if we patiently follow Ogilby's sometimes careless account, it becomes clear that the inscription *En quo discordia cives* above the painting "representing the disorder the Kingdom was in" is complemented on the corresponding west side by a painting which represents "the Restauration of our happiness by His Majesties Arrival," bearing the motto *Felix temporum reparatio* (happy restoration of times). A further correspondence between the east, engraved side, and the west, unseen side, is that of the inscription *Volvenda dies en attulit ultro* with *Redeunt saturnia regna* which appears "over the Great Table." Assembling these details, a distinct schema begins to emerge.

As we have seen, the king would have approached this arch eastwards from the Tower of London. The disposition of the allegorical figures is such that Monarchy and Loyalty would have been seen beneath the painting of Charles at Dover, while Rebellion and Confusion would have been seen beneath the painting of the trophy of "decollated heads." The initial symmetry is continued in the design of the first arch as a whole. The painting directly behind that of Charles landing at Dover depicts the Lord Mayor "delivering to the King the Keys of the City." The symmetry of design is continued by the four figures standing in the niches, only two of whom are visible in Loggan's engraving. The figure above Charles landing at Dover is a "Woman in pleasant colours; the Emblem on her Shield, a Terrestrial Globe; the Sun rising, Bats and Owls flying to the Shadow: the word *Excoecat Candor*": that above Charles receiving the keys of the city "hath on her Escutcheon a Swarm of Bees, whetting their stings: the Word *Pro Rege Exacuunt*." Opposing these in symbolically dramatic apposition is the figure above the trophy, who "hath on her Shield a Mountain burning, Cities, and Vineyards destroyed, and ruined: the Word *Impia Foedera*. The Covenant: in abhorrence of which villainous Combination, according to this Order of both Houses, it was burnt by the Common Hangman."[78] The fourth and final figure directly behind this, and in apposition to that bearing the inscription *Pro Rege Exacuunt*, "hath on her Escutcheon an Arm as it were out of the clouds; in the hand a naked sword: the Motto, *Discite Justitiam Moniti*." Hence, just as the inscriptions over the visible arches showing the 'ruinous' state of the country complement each other (*En quo discordia cives / Perduxit miseros*), so *Discite Justitiam Moniti* is found in the same satanic context as *Ausi immane nefas ausoque potiti*, from the sixth book of Virgil's *Aeneid*, in the description of the Titans suffering in Erebus. Thus is established a double symmetry—that of the symbolic relationship between back and front, accentuated by the relationship of left to right. Unfortunately, Ogilby's method of interpolating digressions wherever possible tends to obscure the thematic integrity of the design for this first arch, on which the others depend. Inconsistent references to the north, south, east and west of the arches are confusing: it is simpler to refer to the left and right.

By restating the above exposition a distinct symbolic pattern can be seen. This is brought out most readily if we put ourselves in the position of a contemporary—John Evelyn, for example, who spent the evening of the 22nd of April "seeing the severall Arch Triumphals ... some of which though tem[p]orarie, & to stand but one Yeare, were of good Invention & architecture, with Inscriptions."[79] We scrutinize the first arch by beginning at the lower right-hand side, following the design through in an anti-clockwise semicircular movement. Then, having passed through, we repeat this procedure on the other, hidden side, imaginatively reconstructing the façade from the details of the folio, continually paying close attention to the juxtaposition of inscriptions and paintings. This "reading" of a structure with associations of good and evil is not arbitrary. The formal influence of such a comparable artifice as a stained glass window is evident, and reading from right to left (i.e. *stage left* to *stage right*) has a sanction as deeply ingrained in an iconographical tradition as that of hell-mouth itself;[80] the medieval association of left-evil and right-good accepted as prescriptive such lines as Matthew 25:41: "Then shall he say also unto them on the left-hand, Depart from me, ye cursed, into everlasting fire, prepared for by the devil and his angels."

The thematic sequence of the east side, that of the engraving, runs thus:

> Rebellion ("Hell's Daughter"), and Confusion—*Ausi immane nefas ausoque potiti*, Trophy, *Ultor a tergo Deus*—*Impia Foedera*, mountain and city burning—*En quo discordia cives perduxit miseros*, England 'ruinous'—Charles triumphing over Cromwell and the Rump at Hell's mouth, *Volvenda dies en attulit ultro*—*Excoecat candor*, sun rising—*Adventus Augusti*, Charles at Dover, *In solido rursus fortuna locavit*—Monarchy and Loyalty.

Ogilby's details for the west side are rather cursory but they are sufficient to show the continuity of theme:

> Charles receiving the Keys of the City—Escutcheon with bees ("the hieroglyph of a loyal people") *Pro Rege Exacuunt*—*Felix temporum reparatio*, "the Restauration of our Happiness"—*Redeunt saturnia regna*—*Discite justitiam moniti*.

This political Augustanism lies in the effective conflation of the *Aeneid*, book six, the *Fourth Eclogue*, the first and fourth *Georgics* and contemporary English history. Ogilby clearly agreed with the view of his Royalist contemporary, Peter Heylyn, who believed that he who read the stories of "The Commonwealth of Rome ... will judge them rather to contain the acts of the whole World, than a particular Nation."[81] As Charles approaches the first arch his symbolic position is that of Aeneas accompanied by the sibyl viewing the torments of the Titans in Erebus; the English Titans are the rebels of the interregnum. Passing through the arch, Charles becomes the imperial embodiment of the Augustus "promised oft, and long foretold,"[82] prophesied by Anchises to Aeneas in the sixth book of the *Aeneid*, following the retrospective view of the Titans. The fulfilment of the prophecy is anticipated by the sense of Time working in conjunction with Fortune, expressed in the inscription *Volvenda dies en attulit ultro* and *Multa dies, variusque labor mutabilis aevi ... In solido rursus Fortuna locavit*. The inscriptions on the rear of the arch announce the realization of the visionary future vouchsafed to Aeneas and, by a symbolic parallel, to Charles, who, restored and entering his capital, now as the new Augustus, brings back the golden age—*Felix temporum reparatio, Redeunt saturnia regna*.

In studying this symbolism of the first arch one can substantiate the parallel drawn by George Sherburn between Octavius's return to Rome after the civil wars of the triumvirate, and Charles's restoration after the English civil wars and the interregnum.[83] Ogilby's controlling idea is to take this primary parallel of the present with the past, Charles's return to London and Augustus's return to Rome, and extend the points of comparison by entrenching another parallel, the English rebels and the other triumvirs, in the mythopoeic context of the sixth book of the *Aeneid*; that is, a context which was invested with sixteen hundred years of satanic association and messianic aspiration. Ogilby thereby imparts a satanic dimension to the enormity of the rebels' actions, proportionately endowing Charles with the godlike qualities of Virgil's Augustus imbued with the messianic aura tradition had fostered on the *Fourth Eclogue*. The method of superimposing one figure upon another—in this case Aeneas, Augustus, and Charles—is that of the panegyrists *amplificatio*; hence the organising principle of Ogilby's narrative design on the first triumphal arch may be designated as rhetorical. As has been noted, *ut architectura poesis* is often nearer the actual practice of Augustan poets than the professed Horatian formula *ut pictura poesis*.[84]

Ogilby's application of the Virgilian schema, as an evaluation of English history, is the most complete formulation of a politically Augustan framework in the period. It has a thoroughgoingness which makes something like Dryden's *Astraea Redux* seem quite fragmentary, though it is exactly fragments of this kind which preceded Ogilby's formulation. One may consider the Augustan myth as little more than rhetorical compliment, a mere rhetorical gesture acquiescing in Royalist propaganda arbitrarily applied at the succession of a monarch. There is certainly a measure of truth in this, but it is a partial truth which discounts the strength of a traditional concept conveyed generation by generation, and fails to recognize its psychological status within the individual poet's mind and his work. As E. H. Gombrich has written concerning the golden age propaganda of the Medici:

> Propaganda, as we know to our cost, is the art of imposing a pattern on reality, and to impose it so successfully, that the victim can no longer conceive it in different terms. Such a pattern will be more likely to exert its spell the deeper it is rooted in tradition, the more affinity it has with the typical nightmares and dreams of mankind. The Messianic Ruler who brings back the Golden Age is precisely such a perennial dream ... unlike flattery, propaganda need not be cynical. Those who propound it may be its first victims.[85]

Ogilby's propaganda was a formulation of the discrete allusions of a year of tumultuous panegyric and related literature which repeatedly turned to Virgilian themes. This is of such significance that detailed illustration is asked for.

Cowley, considering the poet as recorder of "A Picture of Heroick Worth," advises the choice of "some comely Prince of heavenly Birth ... / No proud Gigantick son of Earth, / Who strives t'usurp the God's forbidden seat."[86] The implicit allusion to the Titans who revolted against Jove is made explicit by Henry Bold to whom Charles, surrounded by his peers at the coronation, is like "Upper Jove," who "Conven'd the Gods / ... when secur'd, and free, / From Heaven assayling—gigantomachie."[87] George Bower, in the Restoration year, executed a medal called "Gigantomachia" in which "The King is ... represented as Jupiter demolishing his foes, the giants a probable allusion to the execution of the regicides."[88] Another contemporary, viewing the Restoration, considered that "All lets and Hindrances which have intervened since his Majesties just Rights, are now so many arguments of his Future fixed and peaceable enjoyment. This the Ancients intimated, when they tell us that *Jupiter* himself was not quiet in heaven, till after a long war with the Gyants."[89]

Ogilby's symbolic application was, however, specifically anticipated by John Boys of Hode Court. Boys, an indomitable spokesman for Kent Royalists, had gone into hiding after presenting, in January 1660, a declaration in favour of a free parliament to the unsympathetic mayor of Canterbury. In hiding, Boys busied himself with a translation of the sixth book of the *Aeneid*[90] and included commentary on some passages. This provided a focus for Ogilby, just at the right time. Let us consider some examples. When Boys reached the passage beginning "The Titans, earths first born ...," he comments on rebellion as,

> set on foot by the Titans, the sonnes of the earth, that is, the common rout, and which, like the Aloides, if not suppressed, heaps Pelion upon Ossa, that is, subverts the fundamentals of Government; which though moddel'd, and put together with the greatest policy and prudence that may be, and as firmly rooted as a mountain, is often-times shaken, removed, and overthrown by the convulsions and earthquakes of popular sedition: But mark its reward, it seldome is successful, but carries its punishment with it, not only in this world, where it usually expires upon a gibbet, but as the blackest of transgressions is punished (as by these examples is clear) in the other, with the worst of punishments, viz. eternal damnation.[91]

This comment might well be read as a description of the import of the relevant part of Ogilby's first arch. For some years Ogilby himself had been well aware of the way in which the passage describing the Titans, particularly the Aloides and Salmoneus, served to express a constantly potential truth of political history. In 1649, the year of the regicide, he published the first edition of his *Aeneid*, translating the passage beginning *hic genus antiquom Terrae, Titania pubes*, thus:

> Here young *Titanians* are, earths ancien race,
> Struck down with thunder to the lowest place.
> There saw I both th' Aloides, those vast
> Gyants, who strove heavens fabricks to have raz'd,
> And *Jove* t'have thrust from heavens high Monarchie.

> And saw *Salmonius* in great tortures lie,
> Whil'st he heavens fire, and thunder imitates,
> Brandishing flames and through the *Grecian* states,
> Borne on fowre steeds, proudly through *Elis* drives
> With fond pretence to heavens prerogatives.[92]

Given the struggle between king and parliament, the royal prerogative and law, "Monarchie" for *regnum* and "prerogative" for *honor* were politically incriminating words to use at the time. *Monarchia* is post-classical Latin deriving from a Greek root with an absolute, theoretical connotation, rather than the territorial meaning of *regnum*; "prerogative" for *honor* needs no comment. Presumably Ogilby translated the *Aeneid* during the years of Charles I's declining fortunes, intending his phraseology as a tacit support for the Royalist cause, and sent it to the press before the disastrous event of early 1649; or, publishing later in 1649, he left the text as it was, as a gesture of defiance. However, when he reprinted a revised edition in larger format, complete with Hollar's engravings, in 1654, he had evidently learnt that discretion is the better part of valour, for the offending passage then reads:

> Here young *Titanians* be, Earths antient Race,
> With thunder sunk down to the lowest place;
> Here I the two Aloides beheld,
> Whose mighty size all Fictions far excelled,
> These, though but mortals, storm'd high heav'n, and strove
> To drive from his Celestial Kingdomes, *Jove*.
> I saw *Salmoneus* as he tortur'd sate,
> Who Lightening could, and Thunder imitate;
> Brandishing Flames, he in a Chariot rode
> Through *Greece* in triumph, honor'd like a God.[93]

In the third edition of 1665, Ogilby reprinted his translation of 1649 – "heavens high Monarchy" and "heavens prerogatives" had returned with Charles II.[94]

John Boys, continuing his translation, arrives at the important passage describing the general torments of those in Erebus (lines 607–27) and translates and italicizes Virgil's

> quique arma secuti
> impia nec veriti dominorum fallere dextras

thus:

> *And 'gainst their King and Lawful sovereign*
> *(In impious broyles engag'd) their swords have drawn.*[95]

In the safer atmosphere of the Restoration, Boys, like Ogilby, uses Virgil in a distinctly partisan fashion. But greater interest lies in the only other italicized lines in the section:

> *When warn'd, learn justice; not, the Gods despise ...*
> *All have bin As happy in success, as bold in sin*[96]

for Virgil's

> discite justitiam moniti et non temnere divos ...
> ausi omnes immane nefas ausoque potiti.

The coincidence with Ogilby's choice of these lines as inscriptions increases further when we read Boys's printed marginal gloss to the last quotation: "Such were, for a time, the late Traitors, to whom this verse may well be applied." The temptation to conclude that, as a translator and publisher of Virgil interested in possible rivals, Ogilby bought Boys's translation at more or less the same time as Thomason, and was in the process of studying its merits or demerits when the city council made their hasty commission for the pageant, is surely inevitable. The verse of 1660 was full of golden age acclamation and a few hints at the possible categorizing of the rebels as the classical Titans, which Boys could not have made more explicit. Furthermore, Boys annotates this passage thus: "The Poet having alledg'd divers particulars, lest he should cloy the Reader with too many instances of the same kind, doth as it were sum up his discourse in these following generals, placing such as are found guilty of these or the like crimes in Hell."[97] Ogilby, commenting on the inscription *ausi immane nefas ausoque potiti*, writes that Virgil "spoke it of those, who were, for the like Crimes condemn'd to the Pains of Erebus."[98] The similarity of phrase, following a like appraisal of the crucial lines from book six, indicates that Boys precipitated just at the right time the retrospective framework entrenching the rebels in the mythic context of Erebus, which Ogilby then applied in the design of the first arch.

It is significant to note the shared Virgilian perspective seen, for example, in Dryden and Rachel Jevone's choice of superscription for their restoration panegyrics—*Redeunt saturnia regna.*[99] Similarly, a 1659 tract of Marchamont Needham's,[100] albeit anti-Royalist, concludes by quoting *En quo discordia Cives/Perducet miseros*, while in the first part of John Rushworth's *Historical Collections*, also published in 1659, on a page following the title and depicting recent European wars, we find the rubric *Sed nulla potentia Longa est, Quo non discordia cives*. Finally, an anonymous tract of April 20th, 1660, entitled *Expedients for Publique Peace* takes the line *En, quo discordia Cives/Perduxit miseros* as its epigraph. It is difficult to claim a direct influence in Ogilby's choice of inscriptions. It is rather a mental habit of applying common Virgilian categories in approximate circumstances. Thus Anthony Dopping, Bishop of Meath, in his private notebook poem on the Restoration, writes of the rebels as "base insulting tyrants; who for gold/Betray'd their King, and their owne conscience sold."[101] This obviously does not translate Virgil's *vendidit hic auro patriam dominumque potentem imposuit*, which occurs in the passage between the lines *discite justitiam moniti ... ausi omnes immane nefas ausoque potiti*, yet the Virgilian resonance is unmistakable. Alternatively, when Dryden, twenty-five years later, took the epigraph *Discite, justitiam moniti* for his opera *Albion and Albanius*, we can be certain that he had Ogilby's application in mind, since at the end of the first act[102] (an allegory of the Restoration) Ogilby's triumphal arches appear as part of the stage machinery.[103]

The insurgents as the vanquished Titans seen by the English Aeneas, Charles Stuart, imposes an epic dimension on English history of the mid-seventeenth century, the action one, entire, and great, encompassing the regicide, Charles's flight from the battle of Worcester, exile, and restoration. All are conducted by the heavenly surveillance of the Deity working providentially through time, whose revolution manifests the divine will. The poetry of the Restoration year celebrated Charles as an epic hero comparable to Aeneas. To Sir Robert Howard, Charles's venture on the battlefield was like that of "the bold Aeneas" who then,

> having left Troy
> In its own funerall flames, scorn'd to enjoy
> Safety alone; But, led by Vertues great
> As were the Dangers he was to repeat,
> Return'd among his ruin'd Friends and State,
> To bring them, safety, or to fetch their fate.

Howard believed "Heav'n sure had designe"[104] in Charles's escape and exile, while in Thomas Higgons's panegyric:

> Thus great Aeneas when his Troy was lost
> And nought but ruins left of all that State,
> Wander'd at Land, and on the Floods was tost
> And hurried up and down by Fate ...
> So must you suffer e'er you could be Great
> For Fortune always does with Vertue strive.[105]

Charles's constant changing of countries during his exile, though perhaps discomforting at the time, ensured his status as epic hero when the panegyrists reviewed their sovereign's past misfortunes, "Still tost and turn'd, still on the wing, / His type Aeneas answering."[106] And, as Neptune sheltered Aeneas from the malevolence of Juno, so the compassionate god performed his kindly office for Charles, who "into the Sea being Cast ... Neptune straight calms the raging of the sea." In Cowley's "Ode," Charles-Aeneas undergoes his stern apprenticeship to Destiny as epic hero:

> He does long *troubles* and long *wars* sustain,
> E're he his fatal *Birth-right* gain
> With no less *time* or *labour* can
> *Destiny build up* such a *Man*,
> Who's with sufficient virtue fill'd
> His *ruin'd Country to rebuild*.[107]

Thus Charles suffers a sea-change; having left as Aeneas he returns "with sufficient virtue" as Augustus, who reestablishes order after civil war "When Rome was ruin'd with intestine hate, / Augustus took the rudder of the State." The poet amplifies further:

> And when Domitian's hated Government
> The distrest world had thrown into despair,
> Trajan by Heaven was in Mercy sent,
> The Ruines of the Empire to repair.

Imperial history is seen as the criterion for postwar England: "What Trajan and Augustus did at Rome, / England expects to see, now You are come."[108]

The rhetorical transformation of Charles-Aeneas to Charles-Augustus is, perhaps, best seen in Thomas Mayhew's lengthy panegyric, the middle section of which[109] is dominated by the consistent allusion to Anchises' prophecy to Aeneas of the future accomplishments of the new emperor, *hic vir, hic est ... Augustus Caesar*. Former stories "of the Grecian Travellor / Or him that wandered from the Trojan wars" are "weak and poor Romances," compared to Charles's. Mayhew begins his trope:

> This, England, this is He, that brings thee now
> After thy flood of woes the Olive-bough.
> To make thee know, that Deluge could not cease
> Till this thy Dove were home return'd in peace.

This initial allusion, in which the figure of Charles as Augustus extends to include Noah, expands then to the bringer of plenty: "This England, This is He, who brings thee back / That Amalthean-horn," and continues the figure of *expolitio* at a dizzy speed: "This is your Oedipus ... Your Theseus this ... Your Hercules ... This, This is he that breaks those iron bands ... This, This is He that all thy Breaches bounds...." All these elements are together contained by the controlling allusion sustained by the Augustan phraseology, which duly subordinates the other figures.

The inscriptions *Volvenda dies en attulit ultro, Multa dies, variusque labor mutabilis aevi ... In solido rursus fortuna locavit*, and *Redeunt saturnia regna* are infused with the sense of an advent in time. This needs to be understood within the context of the Restoration year of public acclaim, with its growing acknowledgement of something approaching the symbolic magnitude of the Platonic year, the phoenix period, or a kind of millenium. The king's cavalcade through the temporary arches was over in a day, but Ogilby and the panegyrists celebrated the Restoration as epochal in all human history.

Volvenda dies

As a fit parallel to the temporal events from the regicide to the Restoration, Plato's great year was thought comparable; that year when "all the eight revolutions, having their relative degrees of swiftness, are accomplished together ... and begin again at their original points of departure."[110] In his prose dialogue *Behemoth*, Thomas Hobbes's simple delineation of the circularity of events shows how rhetorically apposite the cosmological parallel was:

> I have seen in this revolution, a circular motion of the sovereign power through two usurpers, father and son, from the late King to this his son. For (leaving out the power of the Council of Officers, which was but temporary, and no otherwise owned by them but in trust) it moved from King Charles I to the Long Parliament; from thence to the Rump; from the Rump to Oliver Cromwell; and then back again from Richard Cromwell to the Rump; thence to the Long Parliament; and thence to King Charles II, where long may it remain.[111]

John Evelyn made the inevitable comparison "Let it be a new year," he says, "a new Aera to all the future Generations, as it is the beginning of this, and of that immense *Platonick* Revolution."[112] The panegyrists took up the theme. Henry Bold exclaims:

> Revolution! Revolution!
> Our King Proclaimed! Restor'd! And Crown'd! A Year
> Like Plato's, set us even as we were.[113]

While Abdiel Borfet's very evident lack of imagination shows how related ideas could come together, yet not coalesce:

> No, though among those Stars, which did appear
> At his renew'd Nativity this year,
> The true Platonick, when the sphere's are rowl'd
> Back to the Loyall points they kept of old.
> Although among those Stars whose glorious train
> Was in conjunction with Charles his Wain....[114]

Though Borfet ruminates confusedly, the sophisticated mind of Abraham Cowley expresses the subdued calm after civil turmoil, the personal involvement of an individual caught up in his country's misfortunes, finding relief in acknowledging the vast impersonal acronychal of an objective but not disengaged universe:

> Now *Blessings* on you all, ye peaceful *Starrs*,
> Which meet at last so Kindly and dispence
> Your universal gentle *Influence*
> To calm the stormy *World*, and still the rage of *Warrs*.[115]

Cowley, like Bold, takes the lines from the ninth book of the *Aeneid*, which include the line *Volvenda dies en attulit ultro*, as the epigraph to his poem. In 1663, James Heath prefixed to his history *A Brief Chronicle of the Late Intestine Warr in the Three Kingdoms* a frontispiece in which Janus stands above a globe, his foot staying its motion at the point where bishops and judges rise and the rebels fall; below the globe are the words *Volvenda dies*. It is likely that Heath was borrowing directly from Ogilby's festival,[116] but we cannot assume that Ogilby (like Cowley and Bold ignoring the reference to Turnus) drew from a secondary source. Again it is a question of a common literary tradition supplying both Ogilby and the panegyrists with a series of concatenated themes. The painting of Charles II as a child in the centre of the second arch is a successful reminder of the revolution of time which has restored monarchy. As the Royalist Peter Heylyn had written years before:

> For questionlesse it fareth many times with a Common-wealth as with the
> Sunne: which runneth through all the signes of the Zodiack, till it return to
> the place where its motion first began. And the *Platonicke* year of reducing all
> things to the same begining, continuance and period, how false soever in the
> bookes of Nature, is in some sort true in the change of Government.[117]

Illegitimate government gave way to a restored legitimate monarchy; "our shaken Republic rushed at once into your Princely arm," said Evelyn.[118] Dryden's famous lines from *Astraea Redux*:

> And now times whiter series is begun
> Which in soft centuries shall smoothly run
> ....
> Oh Happy Age! Oh times like those alone
> By Fate reserv'd for Great Augustus Throne
> (lines 292–93, 320–21)

are just a few among very many alluding to the same theme which Ogilby, following the poets, incorporated into his design.

The related ideas of the Platonic year and golden age, deriving from a circular concept of history as ancient as Hesiod, bore, paradoxically, incipient seeds of their own decay, which the panegyrists were not entirely insensitive to. The *topos* of *translatio imperii*, drawing on this circular idea of history, lamented an interminable rise and fall of empires, indirectly suggesting that the restored emperor of Britain would be caught in the process. Heylyn's *Cosmographie*, a much reprinted volume in the seventeenth century, bemoans "that such is the condition and vicissitude of humane affairs that there is nothing permanent, and much less of certainty. The greatest Monarchies of the world, the Babylonian, Persian, Grecian, Roman, have all had their periods, nothing remaining of them now but the name and memory."[119] In 1661, Evelyn echoed the theme in his *Panegyric*: "Empires passe, Kingdomes are translated, and dominions cease."[120]

To counter this some panegyrists adapted the apocalyptic pronouncement of the impending suspension of all time ("And the angel ... sware by him that liveth for ever and ever ... that there should be time no longer" [Revelation 10:5–6]) by viewing the Restoration as a new monarchical millenium, which Charles inaugurates. A startling example of the way this conversion of ideas was spontaneously seized upon can be seen in the triumphal days immediately following Charles's re-entry into London, on May 29th. On June 3rd appeared a poem in which "a person of honour" avers "till time shall be no more ... Princes shall rule."[121] Similarly, on June 4th, the well known Royalist poet, Alexander Brome, solemnly adjures Charles to "Govern the nations ... Till time shall be no more."[122] Lastly, Arthur Brett published the following day his rather prolix poem in which he relates both Platonic and apocalyptic ideas:

> Such is Our Prince who dothe returne
> The Phoenix of the Royal Urne,
> With him returns that beauteous Dame
> We Ecclesia Anglicana name,
> The Hierarchy is getting ground
> (Its Platonic year's come round).

The symbolic phoenix is associated with the Platonic year which, to Brett, concludes with the coronation "When he is crown'd in all your sights ... ," and then, "Believe a Resurrection / A time when time shall be no more."[123]

The mystical phoenix, further enhancing the religious interpretation of the *Fourth Eclogue* as a familiar emblem of Christ's Passion and contributing to the significant idea of an advent in time, was directly used in the panegyrics of 1660–1661 and was almost certainly included by Ogilby on the first arch above the motto *Felix temporum reparatio* (happy restoration of times). The panegyrics, the motto's derivation, the phoenix appearing on contemporary coins, and above all the earlier established symbol of Charles as phoenix, make this conclusion inescapable. The motto *Felix temporum reparatio*, which adorns the rear of the first arch with *Redeunt saturnia regna*, was the legend which Constantine had inscribed on a series of bronze coins struck in A.D. 348 to celebrate the eleven hundredth year of Rome's foundation.[124] In A.D. 334, during Constantine's reign, the phoenix was rumoured to have made its fifth appearance in Egypt. The earlier four appearances were during the reign of Sesostris (866 B.C.), Amasis (566 B.C.), Ptolemy Philadelphos (266 B.C.), and a few years before the death of Tiberius, in A.D. 34—the year of the death and Resurrection of Christ. Between each date spanned the period of three hundred years which was thus believed to constitute the phoenix period or cycle.[125] To Evelyn, at the Restoration, "that Northern Star began the dawning of the day, till your nearer approach did guild our Horizon, brighter then the rayes of the Easter sun, from whose spicy coast, like a true Phoenix you were to come; For so at the sight of that Royal Bird was the memory of Sesostris, of Amasis and Ptolemy ever fortunate, and so was yours to us."[126]

Constantine, translator of and commentator on *Eclogue* IV, deriving the motto FEL TEMP REPARATIO from *magnus ab integro saeclorum nascitur ordo* (line 5), chose the mystical bird of the East, whose reappearance in his own reign three hundred years after the death of Christ confirmed its revelatory nature, as one of the appropriate emblems to embellish the reverse side of his medals. Though Ogilby places the motto directly behind *En quo discordia cives perduxit miseros*, above arches no longer "ruinous," but "finished, to represent the Restauration of our Happiness by His Majesties Arrival," it is almost certain that the phoenix emblem was included.[127]

The application of this symbol to Charles can be seen as early as Wenceslas Hollar's fine engraving of Charles's escape from the battle of Worcester, in part of which he depicts the phoenix in the simultaneous act of self-immolation and regeneration.[128] The phoenix allusion appears only in part of Ogilby's 1661 *Relation*, where he interpolates an entertainment "designed and the speeches made by a person of quality," presented in the front of East India House in Leadenhall Street, after the king had passed through the first arch. The following lines occur in the main speech (p. 10), after an initial display of camels, spices, and "blackamoors":

> *We'l blame that Fire no more, that scorch'd our nest*
> *Of Spicy Trade, since we see You, the Best*
> *Of Kings, Rise from the ashes of that Flame,*
> *That burnt our First Right* Phoenix *of Your Name*
> *For you have outdone* Solomon, *and made*
> *Provision for more than* Ophir *Trade.*

The same attitude, converting the mystical into the mercantile, could echo *Redeunt saturnia regna* in *Redeunt commercia Flandris*,[129] stamped on a medal to celebrate peace and renewed trade after one of the Dutch wars. However, different attitudes coexisted. In the usually circumspect John Evelyn we find an ardent apostrophe in which the conscious application of the phoenix symbol is as touching as history has shown its mystique was inappropriate. Running through the obligatory "partitions of the Demonstrative," Evelyn's rhetoric brings him to Charles's "early Piety" to his father:

> no sooner did that blessed martyr Expire, then our redivive Phoenix appear'd; rising from those Sacred Ashes Testator and Heir; Father and yet Son; Another, and yet the same; introsuming as it were his Spirit, as he breath'd it out, when singing his own Epicedium and Genethliack together, he seem'd prodigal of his own life to have it redoubled in your felicity: Thus, *Rex nunquam moritur* O admirable conduct of the Divine Providence, to immortalize the image of a just Monarch: *Ipsa quidem, sed non eadem, quis et ipsa, nec ipsa est.*[130]

Ernst Kantorowicz, in discussing the juristic significance of the notion *dignitas non moritur*, calls the phoenix "a paragon of royalty on account of its uniqueness or singularity."[131] The Fathers he cites would evidently have been familiar to the pious Evelyn, who cites Lactantius's *Carmen de ave phoenice* from which part of Elizabeth I's personal motto was taken—*Est eadem sed non eadem, quae est ipsa nec ipsa est*. Frances Yates has pointed out "how close is the connection between Elizabeth as the Phoenix and Elizabeth as Astraea. Both are symbols of imperial *renovatio*, implying the return of that best rule under the One, when the world is most at peace, and justice, together with all other virtue, reigns."[132] One can see how equally appropriate the symbols were when applied to Charles: Charles as the new Augustus accompanied by the ubiquitous Astraea, Charles as the "redivive Phoenix," the mortal incarnation of immortal kingship, and Charles as the Christian emperor restoring the true Church of England. Carew Reynall put it simply: "For we are pure in Doctrine," he says, "You are a second Constantine to stay / Our Holy Church from falling to decay."[133] The implicit argument here had been formulated, among others, by Charles I's chaplain in ordinary, Isaac Basire, and was translated and published, significantly in 1661, adumbrating once again the superiority of king over priest in Old Testament and early church history, "from Moses to Constantine the Great."[134]

The messianic aspect of Charles's return in Ogilby's *Entertainment*, though slight, is unmistakable. On leaving the third arch, the temple of Concord, Concord, Love and Truth sing to the king thus:

> Comes not here the King of Peace,
>   Who the Stars so long foretold,
> From all Woes should us release
>   Converting Iron-times to gold?[135]

In the combination of classical and Christian allusions the view of the fourth *Eclogue* as messianic is undisguised. Similarly, in the song at the final arch of Plenty, Ogilby verges on what is implied above, the extreme Royalist cult which saw Charles I as a Christlike figure and then, at the Restoration, transferred this notion to Charles II as Christ the redeemer of a fallen land. Latent in this final song is the comparison of the star at Charles's birth to that of the star at Bethlehem:

> Great Sir, the Star, which at your Happy Birth
> Joy'd with his Beams (at Noon) the wandring Earth,

> Did with his auspicious lust, then pressage
> The glitt'ring Plenty of this Golden Age.[136]

External evidence has survived which indicates that the notion of a monarchical millenium was part of Ogilby's design. Mistakenly assuming that the purchaser of his expensive volume would be satisfied to learn more about Loggan's arch engravings, Ogilby says little of the unengraved sides, leaving his account incomplete. However, an important detail survives in the diary of Ralph Josselin.[137] Noting accurately "divers sad particulars on ye face of ye arch. The high motto being En quo discordia cives &c," he then includes among diagrammatically laid out details the motto *Imperium sine fine dedi* as corresponding to *Volvenda dies en attulit ultro* on the front of the arch.[138]

Ogilby's details for the unengraved side (pp. 37–40) indicate that *Redeunt saturnia regna* was over the Great Table in which was depicted another oak and statue of Charles I, corresponding to the front. On the oak we find *Robur Britannicum*, while underneath the statue, *Restitutor Urbis*, presumably inscribed on a supporting pedestal. Thus the base panel of the Great Table, corresponding exactly to the front side's *Volvenda dies en attulit ultro*, is unaccounted for. The inscription noted by Josselin would fit Ogilby's Augustan schema perfectly. The line is taken from that passage of the first book of the *Aeneid* where Jupiter mollifies the importunate Venus by revealing to her the predestined glories of the Trojan exiles, from Aeneas's colonizing of Latium to the achievements of the Roman people, to whom he has granted a perpetual empire without temporal or territorial bounds, *his ego nec metas rerum nec tempora pono, / imperium sine fine dedi* (lines 278-79). *Imperium sine fine dedi* is also found as a leading inscription celebrating empire on the *Arcus Philippei* of Gevaerts's *Pompa Introitus*.[139]

Further evidence supporting this reading is found in a detail of the second arch. "The Painting on the South-side, over Mars," Ogilby relates (p. 66), "shews the Tower of London; the Inscription *Clauduntur belli portae*," which, with *Generis lapsi sarcire ruinas* in the corresponding panel above Neptune, Loggan has neglected to include in his engraving. *Clauduntur belli portae*, Ogilby explains, "is in reference to the Temple of Janus, never shut, but in the time of Peace; not opened, but in time of War." This is followed by a note concerning Juno opening the gates after Latinus's refusal, which is illustrated by citing from the *Aeneid* book seven (lines 616-22). However, we find the words *Claudentur Belli portae* as part of that promise for the future which Jupiter reveals to Venus in book one (line 294), after, that is, his revelation *imperium sine fine dedi*. Thus the change of tense—"the gates of war will be closed" to "the gates of war are closed"—describes the *present* Augustan achievement of peace and empire which Charles has symbolically inaugurated in passing through the first arch. Among the sources for the towering figure of Atlas "bearing a Terrestrial globe" (p. 91), Ogilby cites that passage in book six of the *Aeneid* where Anchises prophesies of Augustus as Roman emperor *ubi coelifer Atlas / Axem humero torquet stellis ardentibus aptum* (lines 789-97). The whole passage is rendered memorably by Dryden:

> But next behold the youth of form divine—
> Caesar himself, exalted in his line—
> Augustus, promised oft, and long foretold,
> Sent to the Realms that Saturn ruled of old;
> Born to restore a better age of Gold.
> Afric and India shall his power obey;

> He shall extend his propagated away
> Beyond the solar year; without the starry way,
> Where Atlas turns the rolling heavens around.
>
> (lines 1077–85)

It is in the second arch, where Ogilby celebrates Charles as the British Neptune, that mythological and mercantile notions of empire are combined in a symbolic comment on the history of rivalry for maritime power between England and her neighbours.

Neptuno Britannico

The first two arches acclaim Charles as the English Augustus whose return has restored the golden age and brought peace both on land and sea, thereby anticipating territorial and maritime empire. The third and fourth arches depict the necessary corollaries, Concord and Plenty. As Samuel Pordage phrased it in his *Heroick stanzas* on the coronation day:

> Caesar crown'd, the world indues a peace;
> The fane of Janus now is locked up fast,
> Soft peace and plenty, rest, and arts embrac't.

The poet anticipates Ogilby's dedicatory inscriptions, ... BRITANNIA TERRA MARIQ. PACATA ..., and UBERITATI AUG: EXTINCTO BELLI CIVILIS INCENDIO CLUSOQUE IANI TEMPLO. The characteristically felicitous juxtaposition of the Tower of London with the Temple of Janus—once again seeing the actual in a mythic context—is repeated in Ogilby's consideration of the dedication of the final arch. Coins of Augustus bearing Uberty or Plenty are the source for the attribution UBERITATI AUG., and, Ogilby continues, "What is meant by *extincto belli civilis incendio*, the extinction of the flames of Civil War is unfortunately known to us all, and may serve to explicate what follows, *Clusoque Jani templo*" (p. 141). Foremost among the examples of those who have closed the gates is Augustus, "once after Actium, about the time of the nativity of our Saviour; and then most justly when there was an Universal peace over the whole world ... And at this time it may be properly said to be shut at the fortunate arrival of our Sacred Sovereign into His Kingdoms, at what time there was a general peace throughout all Christendom" (pp. 142–43). Again Ogilby verges on what is implied in the above song, "Comes not here the King of Peace," thus imparting a millenial resonance to the earlier inscription *imperium sine fine dedi*, seen below the inscription from Virgil's messianic eclogue, *Redeunt saturnia regna*. Just as Heath's frontispiece depicts Janus halting the movement of the globe, and the panegyrists announced a monarchical millenium, so the change of tense from *claudentur* to *clauduntur* announces the realization in an unconditional present free from the contingencies of history apparent in the theme of *translatio imperii* which finally rests in the empire of Britain, as prophesied by James Howell of Charles II:

> 'Twas by a *Charles*, France once the Empire got:
> 'Twas by a *Charles*, Spain also drew that lot:
> Why may not *Britain* challenge the next Call,
> And by a *Charles* be made Imperiall?[140]

By including on the second arch the inscription *Unus non sufficit* and the dedication NEPTUNO BRITANNICO ... CUIUS ARBITRIO MARE VEL LIBERUM VEL CLAUSUM, Ogilby asserts Britain as a maritime imperial power comparable to the Habsburgs and superior to the Dutch, a power echoed by Evelyn a few years later, viewing Charles as "a Prince, to whom God had design'd the Dominion of the Ocean, which renders Your Majesties Empire Universal."[141]

The imperial theme had been predictably proclaimed by Rubens throughout the Antwerp festival, not only on the aforementioned *Arcus Philippei* surmounted by an inscription including *Imperium sine fine dedi*, but in the constant representation of the Habsburgs' proud impresa of the pillars of Hercules flanking the motto *Plus ultra*, thereby acknowledging the new-found lands discovered by the maritime adventurers beyond the Mediterranean, and colonized as the Spanish Empire. Ironically, Antwerp at that time was excluded from mercantile contact with the outside world, as parts of the Scheldt were blockaded. Thus Rubens's pageant, *Mercurius arbituriens*, strategically sited near the river, importunes Ferdinand to ensure trade once more, protesting the former glories of worldwide commerce facilitated by that pride of the Renaissance, the compass, which is depicted above the topmost inscriptions of the façade, *Polus non sufficit unus*.[142] The inscription *Unus non sufficit* beneath Atlas and between the two hemispheres, on Ogilby's second arch, is clearly an affirmation of the rival English claim to universal mercantile empire.

Significantly, though the traditional cardinal virtues are represented on the third arch, the seven liberal arts also usually depicted are replaced on this second arch by a *tableau vivant*, depicting "Arithmetick, Geometry, Astronomy, and Navigation" (p. 96) — a notable shift in emphasis from the *studia humanitatis* to techniques of calculation well adapted to the new golden age, in which the Royal Society flourished. As one anonymous panegyrist put it: "The Seamans Art, and his great end, Commerce [are Charles's delight], And even machanick Arts do find from you / Both entertainment and improvement too."[143] Charles as the British Neptune determines whether the seas are "open" or "closed," *cuius arbitrio mare vel liberum vel clausum*. "If any Nation may plead prescription for this Title," says Ogilby, "the King of England may, having had a longer uninterrupted Succession in the Dominion of the British Seas, then the Romans in the Mediterranean, or any other Nation, that History has acquainted us with, the Antiquity whereof being purposely and at large declared by Mr. Selden" (p. 52). Charles as Neptune; the representation of the *Sovereign of the Sea* in the centre table; the choice of words for the dedication and the reference to John Selden — all point to one of the most important diplomatic and juridical controversies of the seventeenth century, that of the dominion of the sea.[144]

The Dutch jurist, Hugo Grotius, had claimed that according to Roman law the seas were open and not exclusively the property of any one nation. His anonymously published book *Mare Liberum* (1609),[145] intending to counter the Portuguese pretensions to a monopoly of navigation and commerce in the Indies, was thought to glance obliquely at English claims for fishing rights concerning the "assize-herring." Though Grotius achieved his immediate object in securing rights for the Dutch to trade with the East Indies, in the treaty of Antwerp, his book was not forgotten. A controversy ensued, culminating, in England, in John Selden's *Mare clausum*, originally written for James I and published in an expanded and corrected edition at the request of Charles I in 1635. Selden claims absolute maritime sovereignty for the English monarch in arguments largely based on the sanction of historical precedent going back to the ancient Britons, the Romans, and the Anglo-Saxons amongst whom, it was claimed, Edgar styled himself "Lord of the Sea." Precedence was even discovered in the shadowy myths of prehistory.

Sir Winston Churchill, considering the mythic history of England, regarded Neptune as:

> Lord of the Seas, which (figuratively speaking) was as much as Lord of the whole Earth. It being from that time believ'd, that who so rul'd the Seas must by consequence have the dominion of the Land, whereupon *Homer* salutes him by way of Sanction with the Attribute of κράτος ωαλάσσης which we may english, *Sovereign of the Seas;* And accordingly the first Writers of our History have been willing the World should believe, that old *Albion* who first gave name to this Isle, was himself Sirnamed *Mareoticus,* for that he did by right of his descent from *Neptune* ἐωαλασσοκρατεῖ (as Polybius expresses it) i.e. claim the dominion of the Sea.[146]

Churchill, writing after the launching of the *Sovereign of the Sea* (two years after the publication of *Mare clausum*), was obviously influenced in his rendering of the Homeric epithet (more properly "ruler of the sea"). The name of Charles's great ship, however, was as much a part of the controversy as Selden's book: fixed menacingly to the beakhead was an effigy of Edgar, the Saxon "Lord of the Seas," while on every one of the *Sovereign of the Sea*'s guns was inscribed *Carolus Edgari sceptrum stabilivit aquarum*[147] Ogilby's second arch manifestly embodies that self-defensive nationalism and maritime imperialism which the first Dutch war had increased. That scorn of his fellow islander, Andrew Marvell, for "their *mare liberum,*"[148] was shared by Ogilby in his design, and by Elkanah Settle in his poem against the Dutch, at the height of the second war, entitled *Mare clausum: or a Ransack for the Dutch* (1666).

The *Neptuno britannico* theme is developed by the central inscription of the second arch which proclaims the alliance of the elements with the restored emperor:

> O nimium dilecte deo, cui militat aequor
> Et conjurati veniunt ad classica venti.

This is rendered by Ogilby:

> For thee, O Jove's delight, the seas engage,
> and mustred Winds, drawn up in Battel, rage.

The inscription derives from Claudian's *Panegyric on the third Consulship of the Emperor Honorius:*

> O nimium dilecte deo, cui fundit ab antris
> Aeolus armatas hiemes, cui militat aether
> et coniurati veniunt ad classica venti
> (lines 95–97)

which Platnauer translates, "Verily God is with thee, when at thy behest Aeolus frees the armed tempests from his cave, when the very elements fight for thee and the allied winds come at the call of thy trumpets."[149] Claudian is Ogilby's most favoured source but the choice of this inscription is quite complex. Though the panegyric suitably concludes with a prophecy of mercantile empire, an examination of the verses shows that Ogilby probably had in mind a parallel between Roman and English political history.

Evidently Ogilby has formed his couplet by combining the first and second halves of the first and second lines with the third line. *Aether* is replaced by *aequor* to agree with the maritime theme. The omission of the source would appear to be no more than a mere oversight were it not for a curious history of the lines *o nimium dilecte deo, cui militat aether / et coniurati veniunt ad classica venti*. Orosius, a Spanish Christian of the late Roman Empire, in *Adversos Paganos Historiarum Libri Septem* sought to demonstrate the reality of divine providence in man's affairs by citing the bloodless victories of his contemporary Theodosius I and his son Honorius. He singles out the battle between Theodosius and Eugenius in which there were neither heavy losses, nor Theodosius's "bloody revenge." Orosius finds evidence of God's providence witnessed even by "a most obstinate pagan," Claudian, and then quotes "o nimium dilecte deo, tibi militat aether et coniurati veniunt ad classica venti." Orosius's *Libri septem* had appeared as part of La Bigne's *Magna bibliotheca veterum patrum*[150] which was reprinted at Paris in 1654, the period after civil wars when to Englishmen bloodless victories would have seemed far removed from the bitter reality. The actual bloodless victory of Charles's restoration — celebrated as such incessantly in panegyric — would have seemed an incontrovertible token of God's providence.

Again, in the writings of Ciriac of Ancona, the fifteenth-century Italian humanist, we find another striking appearance of this enigmatic couplet. The Italian bibliophile, recording the inscription on an obelisk erected in the hippodrome at Constantinople, inserted as a marginal gloss beside a puzzling *lacuna* the above couplet which Mommsen believes,[151] presumably in view of the substitution of *tibi* for *cui*, was taken from Orosius rather than Claudian. The inscription in question reads:

DIFFICILIS QVONDAM DOMINIS PARERE SERENIS
IVSSVS ET EXTINCTIS PALMAM PORTARE TYRANNIS
OMNIA THEODOSIO CEDVNT SVBOLIQVE PERENNI
TER DENIS SIC VICTVS EGO DOMITVSQVE DIEBVS
IVDICE SVB   PROCLO   SVPERAS ELATVS AD ARAS

The couplet, which was intended to follow the fifth line, again refers to a context in which, though obscure, *omnia Theodosio cedunt*. And equally significant is a context in which the name of Proclus (the prefect of Constantinople beheaded by the vanquished tyrant Rufinus) is vindicated. If we recall that the name Theodosius in Greek means "god-given," we can see a number of allusions most apposite to the year 1660. Perhaps Ogilby had an unresolved parallel in mind between Theodosius, his sons Honorius and Arcadius, Stilico the general and Rufinus the tyrant, and Charles I, Charles and James, General Monck and Cromwell?

However, did Ogilby know the relevant passage in Orosius and had he seen Ciriac's gloss which only appears in inferior manuscripts from which it was taken by other commentators? Ogilby uses over a hundred and thirty sources, both ancient and modern, for his *Entertainment*: not once are the names of Orosius or Ciriac mentioned (the couplet is not found in Gevaerts), while Claudian is cited almost fifty times, closely followed by Virgil and Ovid (see Index of Sources). On these grounds one would be inclined to cite Claudian as the sole source, though Ogilby's redaction of the three Claudian lines — so close to that of Orosius and Ciriac — and the omission itself of such a well-used source indicate that Ogilby drew on either of the latter. Janus Gruterus, Ogilby's acknowledged source for details of inscriptions, includes in his *Inscriptiones antiquae totius orbis romani* the obelisk inscription;[152] similarly George Sandys in his *Travailles*;[153] but neither include the Claudian couplet. Finally, one can only conjecture that the couplet was included as a fit allusion to his own times which would have needed too much explanatory material in an already encumbered folio. Ogilby must have known that it was a corruption of Claudian's III *Honorius* which concludes, aptly, with a triumphal prophecy of mercantile dominion, *vobis Rubra dabunt pretiosas aequora conchas / Indus ebur, ramos Panchaia, vellera Seres*, "To you the Red Sea shall give previous shells, India her ivory, Panchaia perfumes, and China silk."[154] The classical golden age of Virgil and Ovid was inimical to trade, and particularly maritime trade. As Dryden put it, "The greedy sailor shall the seas forego / No keel shall cut the waves for foreign ware." The "plenty" of Saturnian times was natural and spontaneous. Those city senators with a vested interest in all things mercantile would have been uneasy with the lines from the fourth *Eclogue*, "pauca tamen suberunt priscae vestigia fraudis, / quae temptare Thetim ratibus ...," rendered by Dryden, "Yet, of old fraud some footsteps shall remain: / The merchant still shall plough the deep for gain."[155] Ogilby's couplet reinforces the claim to maritime power in an appeal to nature mythologized in a pathetic fallacy, rather than making a direct political point as in the inscription below it referring to the *mare clausum* controversy. On the other hand, a more sophisticated response which recognised the couplet could have imaginatively applied the historical parallels. At its simplest, another view, which must be faced, is that arch merely sublimates mercantilism.

Pro rege exacuunt

On the second arch, alongside the figure of Europe bearing a pendant depicting the myth from which her name derives, are the figures of Asia, Africa and America supporting pendants "bearing the Arms of the Companies trading into those parts," the Turkey Company, the East India Company, and the Merchant Adventurers.[156] The men of these companies wished to see London as 'This Empory the Magazine of all That's Rich.'[157] It is in the emblem of the bee that Ogilby makes the unconscious compromise between the classical thematic iconography and the self-justifying commercialism of those paying for the festival. The emblem of the bee first occurs on an escutcheon of the first arch depicting "a Swarm of bees, whetting their stings with the motto *Pro rege exacuunt*" (p. 39), a compression of the passage in the fourth *Georgic* in which the bees urgently prepare for war, and the defence of their king:

> tum trepidae inter se coeunt pinnisque coruscant
> spiculaque exacuunt rostris aptantque lacertos,
> et circa regem atque ipsa ad praetoria densae
> miscentur magnisque vocant clamoribus hostem.
>
> (lines 73–76)

This is rendered by Ogilby as:

> They list proud troups in haste, their Spears they whet,
> Their light shields furnish, and their arms they fit,

> Guarding their *King* thick to the Court they goe,
> And with loud clamour challenge out the foe.[158]

On the second arch the inscription *Generis lapsi sarcire ruinas* appears between the figure of Neptune and the painting of the exchange (as noted earlier, Loggan has neglected to include this in his engraving). The context, again that of the fourth *Georgic* (lines 248–50), is translated by Ogilby in the *Entertainment* (p. 66):

> How much by Fortune they exhausted are,
> So much they strive the ruins to repair
> Of their fal'n Nation, and they fill th 'Exchange
> Adorning with the choicest flow'rs their Grange.

The bee reappears twice on the third arch: the figure of Peace "hath her Shield charged with an Helmet, and bees issuing forth ... the Word *Pax bello potior*." Lastly, an unseen figure is described as bearing "a Shield, the King of Bees flying alone; a swarm following at some distance: the Word *Rege incolumi mens omnibus una*" (p. 133). Again the fourth *Georgic* is used, and Ogilby translates the line, "Whilst their King lives, they all agree in one."[159]

Though the bee may be regarded as a joint emblem of loyalty and industry, antiquity tended to regard the latter as subsidiary to the political application of the former. Explaining his sources for the first citation, Ogilby quotes Pliny and Claudian's references to the bee as an emblem of Loyalty, concluding that "the Aegyptians made a Bee the hieroglyph of a loyal people" (p. 39). Doubtless, here, Ogilby draws on the *Hieroglyphics of Horapollo*,[160] a source used by Gevaerts.[161] The bees issuing from the helmet is included by Alciati in his *Viri Clarissimi*,[162] and was included as a verbal image by Dekker in his speech for the *Genius loci* at the 1604 James I entry.[163] But in the translation of exchange for *horreum* (granary or storehouse), Ogilby tends to bring to the fore the idea of industry or simple commercial drive which distinguished itself from loyalty in a most pointed way in Cibber's bas-relief for the monument. Here, among other figures, are found Peace, Plenty and Industry—given in this order in an early print.[164] The emblem of Industry is a beehive at the foot of the figure of the city of London which reappeared in a later Lord Mayor's pageant[165] and was included in the 1709 English translation of Ripa's *Iconologia*, though it is not part of the first Italian edition.[166]

Ogilby stresses Loyalty, in the setting of a new golden age, on the first arch in the painting below the figure bearing the inscription *Pro rege exacuunt* showing the city fathers presenting the keys of the city to Charles, while Industry correspondingly matches the commercial bias of the second arch in the inscription *Generis lapsi sarcire ruinas* below the painting of the Royal Exchange. The difference between these emblems of the bee is exactly illustrated if we compare two citations, one at the beginning of the century, the other after the Restoration. John Donne, delivering in 1622 an anniversary sermon on the Gunpowder Plot, declared the Parliament "that house, which is the hive of the Kingdome, from whence all her honey comes."[167] In 1668, Josiah Child in his *Brief Observations concerning Trade* spoke of idle men as "Neither scattering by their expences, ... nor working with their hands or heads to bring either Work, or Honey to the common Hive of the Kingdom" (p. 14). Donne's context is that of a loyal parliament endangered by traitors, while Child's is concerned with an industrious country encumbered by idlers.

In June 1660 a broadsheet had appeared bearing an engraved emblem of Fame above a beehive surrounded by swarms of bees; a poem by John Lawson explains:

> Heav'n had the Angels cry aloud to *Fame*
> To blow the Trumpet in our Sovereign's Name.
> Just *Fame* obeys and sounds it in the Eares
> Of *Englands* Commons and the Noble Peeres.
> Both Houses meet, and Vote the Droven Bees
> With their Great King, are welcom when they please.
> White-Hall and all the Palaces do strive
> To be unto this honey-dew a Hive.[168]

The loyalty of the courtier-exiles is emblematized by the activity of the bee, whereas to John Crouch it is action of the readmitted secluded members which earns the symbolic attribution:

> *Secluded Members* Act, Vote their consent
> For the just freedom of a *Parliament*
> They rise, when forthwith from their burdned *Hives*,
> *Ripe Bees* swarm out, all prodigall of their *Lives*,
> The Bells to their new *Hive* these clusters *Ring*,
> Where, with one *humming Vote* they call their *King*.[169]

Crouch continues by invoking a new age of gold, anticipating Ogilby's linking the ideas in his designs, and then makes quite plain the vested interest of the city in the king's restoration:

> The City now long squeez'd and wire-drawn, made
> The *Citadel*, and *Mart of Europe-trade*:
> The Ship-wrackt Merchants in full *Change* resort,
> Conceive both *Indies* brought home with the *Court*
> For ever, *London*, shut thy Heart and *Hands*
> Against all factions and rebellious *Bands*:
> Twas time to *King* it, when thy purse and fame
> Lore'd [*sic*, "lowered"] to the Imperious Bank of *Amsterdam*.[170]

The poet inadvertently reverses Ogilby's pattern; here loyalty is a necessary subsidiary to industry, rather than the reverse. This self-interest of the city did not go unnoticed:

> What need the Citizens such Fabricks rear,
> As if they'd make them touch the very sphear,
> As if they would the starres out-vie,
> And make St Pauls Church not seem high.
> 'Twould be far better, could they boast
> They sacrific'd their loves, and not their cost:
> But we'el not blame them, since such is their joy,
>   they cant' withold,
> To offer up to it, the God they most adore, their gold.[171]

The anonymous poet is a delicate remove from the scepticism of the much maligned and incarcerated George Wither who, in the year of England's jubilee and self-congratulation, denounced the self-interest of all classes of society, including the merchants of the city which,

> If ... we our *Trustee* made,
> She, to enlarge her *Charters*, and her *trade*,
> To make herself more powerful, and more rich.
> Hath ever been inclin'd so over-much:
> And, to and fro, her self so often windes,
> To *this* and *that*, as she occasion findes,
> That, when in her we do repose our trust,
> We shall have *Charters* written in the Dust.[172]

Wither was one voice while the panegyrists were many, and the formal public image of restored kingship was that of the panegyrists' aspiration – evidently shared by Ogilby – which never reached such an adulatory pitch again.

Conclusions

The ostentation of an economic paradise expressed in terms of the traditional golden age had certainly worn thin by 1673 when John Hodges published a broadsheet entitled *How to Revive the Golden Age*, which is an epitome of the mercantilism advocated by Carew Reynell in his book advertised at the foot of the broadsheet, *The True English Interest*. Yet the phrase "golden age" remains as a conceptual category of expression. Its persistence even as a commonplace, as Hodges uses it, derived from an innate conservative compulsion to sanction future economic progress by an appeal to a past idyllic criterion, however incompatible.

Although the idea of the golden age had an inflexible grip upon the imagination, a number of related ideas would be spun out of it by amplification on a given *topos*, according to epideictic prescriptions. Biblical and classical traditions are inextricably interwoven in the idea of creation, providing for the seventeenth-century concatenated metaphors linking the golden age with Eden,[173] chaos and satanic rebellion with the Flood and terrestrial insurrections. Charles, hailed as Augustus, was also unfallen Adam and Noah, surviving the Flood, as well as the Sun King – the god who brings order out of chaos, light out of darkness.[174] The gradual formulation of a metaphysical system in which nothing could be redundant because everything was linked in the familiar great chain of being provided a number of significant analogies readily adaptable to the rhetoricians' exhortation to continually amplify and embellish.

Thus the Rump, apart from the satanic correspondence discussed above, was also continually exploited for the macro-microcosmological body politic correspondences with Charles as the exiled head.[175] Similarly Charles was *medicus regni* and *salus populi*, the healing Christ-king of a languishing country.[176] Continual amplification on the *pater patriae* figure (Aeneas, Augustus, Adam, Noah, and so forth) not only shows how a literary method reflects a hierarchical creation, but it also induces a mental habit of rhetorical association.

It has been shown that the design of the first triumphal arch is rhetorical in so far as it visualizes the progressive amplification of the panegyrists. The second arch, though not rhetorical in this overt sense, is nevertheless an example of the duality by which two seemingly disparate ideas could coexist in the mind of Ogilby and his contemporaries as imagistic corollaries, each implying the other by an almost automatic habit of rhetorical association, though only one may be expressed verbally or visually. Two contexts in John Evelyn's writings clarify this. In both his *Panegyric* and the dedication to his translation of Freart's work, *A Parallel of the Ancient Architecture with the Modern* (1664), the contexts are primarily Augustan. The first is concerned with the inadequacy of the temporary triumphal arches in which Charles is a symbolic Augustus, the second with Charles as an "architect" of the new "Augusta" – London. In the former Charles is seen as bringing order out of chaos, guiding the ship of state to safe harbour. In the latter Charles is "a Prince, to whom God has designed the Dominion of the Ocean" after guiding "this giddy Bark through such a storm."[177]

The *Panegyric* intimates what is made plain in the *Parallel*, that the "giddy bark" theme is a rhetorical corollary to the maritime, imperial attribution preceding it: the contiguity of the two ideas effectively overlaps their range of meanings, and mercantile imperialism takes on part of that religious providential aura which invests the Noah-Aeneas giddy bark image. One example may be taken from Restoration panegyric. Concerning Charles's return by sea, one anonymous poem exclaims:

> Triumphant Navy! Formerly your Freight
> Consisted but of Laurel, or of Plate;
> But to your happy Country now you bring
> More then both Indies in our Matchless King
> Twice has the World been trusted in a Barque;
> The New, the Charles contain'd, the Old, the Ark;
> This bore but those who did the World rebuild
> But that bore you, to whom the World must yield.[178]

As in Evelyn's *Parallel* the historical "Barque" is a contiguous rhetorical corollary of the contemporary "Triumphant Navy," amplifying by a commonplace on the import of Charles's return.[179] Thus the second triumphal arch, while to us evincing an overt mercantilism, would have had for Ogilby and his contemporaries a further qualifying association induced by the habit of rhetorical association, though the corollary is not visually depicted. A further parallel supporting this view may be made by comparing the design of seventeenth-century frontispieces (which were influenced by that of triumphal arches)[180] with Ogilby's second arch. Joshua Sylvester's translation of Du Bartas's *Divine Weekes* and Peter Heylin's *Cosmographie* were extremely popular in the seventeenth century.[181] The *Divine Weekes* is a religious poem concerned with the creation of the world while the *Cosmographie* is primarily a work of geography, yet the frontispieces of both are designed around a fourfold division (four pillars, four continents) surmounted by globes and finally topped by the Hebrew Tetragrammaton and quotations from Genesis. Clearly, geography is seen as a branch of sacred learning, the earth as nature's book complementing the revealed truth of the Bible. Hence, to an observer of the Ogilby festival and a reader of his book, the depiction of the four figures representing Europe, Asia, Africa, and America, on the second arch beneath Atlas, though to us ostensibly mercantile, would have had further associations as an emblematic artifice. Man's "fabrick" depicts "Great Nature's Fabrick,"[182] the world shown by Sylvester and Heylin. God's creation from chaos survived a second chaos, the Flood, which providentially bore Noah, as Charles survived

England's chaos, the civil war, by the same providence to return with his triumphant navy—returning the "giddy Barque" to safe harbour.

Royal entries of the Renaissance were the most socially and artistically inclusive forms of spectacle. Architecture, music, poetry and painting were combined in the dramatic encounter of monarch, nobles and populace, all of whom were involved in a celebration in which the historical and the mythological, the real and the symbolic were integrated. Ogilby's conception in the triumphal arches provided a most intensive symbolic spectacle of the Restoration. In hailing Charles as a new Augustus who brings back a golden age of peace and the plenty of maritime imperialism, Ogilby inaugurated what was to become an evaluative term for an entire period—the Augustan age.

Ogilby's festival was the last of its kind in England, lying just outside that period of European culture between the dates of the two quotations I have taken as epigraphs to this introduction. The observations of the Italian humanist Giovanni Pontano in attendance at the Court of Naples and the English aristocrat, William Cavendish, Earl of Newcastle, courtier of Charles I and tutor to his son, typify that Renaissance awareness of the significance of spectacle and pageantry.[183] Although the approach taken here particularly stresses the topicality of Ogilby's *Entertainment*, the festival is closely related to the iconography of English and European royalist spectacle. Jacobean and Caroline themes are clearly asserted as a restoration of the ideology of kingship. The 1604 entry had welcomed James I as the new Augustus bringing peace and restoring the golden age.[184] In Ben Jonson's *Neptunes Triumph* (1624) Prince Charles as Albion is cared for by Neptune, "the familiar persona of King James."[185] Davenant's *Britannia Triumphans* (1638) features the royal flagship, the "Sovereign of the Seas." The nationalist idea "that every monarch *est in patria sua imperator*, is emperor in his own land" led to an appropriation by the Habsburgs, Valois and Stuarts of the symbolism of empire, a humanist amalgam of the Roman, universalist and messianic.[186] However, the previously quoted remark of Sir William Petty, casting a cold eye on "these mistaken and distasted vanities" of Ogilby's festival, anticipated the views of Whig historians represented by James Ralph's observation on the Restoration year: "tho' outside Shew serves to dazzle those who regard Outside only, it will not convince those who carry their enquiries to the Heart."[187]

James II, though crowned on St. George's day, did not follow the example of his brother's coronation cavalcade. Until the beginning of the eighteenth century the Lord Mayor's pageant, partly appropriating the spectacle of a royal progress, satisfied the Londoners' love of pageantry. Nearly a year after Charles's cavalcade through the triumphal arches, a severe storm partly blew down one arch and sent the royal coat of arms toppling from the first—an ominous sign for the future, it was covertly pointed out.[188] Then, like an insubstantial pageant faded, Ogilby's arches were dismantled and not a rack was left behind: the materials were sold to the master carpenters who had erected them.[189]

Having received the sceptre bearing the symbolic dove, the newly crowned king duly began his sacred office. The previous evening, following the cavalcade, and after observing the pyrotechnic water triumphs on the Thames,[190] the king found refreshment beneath the glories of Rubens's apotheosis of Stuart kingship at the Whitehall Banqueting House. A detail of the fourth arch dedicated to Plenty depicts "Bacchus a Youth in a Chariot drawn by Tigres; the Reins, Vine-Branches; his Mantle, a Panthers skin; his Crown, of Grapes, and Ivy; A Thyrsus in his left hand, a cup in his Right: underneath *Liber Pater*. The painting over this represents Silenus on his Ass, Satyres dancing round about him, in Drunken and Antick Postures: the Prospect, a Vineyard" (p. 143). Shades of Charles, Buckingham, Rochester and all the merry gang! If Ogilby had added "Priapus in the shrubbery" as an intimation of Charles in his gardens at St. James's, perhaps we could say that this would have more truly represented the advent of the new saturnalian epoch in England's history which ensued. But this would discount the significance of a sober and circumspect man like John Evelyn who, at Charles's re-entry into London, had piously "stood in the Strand and beheld it, and blessed God."[191] Evelyn had composed the most impressively hieratic panegyric of all—at its presentation Charles had asked "if it were in Latin," and "hoped it would not be very long."[192] Bacchus was more in evidence in those words than Augustus, but, however briefly, in 1660–1661, "little children did much rejoice, and antient people did clap their hands, saying, golden dayes began to appear."[193]

Notes

Unless otherwise stated, the place of publication is London. Where a month date is given this indicates that the reference is part of the Thomason Tract collection in the British Library.

1. *Memoirs*, ed. Andrew Browning (Glasgow, 1936), p. 38.
2. J. G. Nichols, *London Pageants* (1831), pp. 74–76; F. W. Fairholt, *The Civic Garland*, Percy Society, vol. 19 (1846), p. 31; W. Jones, *Crowns and Coronations: A History of Regalia* (1883), p. 233.
3. *Chapters on Coronations* (1838), p. 84.
4. P. E. Schramm, *A History of the English Coronation* (Oxford, 1937), refers to the triumphal arches, drawing on L. G. Wickham Legg's selection (*English Coronation Records* [1901], pp. 276–86) from Walker's *Circumstantial Account* (see n. 40); R. Withington, *English Pageantry* (Cambridge, Mass., 1918–20), 1: 241–47.
5. I. Fletcher Kyrle, "The Literature of Splendid Occasions," *The Library*, 5th ser. 1 (1946–47): 192; Eric Halfpenny's "*The Entertainment* of Charles II" in (*Music and Letters* 38 [Jan. 1957]: 32–44) is concerned with the organization of the musicians during the cavalcade through the city, while his later article, "The Citie's Loyalty Display'd," (*Guildhall Miscellany* 10 [1959]: 19–35), deals primarily with the orders of precedence observed in the procession, though usefully printing for the first time the city's accounts for the *Entertainment*.
6. Earl Miner, *Dryden's Poetry* (Bloomington and London, 1967), p. 81, where the first triumphal arch is used to illustrate an argument concerning *Mac Flecknoe*; again the first, with the fourth arch, appears in Glynne Wickham, *Early English Stages* (1963), vol. 2, pt. 1, plates 18–19, to illustrate discussion concerning the continuity of festival artefacts.
7. R. C. Strong, "A Note on Charles II's Coronation Entry," *The Coat of Arms* 6 (April 1960): 43–48, and Gerard Reedy, S.J., "Mystical Politics: The Imagery of Charles II's Coronation," in *Studies in Change and Revolution*, ed. Paul J. Korshin (Menston, 1972).
8. Katherine S. Van Eerde, *John Ogilby and the Taste of His Times* (Folkstone, 1976); Howard Erskine-Hill, *The Augustan Idea in English Literature* (1983). In all that follows concerning English Augustanism and Ogilby's *Entertainment*, I am deeply indebted to Howard Erskine-Hill and to the scholar who virtually established English festivals as a subject meriting serious study, Sydney Anglo. I thank both, my early teachers, for the liberality of their knowledge and the generosity of their encouragement.
9. *Mac Flecknoe*, lines 102, 104; *The Dunciad*, Bk. I, lines 141, 328.
10. Katherine S. Van Eerde *John Ogilby*, chap. 3. For Ogilby in Ireland see particularly William Smith Clark, *The Early Irish Stage* (Oxford, 1955), chaps. 2–3.

11. "Ogilby's Coronation *Entertainment* (1661–1689); Editions and Issues," in *Papers of the Bibliographical Society of America* 47 (1953): 339–55. See Van Eerde chap. 3 also for Wenceslaus Hollar's contribution to the engravings.

12. Godfrey Davies, *The Restoration of Charles* II (San Marino, 1955). J. R. Jones, ed., *The Restored Monarchy* (1979), provides a useful bibliography for the period.

13. James I's was the most recent royal progress from the Tower, although postponed because of plague which later cancelled that of Charles I. David M. Bergeron, "Charles I's Royal Entries into London," *The Guildhall Miscellany* 3 (April 1970). For a full background to the topic, see also Bergeron's *English Civic Pageantry (1558–1642)* (1971).

14. *Remembrancia*, 9: 20. Letter from the Earl of Manchester, Lord Chamberlain, of the Household, to the Lord Mayor (dated February 9, 1660 o.s.).

15. Eric Halfpenny conjectures that "it seems most unlikely that Ogilby was brought in before this date" ("*The Entertainment* of Charles II," p. 20).

16. *The Relation*, p. 39.

17. *The Diurnal of Thomas Rugg 1659–1661*, ed. William L. Sachse, Camden 3rd ser., vol. 91 (1961), p. 152.

18. Others were John Scot, William Pope, Thomas Wratton, Roger Jerman (carpentry); William Lightfoot, Andrew Dacres (painting); Thomas Whiting (joinery); Richard Cleer (carving). Lastly, "*The Principal Parts of the Musick*, by His Majestie's Servants: All Composed by Matthew Lock, Esq: Composer in Ordinary to His Majesty." *The Relation*, p. 39.

19. Hugh Ross Williamson, "Sir Balthazar Gerbier" in *Four Stuart Portraits* (1949), pp. 26–60; D.N.B. and Edward Croft Murray and Paul Hulton, *Catalogue of British Drawings* (Trustees of the British Museum, 1960), 1: 328–30.

20. *An Humble Remonstrance concerning expedients whereby his sacred Majesty may increase his revenue, with great advantage to his loyal subjects.*

21. *C.S.P. Dom.* (1660–61), p. 415.

22. *C.S.P. Dom.* (1660–61), p. 522.

23. *C.S.P. Dom.* (1660–61), p. 412, as late as December 13 mentions February 6th as the prospective date.

24. See Prosper Arents, "Pompa Introitus Ferdinandi. Bijdrage tot de Rubensbibliografie," *De Gulden Passer* (1949, nos. 2, 3 and 4), pp. 341–44, where it is noted that as Ferdinand died suddenly on November 9th, 1641, the Antwerp authorities pre-dated the dedication. It appears that the book was finally published after 1641. See J. R. Martin, *The Decorations for the Pompa Introitus Ferdinandi* [corpus Rubenianum Ludwig Burchard XVI (London and New York, 1972)], and Elizabeth McGrath, "Le Déclin d'Anvers et les decorations de Rubens pour l'entrée du prince Ferdinand en 1635," in Jean Jacquot, ed., *Les Fêtes de la Renaissance* III (Paris, 1975), pp. 173–86.

25. *P. Virgilii Maronis Bucolica, Georgica, et Aeneis* (Venetiis, 1556). After citing Rhodiginus, which Ogilby obviously borrows, Erythraeus notes "Duae Harpyae basi cuidā veteri opere incisae, Venetiis in templo D. Martini, certū hodie statuariis et pictoribus figurandi monstri praebēt exemplar" (p. 171).

26. For Gerbier's correspondence see under the index in W. Sainsbury, *Original Unpublished Papers Illustrative of the Life of Sir Peter Paul Rubens* (1859), where the following details are substantiated.

27. Williamson, p. 38.

28. "Today I am so overburdened with the preparations for the triumphal entry of the Cardinal Infante ...," the artist wrote, on December 18th: *The Letters of Peter Paul Rubens*, trans. and ed. R. S. Magurn (Cambridge, Mass., 1955), p. 393.

29. Sainsbury, p. 187, no. 251.

30. These engravings were reprinted by William Morgan to complement a 1685 version of the *Relation*, though these include lettering in the arch-spaces (see Bowers, p. 355). It ought to be pointed out here that this 1685 edition, which was reprinted at Edinburgh in 1689, must explain Anthony Wood's remark that Ogilby's coronation book "hath been much made use of in succeeding coronations." *Athenae Oxoniensis*, ed. Philip Bliss (1817), 3: 742.

31. See the D.N.B. entry under both Sir Balthazar and George Gerbier D'Ouvilly. It would appear that George was not residing in London during the Restoration, since the *C.S.P. Dom.* (1660–61), pp. 589–90,

contains an aggrieved petition from "George St. George, the supposed son of Sir Balthazar Gerbier," denying any filiation and accusing Gerbier of fraudulently acquiring an estate left him by the Duke of Buckingham who had placed him, he claims, as a child, under the wardship of Sir Balthazar. The petition is dated "Venice, May 17, 1661."

32. Giavarina witnessed the coronation, *Entertainment*, p. 175.

33. Gerbier, *The None-such Charles his Character* (1651), passim.

34. Ogilby's petition of March, 1661, *C.S.P. Dom.* (1660–61), p. 553. *The Relation* (sig. A1) prints the king's grant of copyright to Ogilby.

35. *Medallic Illustrations of the History of Great Britain and Ireland*, ed. E. Hawkins, A. W. Franks, and H. Grueber (1969 ed.), 1: 460.

36. Respectively, the notes of Edward Barlow, cabin boy (*Barlow's Journal*, ed. Basil Lubbock [1934], 1: 43), and Edward Montagu, First Earl of Sandwich and Admiral of the Fleet, both on the "Charles." (*Journal*, ed. R. C. Anderson [1929], p. 78).

37. *Englands Joy or a Relation of the Most Remarkable passages, from his Majesties Arrivall at Dover, to His Entrance at Whitehall* (1660), pp. 4–5.

38. "Ode Upon his Majesties Restoration and Return" (May 31, 1660), in *The English Writing of Abraham Cowley*, ed. A. R. Waller (Cambridge, 1905), p. 421. All references to Cowley are from this edition.

39. 12 Car. 11 c. 14.

40. Sir Edward Walker, the Garter's enigmatic phrase in *A circumstantial account for the preparations for the Coronation of His Majesty King Charles II* (first published 1820), p. 28.

41. *A Perfect catalogue of all the Knights of the most noble order of the Garter ... by J. N.*, sig. A2^r.

42. *The Continuation of the Life* (Oxford, 1759), p. 99. During the interregnum the traditional coronation regalia had been destroyed.

43. *C.S.P. Venetian* (1660–61), pp. 244, 286.

44. For this cumulative transformation see *The Rump: or an exact collection of the choycest Poems and Songs relating to the late times ...* (1662), passim. (This volume has been studied by H. F. Brooks who provides a title and first line index, identifying many of the authors, in "Rump Songs: An Index with Notes," *Oxford Bibliographical Society, Proceedings and Papers* 5 (1936–39): 281–304). For the "Scarlet Beast" and Monck rescuing the Virgin, see respectively *The Key of Prophecie* (January 28, 1660), and *A Panegyrick* (May 22, 1660), by Richard Farrar.

45. R. C. Strong, "Queen Elizabeth I and the Order of the Garter," *The Archaeological Journal* 119 (1964): 264.

46. *A Poem upon his Majesties Coronation* (April 23, 1661), p. 3.

47. In the 1620s Gerbier had supervised the casting of Le Sueur's equestrian statue of Charles I and after the regicide had purchased both the Titian and Van Dyck formerly in the king's possession (see *Catalogue of British Drawings*, pp. 329–30). Lastly, in his old age, Gerbier recommended the traveller in Rome to "go to the Capitol and there see *Marc Aurelius* on Horse-back" (*Subsidium Peregrinantibus. Or An Assistance to a Traveller* [Oxford, 1665], p. 96). For full discussion see Roy Strong, *Van Dyck, Charles I on Horseback* (1972).

48. *A Perfect Catalogue...* see above, n. 41, and *The History of that most famous Saint and Soldier St. George of Cappadocia* (April 19, 1661).

49. Walter George Bell's *Unknown London* (1920), pp. 168–69, recounts two stories associated with this notorious statue's uncertain provenance.

50. *An Hymn to be sung in the procession at St. George's Feast instead of the Letany; Composed by an order of the Sovereign* (April 17, 1661).

51. *C.S.P. Dom.* (1660–61), p. 606.

52. "*The Entertainment* of Charles II," p. 23.

53. *C.S.P. Dom.* (1661–62), p. 350.

54. *P.R.O. State Papers Domestic* 29, v. 34. (Listed in the *Calendar* [1660–61], p. 571.)

55. Fredson Bowers, p. 353.

56. *Elias Ashmole (1617–1692)*, (1966 ed.), 3: 823, n.5.

57. *Diary*, ed. H. B. Wheatley (1904), 2: 22 (see n. 2. where Wheatley gives White Kennet's relation of the incident).

58. *C.S.P. Venetian* (1659–61), p. 286.

59. Ed. cit., 2: 16.

60. Ibid.

61. *The Diary of The Rev. Ralph Josselin. 1616–1683*, ed. E. Hockliffe, Camden 3rd ser. vol. 15 (1908), p. 138.

62. Halfpenny, p. 34.

63. *A Detection of the Court and State of England during the Four last Reigns* (1694), 2: 103. Coke conflates the festivities for Charles's May entry with those for his coronation.

64. "A Treatise of Taxes and Contributions" (1662), in *The Economic Writings of Sir William Petty*, ed. C. H. Hull (Cambridge, 1899), 1: 33.

65. William Smith to John Langley (April 13, 1661, Drury Lane), *Royal Commission on Historical Manuscripts* (1876), 5th Report, p. 175, fol. 101.

66. The Thomason copy is dated April 19th, 1661.

67. Loc. cit., n. 61.

68. *A True Discovery of a bloody Plot contrived by the Phanaticks* (April 17, 1661).

69. Op. cit. Smith's earlier observation is pertinent to his expectations: "The Presbyterians would not yet be quiet if they durst stir, nor are they content, though they have the best offices in Court and City, while we poor Cavaliers are ready still to starve" (August 18, 1660, p. 174).

70. I have desisted from giving page references in the following exposition of the first arch unless a point is controversial, as this would disrupt any continuity, the reader having to turn from the introduction to Ogilby's text, then to Loggan's engraving, and finally back to the introduction. Ogilby's practice is to distinguish his description of the arches as distinct from his account of the sources, by insetting his italicized narration enclosing every line with inverted commas.

71. William Davenant's *Salmacida Spolia* (1640) is perhaps the best example; Allardyce Nicoll, *Stuart Masques and the Renaissance Stage* (1937), pp. 117–26. For a survey of the "Monarch as Masquer" primarily in the Tudor period, see Stephen Orgel, *The Jonsonian Masque* (Cambridge, Mass., 1965), pp. 19–36.

72. The following context of the inscription (*Aeneid* 11. 425–27) is taken from the 1661 *Relation* (p. 4) which, infrequently, has passages which were left out of the expanded 1662 edition. Where line references to Virgil are given, the edition used is that of Teubner (Leipzig, 1881).

73. *The Entertainment*, p. 21. This quotation is not from Horace. I have been unable to trace it.

74. *Aeneid* 6. 624.

75. Sir Winston Churchill has this parallel of the Caesars in mind in his *Divi Britannici* (1675), "begun when every Body thought that Monarch had ended, and would have been buried in the same grave with [Charles's] Martyr'd Father" [sig. A1ᵛ], when he asked "what have we more to wish, but that you may prove as like the second, as he was to the first Caesar, Et ut Nomine SECUNDUS, sic Majestate AUGUSTUS ..." [sigs. A2ʳ⁻ᵛ].

76. Thus from your Royal Oke, like *Jove's* of old,
  Are answers sought, and destinies fore-told:
  Propitious Oracles are beg'd with vows,
  And Crowns that grow upon the sacred boughs.   (lines 129–32)

See *The Works of John Dryden* ed. E. N. Hooker and H. T. Swedenberg, Jr. (Berkeley and Los Angeles, 1956), 1: 36, 234–41.

77. The crucial passage is, *hic quibus invisi fratres ... omnia peonarum percurrere nomina possim* (6. 608–27), containing two of Ogilby's inscriptions:

  "discite justitiam moniti et non temnere divos."
  vendidit hic auro patrium dominumque potentum
  imposuit, fixit leges pretio atque refixit;
  hic thalamum invasit natae vetitosque hymenaeos;
  ausi omnes immane nefas ausoque potiti.   (lines 620–24)

78. "The Covenant has been burnt by the public executioner, to the satisfaction of all good people, and even of many of its former partisans," in *C.S.P. Dom.* (1660–61), p. 595. Secretary Nicholas to Sir William Curtis, from Whitehall, May 24.

79. *Diary*, ed. E. S. de Beer (Oxford, 1955), 3: 276.

80. Émile Mâle, *The Gothic Image* (1961) pp. 365–83.

81. *Augustus, or, An Essay of those Meanes and Counsels, whereby the Commonwealth of Rome was altered, and reduced unto a Monarchy* (1632), p. 3.

82. Dryden's phrase, *Aeneid* 6. 1079, vol. 3, line 1229. *The Poems of John Dryden*, ed. James Kinsley (Oxford, 1958).

83. "The Restoration and the Eighteenth Century," *A Literary History of England*, ed. A. C. Baugh (1948), p. 699. For the general cultural application of Augustanism see Howard Erskine-Hill, "Augustans on Augustanism: England, 1655–1759," *Renaissance and Modern Studies* 11 (1967): 55–83.

84. See Paul Fussell, *The Rhetorical World of Augustan Humanism* (Oxford, 1965), chap. 8, "The City of Life and the City of Literature," particularly p. 189. A valuable contribution to the study of rhetoric and culture is James D. Garrison's *Dryden and the Tradition of Panegyric* (Berkeley and Los Angeles, 1975).

85. "Renaissance and Golden Age," *Journal of the Warburg and Courtauld Institutes* 24 (1961): 307.

86. "Ode," ed. cit., n. 38, p. 428.

87. *St. George's day Sacred to the Coronation* (April 1660), p. 1.

88. H. A. Grueber's editorial comment on pl. 43, *Medallic Illustrations of The History of Great Britain and Ireland* (1911).

89. James Heath, *The Glories and Magnificent Triumphs of the Blessed Restitution of His Sacred Majesty ...* (1662), p. 132.

90. *Aeneas his descent into Hell ... Together with an ample and learned comment apon the same* (December 30, 1660).

91. Ibid., pp. 22, 121–22.

92. *The Works of Publius Virgilius Maro*, p. 142.

93. Ibid., p. 353.

94. Ogilby reprinted the key terms under discussion here, but there are some slight stylistic differences between the two editions: for example, the 1649 "all dar'd bold crimes" has been altered to "All dar'd strange crimes," indicating conscious deliberation in the choice of "Monarchy" and "prerogatives" rather than merely incidental repetition.

95. Op. cit., n. 90, p. 23.

96. Ibid.

97. Op. cit., n. 90, p. 124, n. 62.

98. *The Entertainment*, p. 27.

99. *Astraea Redux* (June 19, 1660), *Exultationis Carmen* (August 20, 1660). See H. T. Swedenberg, "England's Joy: *Astraea Redux* in its Setting," *SP* 50 (1953): 30–44.

100. *Interest will not Lie. Or, a View of England's True Interest*.

101. Add. MS. 711 (Cambridge University Library), fol. 127.

102. The stage directions, *Part of the Scene disappears, and the four Triumphal Arches, erected on his Majesty's Coronation, are seen*, follow the lines of Augusta and Thamesis: "... The royal squadron marches, / Erect triumphal arches, / For Albion and Albanius." See *The Works of John Dryden*, ed. cit., (1976) 15: 29, 273. *Discite justitiam moniti, et non temnere divos* also appears "Over the King, in a scroll" in Dryden's explanation of the theatre frontispiece.

103. After the trials arising out of the Popish Plot a tract appeared entitled *The Triumphs of Justice over unjust judges* (1681), with the epigraph *Discite justitiam moniti, et non temnere Leges*. The following year a Whig poem was published, obviously aligning itself with the Titans, entitled *TITANTOMAXIA, or a full and true Relation of the Great and Bloody Fight between three Pagan Knights and a Christian Giant*.

104. "A Panegyrick to the King," in *Poems* (June, 1660), p. 7.

105. "A Panegyrick to the King," p. 9.

106. Arthur Brett, *The Restauration* (June 5, 1660), p. 16.

107. Ed. cit., n. 38, p. 428.

108. Thomas Higgons, *A Panegyrick to the King* (June 10, 1660), p. 5.

109. *Upon the joyful and welcome return ...* (May 29, 1660), pp. 6–8.

110. *Timaeus*, 39, in *The Dialogues of Plato*, trans. B. Jowett (Oxford, 1875), 3: 621–22.

111. Ed. Ferdinand Tonnies (1889), p. 204. For discussion of this important topic see V. F. Snow, "The

Concept of Revolution in Seventeenth Century England," *The Historical Journal* 5, no. 2 (1962) pp. 167–74, and Perez Zagorin, *The Court and the Country* (1969), introduction, pp. 1–18.

112. *A Panegyric to Charles II*, ed. Geoffrey Keynes, Augustan Reprint Society, no. 28 (1951), p. 4.

113. *St. George's day Sacred to the Coronation* (April, 1660), p. 1.

114. *Postliminia Caroli II. The Palingenesy, or Second Birth of Charles II to his Kingly Life* (June 8, 1660).

115. "Ode," ed. cit., n. 38, p. 420.

116. In his *Glories and Magnificent Triumphs* (ed. cit.) for his account of the cavalcade (pp. 186–89), Heath Draws on Ogilby's *Relation*.

117. *Augustus*, ed. cit., p. 21.

118. *Panegyrick*, ed. cit., p. 7.

119. *Cosmographie in four bookes*, 1652. "To the Reader," sig. A4^v.

120. Ed. cit., n. 112, p. 6.

121. *To the king*, p. 5. For an illuminating overview of the topic see Michael McKeon, *Politics and Poetry in Restoration England* (Cambridge, Massachusetts, 1975), pt. 2, "Eschatological Prophecy."

122. *A Congratulatory Poem*, p. 18.

123. *The Restauration. Or, a Poem on the return of Charles the II to his kingdoms*, pp. 11, 21.

124. See Harold Mattingly, "Virgil's Fourth Eclogue," *Journal of the Warburg and Courtauld Institutes* 10 (1947): 14–19.

125. E. Cobham Brewer, *Dictionary of Phrase and Fable* (1897), p. 972, for this and other versions of cycle and period in phoenix lore; while for a seventeenth-century classification of phoenix allusion see Sir Thomas Browne, "Of the Phoenix," *Pseudodoxia Epidemica* (Bk. 3, chap. 12, pp. 219–26), in *Works*, ed. Geoffrey Keynes (1926), vol. 2.

126. *Panegyrick*, p. 7.

127. Again, medals were cast bearing the emblems discussed here; for 1660 medals with the images of the phoenix and of St. George killing the dragon, see H. A. Grueber (1911 ed.), pls. 40 and 44, respectively.

128. 1651. After the painting by Abraham Diepenbeeck inscribed *Redivivo Phoenici*, which is reproduced as the frontispiece to A. M. Broadley's *The Royal Miracle* (1912).

129. See Joseph Addison, "Dialogues on Medals," in *Works*, ed. Bishop Hurd (1854), 1: 347.

130. *Panegyrick*, pp. 5–6.

131. *The King's Two Bodies* (Princeton, 1957), p. 388, n. 245.

132. "Queen Elizabeth as Astraea," *Journal of the Warburg and Courtauld Institutes* 10 (1947): 62.

133. *The Fortunate Change* (April 23, 1661), p. 8.

134. *The Ancient Liberty of the Britannick Church*, p. 6.

135. *The Entertainment*, p. 135. For the introduction of this central theme into English political panegyric, see Sydney Anglo, *Spectacle Pageantry, and Early Tudor Policy* (Oxford, 1969), p. 46.

136. *The Entertainment*, p. 165.

137. *The Diary*, p. 138.

138. Loc. cit.

139. *Pompa introitus*, p. 33.

140. "A Prophetic Poem (partly accomplished) to his present Majesty then Prince, 1640," in *Poems* (1663), p. 6.

141. From the dedication to Charles of his translation of Freart's work, *A Parallel of the Ancient Architecture with the Modern*, sig. a3^v.

142. *Pompa introitus*, p. 150.

143. *A Poem upon his Majesties Coronation* (April 23, 1661), p. 9.

144. I have limited documentation on this topic in the following discussion, since full details may be found in T. W. Fulton, *The Sovereignty of the Sea* (Edinburgh and London, 1911); particularly pp. 338–77. Edgar Wind notes that the seal of Charles II shows him as ruler of the sea, *Pagan Mysteries in the Renaissance* (1967), p. 226.

145. *The Freedom of the Seas* (New York, 1916), a translation with a revision of the Latin text of 1633 by Ralph Van Deman Magoffin.

146. *Divi Britannici*, pp. 2–3.

147. *C.S.P. Dom.* (1637–38), pp. 367–68.

148. "The Character of Holland," line 26, *The Poems and Letters of Andrew Marvell,* ed. H. M. Margoliouth (Oxford, 1927), 1: 95–99.

149. *Claudian,* Loeb Classical Library (London and New York), 1: 276–77.

150. Cologne, 1618–22; the couplet is on p. 221.

151. *Corpus Inscriptionem Latinarum* (Berlin, 1873), vol. 3, pt. 1, p. 138.

152. Heidelberg, 1602–3, p. 185, no. 7.

153. 6th ed. (1658), p. 26.

154. Ed. cit., n. 149, pp. 284–85, lines 197–211. See Garrison op. cit. p. 163 for the tradition of the "two-Indies" *topos.*

155. Respectively, Dryden, ed. cit., vol. 2, lines 46–47, 37–38; Virgil ed. cit., lines 31–32.

156. Note the significant alliance of commerce and empire in the title of the volume used to identify these pendants: *The Emperiall achieuement of our dread Soueraigne King Charles together w^t ye Armes Crests Supporters & mottowes of all ye severall Companies & Corporations of ye severall Companies & Corporations of ye famous City of London* (1630?), Harleian MS. 1049 fol. 1.

157. *The Relation* (1661), p. 11. Compare the order of the terms used in *A Speech made to the Lord General Monk at the Clothworkers Hall in London* (March 13th, 1660): "Our truth, our trade, our peace, our wealth, our freedom." Composed by Alexander Brome, this is included in his *Songs and other Poems* (1661), pp. 199–202.

158. *Works* (1665), p. 81.

159. Ibid., p. 85.

160. See the edition translated by George Boas, "The People Obedient to the King" (New York, 1950), p. 84.

161. P. 47: "inde gemini LEONES, vt Vigiles & Custodes adstant. Horus Apollo lib. 1. de Hieroglyphicis Aegyptiorum Notis."

162. Augsburg, 1531. Sig. C3^v "Ex Bello Pax." Geffrey Whitney included this in his *Choice of Emblems* (Leyden, 1586), p. 138; the emblem of the hive as a commonwealth is also borrowed by Whitney (p. 200); cf. Shakespeare, *Henry V* 1. 2. 183–89, and John Day's 1641 masque *The Parliament of Bees,* in *Works,* ed. A. H. Bullen (1881). For the post-Renaissance fortunes of the bee, J. W. Johnson, "That Neo-Classical Bee," *Journal of the History of Ideas* 22 (1961): 262–66.

163. "soft-handed Peace so sweetly thrives / That bees in souldiers' helmets built their hives." *The Magnificent Entertainment* (1604), sig. B (with contributions by Thomas Middleton). Dekker does not record *Ben Jonson: His part of King James his Royall and Magnificent Entertainment* ... (1604). Both are included in vol. 1 of John Nichols's *The Progresses, Processions and Magnificent Festivities of King James the First* ... (1828). These with Stephen Harrison, *The Archs of Triumph* (1604), constitute the main documents for James's entry.

164. Reproduced by Charles Welch, *History of the Monument* (1893), p. 27.

165. Thomas Jordan, *Londons Glory* (1680), p. 5., where "Industry" bears "in one hand a Shield Vert, Charges with a Bee-hive, and a Swarm."

166. "The Hive declares the *Industry* of the *Bees,* which, being very inconsiderable, are nevertheless, *great* as to their conduct" (p. 7, fig. 27, Artificio-Artifice). Though the 1611 Padua edition does not include this Artifice emblem, it is found in the 1636 Paris and 1644 Amsterdam editions, pp. 28 and 259, respectively.

167. *The Sermons of John Donne* ed. George R. Potter and Evelyn M. Simpson (Berkeley and Los Angeles, 1959), 4: 246.

168. *Upon the Blessed Restoration* (June 6th).

169. *A Mixt Poem, Partly Historicall, Partly Panegyrical, upon the Happy Return* ... (1660), p. 13. On February 21st the members secluded since the Long Parliament of 1648 were readmitted by General Monk, a prelude to the restoration of the king who was proclaimed on May 8th after the deliberations of the Convention Parliament which met on April 25; Godfrey Davies, *The Restoration of Charles II* (San Marino, 1955), pp. 286–89.

170. Ibid., p. 15.

171. *Festa Georgiana or the gentries and countries joy for the Coronation* (April 19, 1661).

172. *Speculum Speculativum* (1660), p. 52.

173. J. M. Evans, *Paradise Lost and the Genesis Tradition* (Oxford, 1968), p. 114.

174. From a vast number of panegyrics I select just one which contains examples of most of these figures: *Britains Triumph for her Unparallel'd Deliverance* by "G. S.," (May 14, 1660). To see how this mode of thought permeated many forms of discourse, compare the language of *A Letter from his Majesty King Charles II to His Peers* (March 20, 1660), *The King's Declaration to all his loving Subjects* (March 30, 1660), and Clarendon's speech at the dissolution of the Convention Parliament on December 24, 1660, in Cobbett's *Parliamentary History* (1808) vol. 4, col. 176.

175. Thomas Forde, "Upon His Sacred Majesties most happy return," in *Fragmenta Poetica*, p. 22.

176. See Abraham Jenings, *Miraculum Basilicon: or the Royal Miracle* (1664), sigs. C 2^{r-v}.

177. See sigs. a2^r–a3^r.

178. *To the King* (June 3, 1660), p. 3.

179. That this idea prevailed in the seventeenth century can be seen in the sermon of John Donne (see above n. 169): "So God hath made us, a little World of our own, This *Iland*; He hath given us *Heaven* and *Earth*, The truth of his Gospel, which is our earnest of Heaven, and the abundance of the Earth, a fruitfull Land; but then he [James I], who is the Spirit of the Lord, he who is the breath of our nostrils, *Incubat aquis*, (as it is said there in the Creation) he moves upon *the waters*, by his royall and warlike *Navy at Sea* ..." (p. 251). This notion of sacrosanct kingship was repeated by Winston Churchill in the Restoration period in his consideration of British kings "being ... more properly like Gods (as *Holy Writ* stiles Kings in general) then any other Princes whatever: For that they do *Incubare Aquis* (as a Divine of great Eloquence has express'd it). Move upon the Waters with such mighty Fleets as seem to give Laws to that indomitable element itself" (*Divi Britannici*, p. 12). Donne is cited in the margin.

180. H. F. Bouchery, "Des Arcs Triomphaux aux Frontispices de Livres." *Les Fêtes de la Renaissance*, ed. Jean Jacquot (Royaumont, 1955), 2: 431–42; G. R. Kernodle, *From Art to Theatre* (Chicago, 1944), pp. 44, 102; Otto Benesch, *Artistic and Intellectual Trends from Rubens to Daumier. As Shown in Book Illustration* (Cambridge, Mass., 1943), p. 13; and Michael Drayton's poem "Upon the Frontispice" which explicitly connects the architectural frontispiece with that of a book frontispiece, in *Works*, ed. J. William Hebel (Oxford, 1933), vol. 4.

181. As B. Rajan testifies for Du Bartas (*Paradise Lost and the Seventeenth Century Reader* [1947], p. 17) and John Locke, for Heylin, "To the reading of history, chronology and geography are absolutely necessary. In geography, we have two general ones in English, Heylin and Moll": *Some thoughts concerning reading and discovery for a Gentleman, Works*, 11th ed., (1812), 3: 273.

182. Loc. cit., n. 178.

183. "De Splendore," *I Trattati delle Virtù Sociali*, ed. Francesco Tateo (Rome, 1965), p. 134. "Letter of Instructions to Prince Charles for His Studies, Conduct, and Behaviour," *Original Letters*, ed. Sir Henry Ellis, 1st ser. 3 (1824): 288–91. I am indebted to Roy Strong for this reference.

184. See Erskine-Hill, pp. 123–32 and Grahame Parry, *The Golden Age restor'd* (Manchester, 1981), pp. 1–21.

185. Parry, p. 56.

186. In large part Roy Strong's *Art and Power* (Woodbridge, Suffolk, 1984) is devoted to these topics in the absorbing survey indicated by the subtitle "*Renaissance Festivals 1450–1650.*" I am particularly indebted to the discussion of "The Idea of Monarchy," pp. 65–74.

187. *The History of England* (1744), 1: 9.

188. *Mirabilis Annus Secundus; Or, The Second Year of Prodigies* (1662), p. 59.

189. Rep. 68, fols, 120, 155 (cited in Withington, *English Pageantry*, p. 247) and Halfpenny, p. 34.

190. John Tatham, *Neptunes address to his most sacred Majesty Charles II* (1661).

191. *Diary*, ed. cit., 3: 246.

192. See Lord Mordaunt's letter to Evelyn, dated April 23, 1661, in *Diary and Correspondence of John Evelyn F.R.S.* (Bohn's Historical Library, 1859), 3: 132.

193. *The Cities Loyalty display'd* (April 19, 1661), p. 5.

Index of Sources

Below are listed the names Ogilby refers to in the *Entertainment*. Where a name cited is not generally used now, it is bracketed, following the accepted usage. Caution shoud be exercised in assuming Ogilby's firsthand knowledge of all his sources—see the introduction, pp. 12-13, concerning his borrowing from Gevaerts.

Aelianus, Claudius ('Aelian'), 43.
Aeschylus, 30, 92, 98, 116.
Ahmad Ibn Sirin ('Achmet'), 115.
Alcaeus, 17.
Anacreon, 130, 132, 147-48.
Antigonus, 125.
Apollonius, Levinus, 91.
Apollonius of Rhodes, 29-30.
Appian, 6, 10, 119, 129.
Apuleius, 98.
Aristophanes, 54, 79, 120.
Artemidorus, 115.
Asconius Pedianus, Quintus, 3.
Athenaeus, 147.
Augustinus, Antonius ('Augustin'), 143.
Aulus Gellius, 57.

Baronius, Caesar, 21, 162.

Callimachus, 95, 153.
Catullus, 90.
Cicero, 20, 153.
Claudian, 3-6, 9, 12, 13-14, 20, 23-24, 32, 34-35, 39, 44-48, 52, 67-68, 77-78, 79, 81-82, 83-84, 86, 87, 90, 91-92, 121, 128-29, 131, 148, 150-51, 152, 154, 160, 161, 163-64.
Cornutus, Lucius Aeneas, 44, 52.

De Acosta, Joseph ('Acosta'), 91.
De Croy, Charles, Duke of Aerschot ('Croyiac'), 20, 21, 46, 89.
Diodorus Siculus, 92-93, 115.
Dion Cassius, 25, 26, 119, 125, 129, 147, 161-62.
Dionysius Halicarnassensis, 2, 51.
Drayton, Michael, 49-50, 59-65.
Du Choul, Guillaume ('Choul'), 19, 26, 94.

Erythraeus, 29.
Euripides, 71.
Eusebius, 17-18, 51, 71, 120, 153.
Eutropius, 18.

Festus, Sextus Pompeius, 81, 94, 158.
Florus, Publius Annius, 24.
Fulgentius, 150.

Gevaerts, Jean Gaspard ('Gevart'), 46.
Goltz, Hubert, 94, 118, 119, 128, 143, 147.
Gruterus, Janus ('Gruter'), 27, 36, 113.

Helvicus, 121.
Herodian, 34.
Herodotus, 71.
Hesiod, 29, 123-24.
Hoelus Dha, 52.
Homer, 16, 54, 78, 92, 117, 122-23, 132.
Horace, 12, 20, 21, 44, 81, 120, 145, 146, 150.
Hulsius, Levinus, 56.

Iraeneus, 97.
Isidore of Seville (Isidorus Hispalensis), 20.

Josephus, 71.
Juvenal, 11, 83, 97, 111.

Lactantius, 17, 120, 156.
Lampridius, Aelius, 83.
Lipsius, 127.
Livy, 2, 7, 8, 25, 87, 141, 142.
Lucan, 19-20, 35, 86, 88, 128.
Lucretius, 163, 164.
Lycophron, 71.

Macrobius, 79, 144.
Manasses, Constantinus, 19.

Mancinus, C. Hostilius, 117.
Manilius, 70–71.
Marcellinus, Ammianus, 17.
Martial, 88–89, 121, 151–52, 157.
Martianus Capella, 100–1.
Meibomius, 98.
Moschus, 70, 72–77, 96.

Nemesianus, Marcus Aurelius Olympius, 150.
Nicharchus, 97.
Nicephorus, 115.
Nicetas, 19.
Nonius Marcellus, 93–94.
Nonnus, 96.
Nymphodorus, 125.

Occo, 120, 125.
Oppian, 132–33.
Ovid, 7, 9, 10, 26, 32, 37–38, 44, 46, 47, 54, 57–58, 94, 95, 99–100, 104–7, 112, 129, 140, 144, 145, 146, 149, 151, 153, 155, 156–57, 158, 159, 162–63.

Pacatus Drepanius, Latinus, 18.
Paeanius, 18.
Palaephatus, 115.
Palladas, 132.
Panvinius, Onuphrius, 157.
Pausanius, 17, 53, 54, 56, 87, 91, 92, 120, 124, 125, 144, 146, 148–49, 150, 155, 159.
Petronius Arbiter, 14, 81, 82.
Philostratus, 42, 146, 164.
Peirius, 21, 120.
Pighius, 3, 119.
Pindar, 16, 44, 94.
Pisander Camirensis, 17.
Piso, Lucius, 141.
Plato, 98.
Pliny, 2, 3, 7, 24–25, 39, 42, 57, 79, 82, 83, 87, 90, 98, 126.
Plutarch, 2, 6, 8, 9, 11, 12, 37, 95, 98, 116, 120, 130, 141.
Pollux, Julius, 79.
Porphyry, 153.
Probus, Marcus Valerius, 44.
Proclus, 94.
Propertius, 10.
Prudentius, 6, 85.

Quintilian, 21, 98.

Richerius, Ludovicus Coelius ('Rhodiginus'), 29.
Ross, Thomas, 8, 10, 59, 70, 118, 127.

Rutilius Namatianus, 30.

Salvian, 84.
Sandys, George, 38, 54–56, 57, 100.
Selden, John, 52, 71, 86, 88, 89.
Seneca, 19, 32, 71, 164.
Servius, 9, 79, 152, 160.
Sidonius Apollinaris, 17, 18, 56, 68–69, 80, 81.
Silius Italicus, 8, 9–10, 58–59, 70, 88, 90, 114, 117–18, 126–27.
Sigonius, 3.
Simonides, 17.
Spartianus, Aelius, 32, 33.
Stanley, Thomas, 72–77, 131.
Statius, 6, 15–16, 22–23, 86–87, 93, 145, 155.
Stobaeus, 25.
Strabo, 17, 57, 88, 99.
Suetonius, 26.
Suidas, 115, 162.

Tacitus, 13, 24.
Tertullian, 17.
Themistocles, 37.
Theocritus, 153.
Tibullus, 144, 146, 153.
Trebellius, 10, 18.

Ulpian, 144.

Valerius Flaccus, 87.
Valerius Maximus, 3, 4, 52, 117, 157.
Valla, Lorenzo, 71.
Varro, 89, 141, 157.
Virgil, 2, 8, 10–11, 15, 17, 22, 27–28, 29, 37, 43–44, 46, 47, 66–67, 69, 71–72, 78, 79, 87, 92, 93, 94–96, 114, 115–16, 124, 128, 141–42, 147, 149, 152, 159, 160.
Vitruvius, 25.
Vopiscus, 18.

The
Facsimile

Bibliographical Note

This facsimile is reproduced, with permission, from the Huntington Library copy, RB 141718. The page or trim size of the original is 11 x 17½ inches; the print area is approximately 8 x 13. The engravings of the first, third, and fourth arch are 12 inches wide, however, while the engraving of the second arch is 19 x 12; these engravings are folded to fit the normal page size. In this facsimile, the arches have been photographed at a reduction ratio slightly different from that of the text.

This copy contains errors in pagination: 84 is printed as *48*; 168–69 are misnumbered *170–71*. There are also minor discrepancies between the Huntington copy and other copies. The British Library copy (N Tab 2024/24 [formerly 603.1.34]) has a frontispiece not found in the Huntington, while the Huntington's engraving of Catherine Regina (after p. 192) is missing from the BL copy; the engraving of Charles's coronation, between 170 and 171 here and in the Society of Antiquaries copy, is found between pp. 165 and 166 in the BL copy.

For fuller bibliographical description, see Fredson Bowers, "Ogilby's Coronation *Entertainment* (1661–1689): Editions and Issues," *Papers of the Bibliographical Society of America* 47 (1953): 339–55.

THE ENTERTAINMENT OF

His Most Excellent MAJESTIE

CHARLES II,

IN

His PASSAGE through the CITY of

LONDON

TO HIS

CORONATION:

Containing an exact Accompt of the whole *Solemnity*; the Triumphal *Arches*, and *Cavalcade*, delineated in *Sculpture*; the *Speeches* and *Impresses* illustrated from *Antiquity*.

TO THESE IS ADDED,

A Brief Narrative of His MAJESTIE's Solemn CORONATION:

WITH

His Magnificent PROCEEDING, and ROYAL FEAST

IN

VVESTMINSTER-HALL.

By *JOHN OGILBY.*

LONDON,

Printed by THO: ROYCROFT, and are to be had at the Authors House in *Kings-Head* Court within *Shoe-Lane*, MDCLXII.

I Have perused a brief Narrative of His MAJESTIES Solemn CO-RONATION, printed by Mr. OGILBY, together with his Description of His MAJESTIES Entertainment passing through the City of LONDON to His Coronation, &c. and, in pursuance of His MAJESTIES Order unto me directed, have examined, and do approve thereof; so as the said Mr. OGILBY may freely publish the same.

From the HERALDS-
COLLEDG this thirteenth
of June, 1662.

EDVVARD WALKER,
Garter Principal King
of Arms.

TO THE
SACRED MAJESTY
OF
CHARLES II,

King of *ENGLAND, SCOTLAND, FRANCE,*
and *IRELAND,* &c.

This DESCRIPTION of the SOLEMNITY of His
Blessed INAUGURATION

Is humbly Dedicated

By

His most Obedient, Dutiful, and

Loyal Servant,

J. OGILBY.

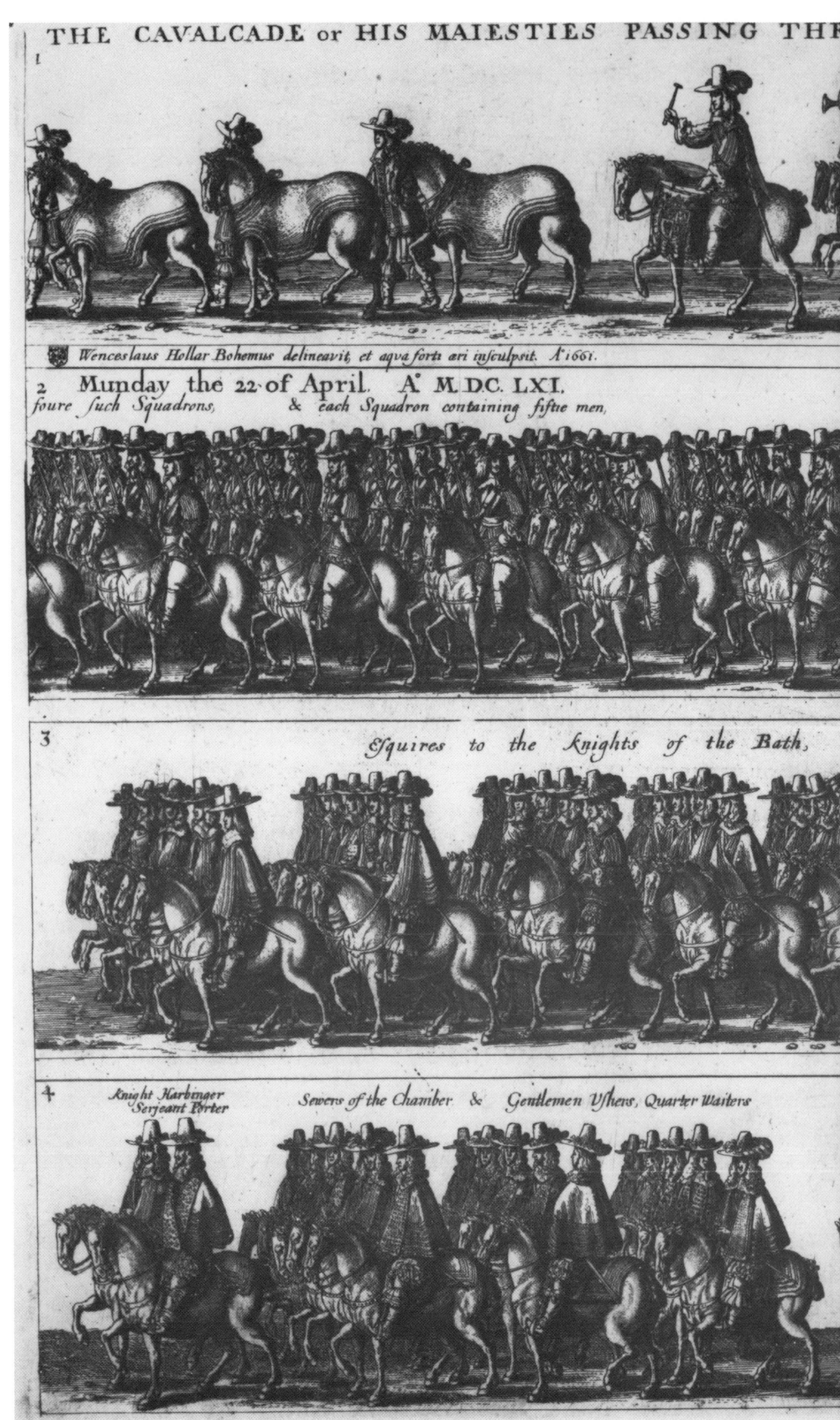

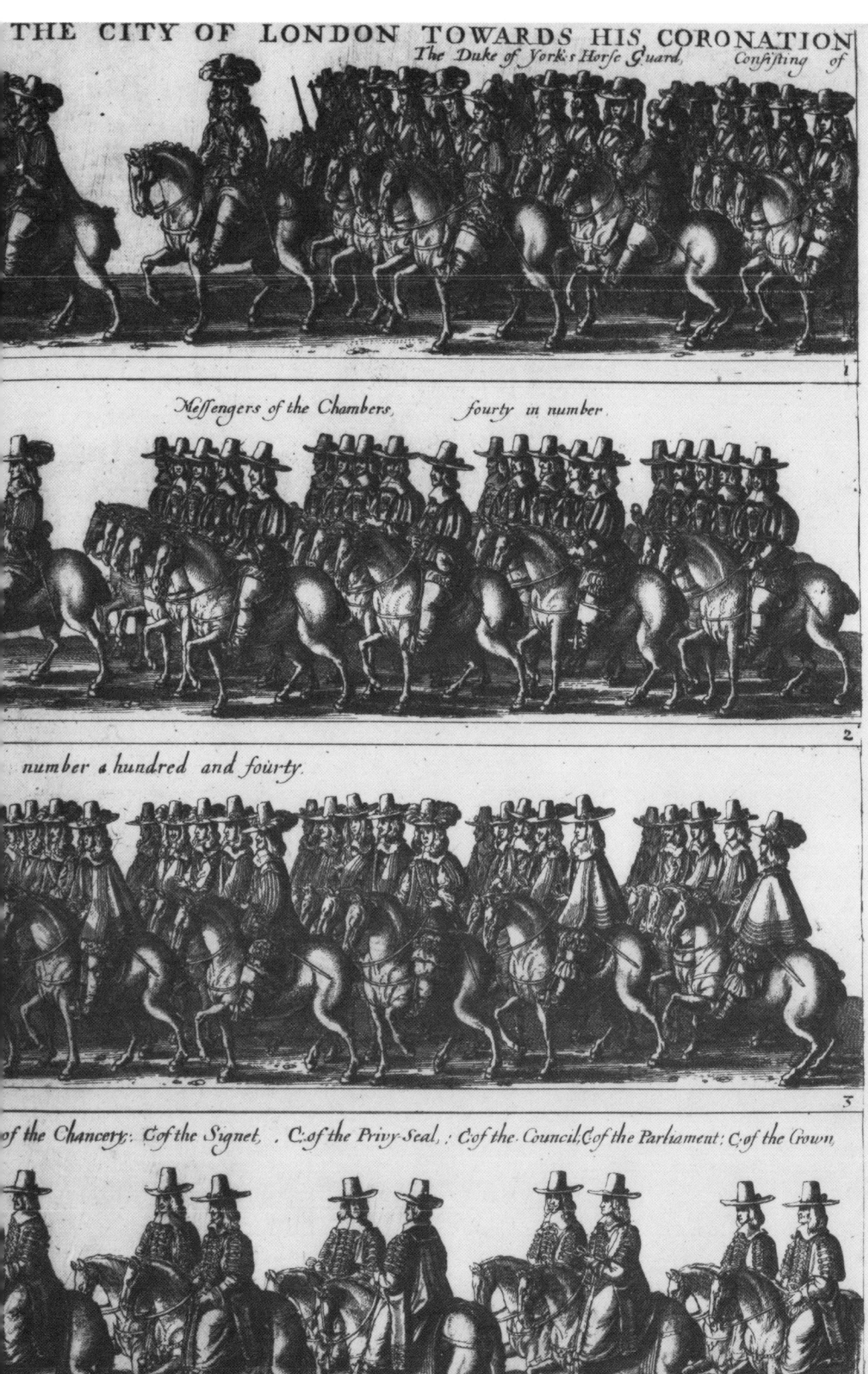

THE CITY OF LONDON TOWARDS HIS CORONATION
The Duke of York's Horse Guard, Consisting of

Messengers of the Chambers, fourty in number.

number a hundred and fourty.

of the Chancery: C: of the Signet, . C: of the Privy Seal, : C: of the Council, C: of the Parliament: C: of the Crown,

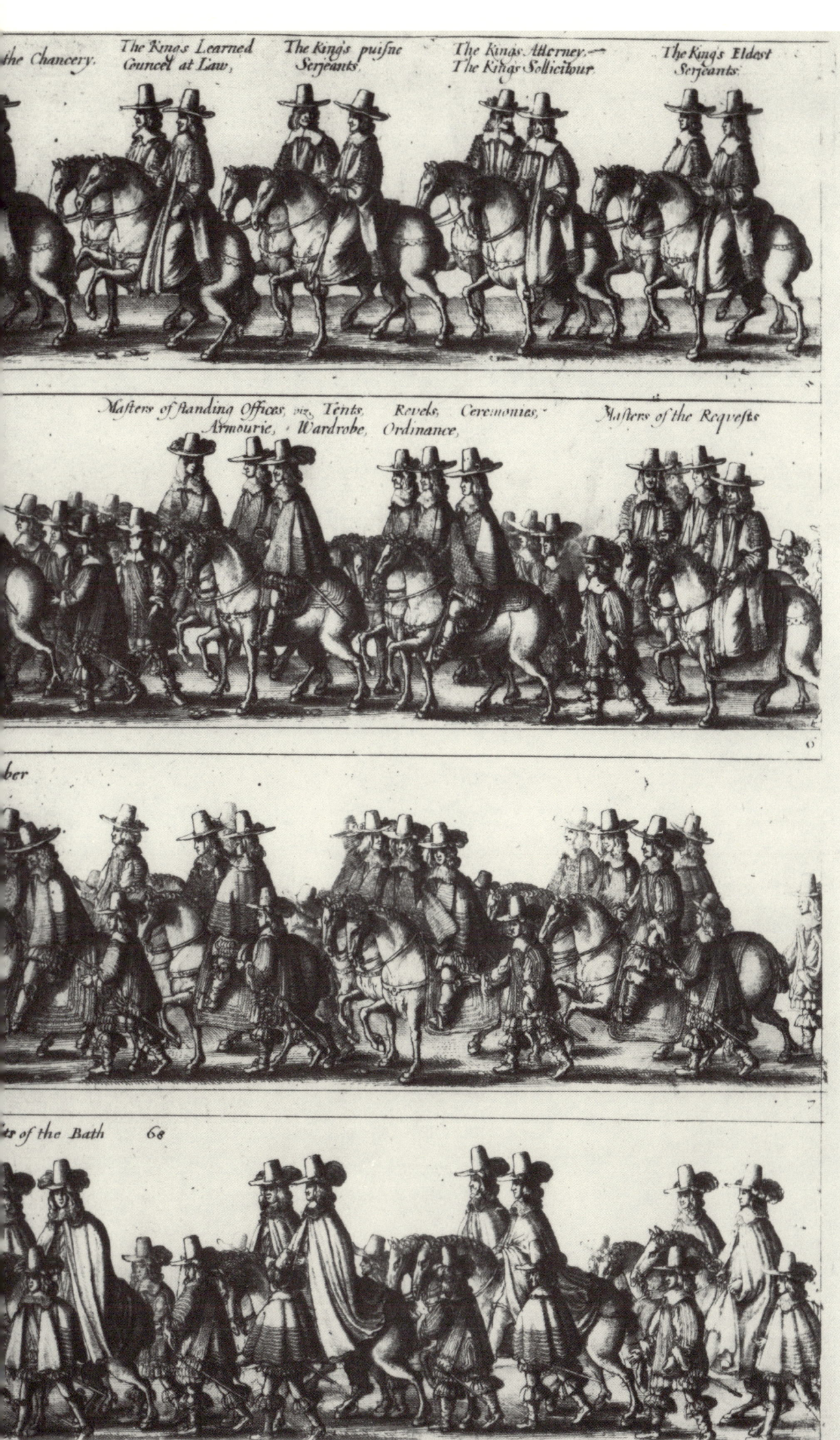

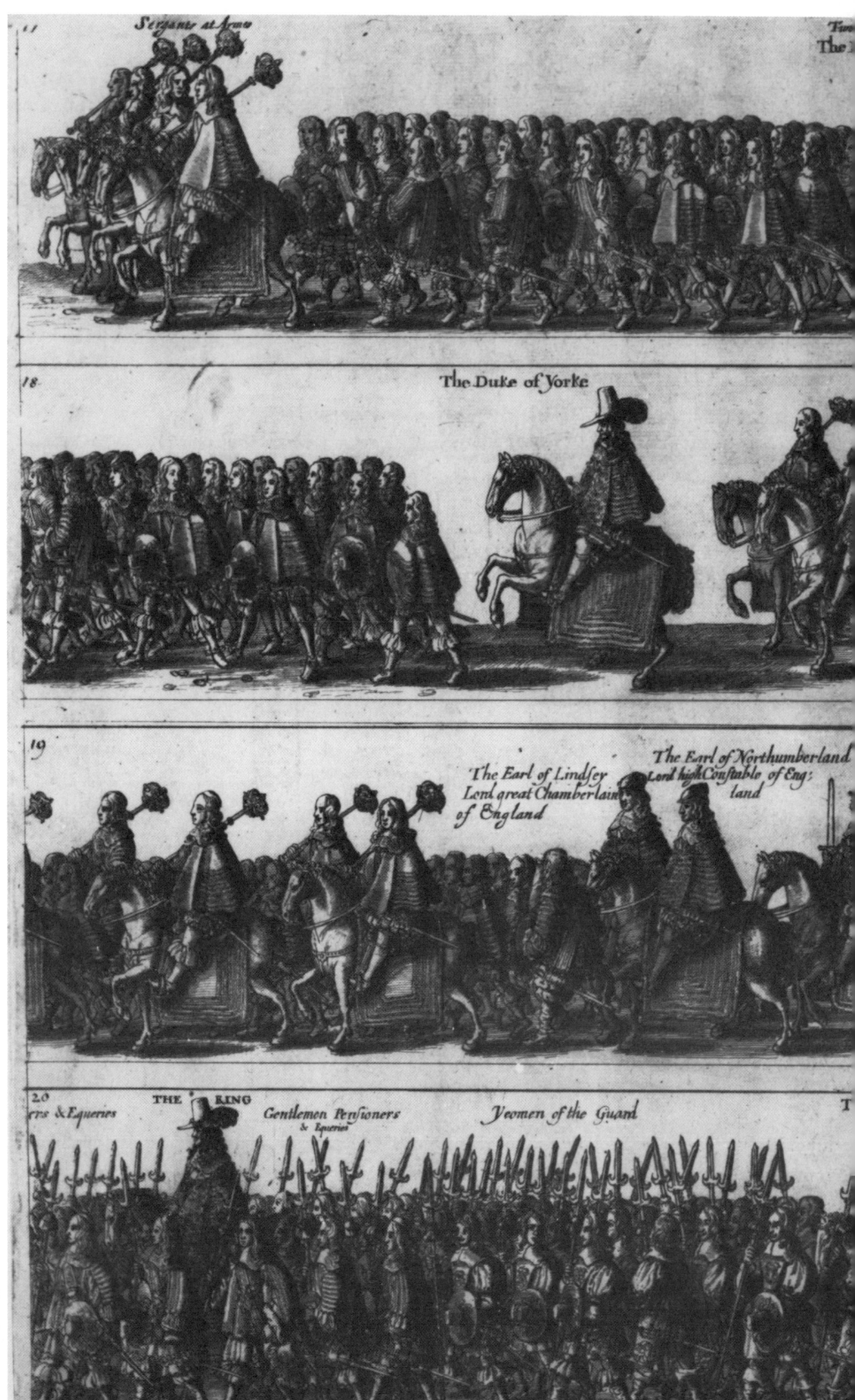

His MAJESTIES ENTERTAINMENTS

Passing through the City of

LONDON

TO HIS

CORONATION;

WITH

A Description of the Triumphal ARCHES, and SOLEMNITY.

THE City of *LONDON*, participating the greatest share of that inexpressible Happiness, which these Kingdoms have received by the glorious Restauration of our Sovereign to His Throne, and of us His Subjects to our Laws, Liberties, and Religion, after a dismal Night of Usurpation, and Oppression, and proportionably exceeding in their Loyalty, took the occasion of His *MAJESTIES* Coronation, to express their Joy with the greatest Magnificence imaginable: imitating therein the antient *Romanes*, who, at the return of their Emperours, erected *Arches* of Marble, which though we, by reason of the shortness of Time, could not

equal in Materials, yet do ours far exceed theirs in Number, and stupendious Proportions.

THE Custom of erecting *Triumphal Arches* among the *Romans* (a thing altogether unknown to the *Græcians*, till their acquaintance with them) most certainly was not coæval with their *Triumphs*, which were within four years as long-liv'd as *Rome* it self. For among the *Greek*, and *Latin* Authours of the *Roman* History, who have been so accurate in enumerating all their Solemnities, especially which concerned their Splendour, and Magnificence, we find not any mention of them till the time of the *Roman Emperours*. Indeed of *Triumphs*, as of all other things, the Beginnings seem to have been but rude. At first nothing more then the Spoils hung up at the house of the Conquerour.

Æneid. l. VII.   *Virgil*, speaking of the Palace of King *Picus*,

> *Multáque prætereà sacris in postibus arma,*
> *Captivi pendent currus, curvæque secures,*
> *Et Cristæ capitum, & portarum ingentia claustra,*
> *Spiculáque, clypeíque, ereptáque rostra carinis.*

> " Besides, on sacred Pillars all along,
> " A World of Arms, Axes, and Chariots hung,
> " Crests, and huge Bars of Gates the Ports adorn,
> " And Spears, and Shields, and Prows from Gallies torn.

Lib. I.
Lib. II.
† in Romulo.

This rudeness of the first *Triumphs*, even among the *Romans*, will sufficiently appear, if we compare the *Triumph* of *Romulus*, mention'd by *Livy*, *Dionysius Halicarnassensis*, and † *Plutarch*, with the excessive Pomp, and Magnificence of the latter, of which we shall give an instance in this Discourse. The greatest Monument of which Magnificence, the *Triumphal Arches*, as we have said, was not heard of before *Julius Cæsar*. 'Tis true, there is still retain'd at *Rome* the memory of *Arcus Romuli*, and *Camilli*. But 'tis certain, it appears not whether they were *Triumphal Arches*, or no; and it is very questionable, whether they bear their true Titles. For *Pliny*, who flourish'd in the time of *Vespasian* the Emperour, calls them *novitium inventum*, *a new invention*: whose Authority much out-weighs those empty Titles of *Arcus Romuli*,

Nat. H.
L. XXXVIII.
cap. VI.

and

and *Camilli*, of which there is no ancient Record. Yet, that they were in use before *Julius Cæsar* almost one Century of years, ha's been conjectured out of these words of *Asconius Pedianus*, an Authour, against whom there is no exception, and who liv'd some years before *Pliny*; *Fornix Fabianus, arcus est juxta Regiam in Sacra via. à Fabio Censore constructus, qui, à devictis Allobrogibus, Allobrox cognominatus est, ibique statua ejus posita propterea est:* The *Fabian* Arch is nigh the Palace of *Romulus* in the Sacred way, built by *Fabius* the Censor, who, from his Victory over the *Allobroges*, had the sirname of *Allobrox*; for which his Statue was placed there. That he triumph'd upon this Victory, we have ample testimony from the Marbles not long since digg'd up at *Rome*, formerly preserved in the *Capitol*. Nevertheless, those words of *Asconius* do evidently conclude the contrary: for he says expresly *built by Fabius Censour.* His Censourship is referred by *Sigonius* and *Pighius* to the Year U.C. DCXLV. his Triumph happened *anno* DCXXXIII. as appears from the Marbles now mention'd,

Q. FABIUS Q. ÆMILIANI F. Q. N. AN. DCXXXIII.
MAXIMUS. PROCOS. DE. ALLOBROgibus
ET. REGE. ARVERNORUM. BETULTO. X. K.

Whence it is clear the Arch was built long after his Triumph. And *I* conceive his Statue was plac'd there rather in regard of his expences, then of his Victory so long before obtain'd. Neither is it strange after the space of above seven hundred years, to find this alteration. We may observe many other, but shall onely take notice of two. First, The ancient *Romans* granted not the honour of Triumph to any, who had not slain in one pitch'd Field five thousand of their Enemies. *Jus triumphi datur ei, qui quinque millia hostium unâ acie ceciderit.* Secondly, They allowed not Triumph for a Victory over their Fellow-Citizens; as *Q. Catulus* triumph'd not over *M. Lepidus*, or *L. Antony* over *Catilin*, or *Sylla* over *Marius*, or *Cinna* over *Carbo*, or *Cæsar* over *Pompey*.

Valer Maximus, Lib 11 cap viii.

Claudian,

De vi. Consulatu Honorii.

— *cùm Gallica vulgò*
Prælia jactaret, tacuit Pharsalica Cæsar.
Namq; inter socias acies, cognataq; signa,
Ut vinci miserum, nunquam vicisse decorum.

Of

>   —— Of *Gallick* Fights oft at his Board
>   Boasts *Cæsar*, of *Pharsalia* not a word.
>   Though sad the case to fall in Civil War,
>   Yet 'tis no honour to the Conquerour.

which he means too in these Verses,

De Bello Getico.

> *Semper ab his famæ petiere insignia bellis,*
> *Quæ diversa, procul tuto, trans æquora virtus*
> *Exercere dabat : currus, Regùmque catenæ*
> *Inter abundantis fati ludibria ductæ.*

> They by such Wars sought Fame in Fields remote,
> Beyond Seas Victory by their Valour got:
> Hence Kings in Chains and Chariots march in state,
> 'Mongst various Sports of their abundant Fate.

Ibid.

L.v. Lib. xl.

De civibus triumphare nefas, saith the same *Valerius Maximus*. In both which particulars the *Roman* History affords exceptions. In the first, in the *Triumph without a War, anno Urbis Cond.* DLXXIII. In the second, in the Triumphal Arch, yet almost entirely standing, of *Constantine the Great*, which the Senate, and People of *Rome* dedicated to him upon his Victory over *Maxentius*, a General of part of the Imperial Forces. The Inscription this,

>   IMP. CÆS. FL. CONSTANTINO. MAXIMO
>   P. F. AUGUSTO S. P. Q. R.
>   QUOD. INSTINCTU. DIVINITATIS. MENTIS
>   MAGNITUDINE. CUM. EXERCITU. SUO.
>   TAM. DE. TYRANNO. QUAM DE OMNI EJUS
>   TACTIONE. UNO. TEMPORE. JUSTIS
>   REMPUBLICAM. ULTUS. EST. ARMIS
>   ARCUM. TRIUMPHIS. INSIGNEM. DICAVIT

passing to His CORONATION.

Three *Triumphs*, of the same nature, in one Century of years, are reckoned by *Claudian*, who makes *Rome* to speak thus, _{De vi. Consulatu Honorii.}

> *His annis, qui lustra mihi bis dena recensent,*
> *Nostra ter Augustos intra pomæria vidi,*
> *Temporibus variis: eadem sed causa Tropæis,*
> *Civilis dissensus erat* ———

> Lustres twice ten, with annual Springs, and Falls,
> Pass'd, since I saw three Emp'rours in our Walls,
> At sev'ral times: each, on sad Scores, did boast
> Triumphs for Civil Broils ———

Both which particulars comprehend this *Triumph* of His most *Sacred Majesty*, which was upon a Victory over the Enemies of His Countrey without a Battle.

These *Arches* generally bore the name of him, that rid in Triumph, and had a Title insculp'd, to testifie for what Victory they were erected: both which appear from this Speech of the City of *Rome* to *Honorius* the Emperour;

> *Ast ego frænabam geminos, quibus altior ires,*   _{Claudian ib.}
> *Electi candoris equos, & nominis Arcum*
> *Jam molita tui, per quem radiante decorus*
> *Ingrederere togâ, pugnæ monumenta dicabam*
> *Defensam titulo Libyam testata perenni.*

> But I put in your Steeds more white then Snow,
> And of your Name design'd a stately Arch,
> Through which you might in Regal Purple march.
> The Battle too, and lasting claim engrav'd
> Attesting Monuments that you *Libya* sav'd.

They were always adorn'd with some Spoils of the Conquered Enemy. *Claudian*,

> ——— *Spoliisque micantes*   _{Paneg. iv.}
> *Innumeros arcus*———

C   Innum'rous

Innum'rous Arches rich with glitt'ring Spoils.

Prudentius,
> *Frustrà igitur currus summo miramur in Arcu*
> *Quadrijugos, stantésque Duces in curribus altis,*
> *Sub pedibusque Ducum captivos poplite flexo*
> *Ad juga depressos, manibusque in terga retortis,*
> *Et suspensa gravi telorum fragmina trunco.*

> We Chariots on the Arch admire in vain,
> In them their haughty Leaders standing see,
> And Captives stooping with low-bended knee,
> Their hands behind them ti'd; of pond'rous Oke
> Huge Truncheons hanging of strong Jav'lins broke.

Sometimes they bore insculp'd the Battle, in which the Conquerour had merited his *Triumph*, as those of *Septimius Severus*, and *Constantine*. In others, the whole pomp of the *Triumph* was represented; as in that of *Vespasian* and *Titus*, where are still to be seen led in *Triumph* the Spoils of the Temple of *Jerusalem*, the Ark of the Covenant, the Candlestick with seven Branches, the Table of the Shew-Bread, the Tables of the Decalogue, with the Vessels of pure Gold for the use of the Temple, the Captives chain'd, the Emperour riding in his *Triumphal* Chariot, &c. The order, and method of a *Triumph*, among the *Romans*, we will here briefly, but distinctly deliver, chiefly out of *Plutarch*, in the Life of *P. Æmilius*.

In Romulo. The captivated Statues, Pictures, and Colossusses, lead the Van. *Plutarch*, of the Triumph of *P. Æmilius*, *The first day* (for this Triumph lasted three) *scarce sufficed for the passing of the Statues, Pictures, and Colosses, lead in two hundred and fifty Carriages.* *Appian* says, that *Pompey* carried the Statues of the Forreign Gods in Triumph.

The next followed the choicest Arms and Spoils of the Enemy. *Plutarch*, *The next day were carried the fairest and richest of the* Macedonian *Weapons upon several Carriages, glistering with the Brass and Iron new scowr'd: artificially plac'd, (yet that they seem'd to have been thrown together promiscuously without any order) the Head-pieces upon the Shields, the Corslets upon the Buskins, &c. which striking constantly against each other, made so terrible a noise, that the sight of them, though now overcome, was a terrour to the Spectatours.* Statius,

Ante

passing to His CORONATION.

> *Ante Ducem spolia, & duri Mavortis imago,*   Lib. xii.
> *Virginei currus, cumulatáque fercula cristis;*
> *Et tristes ducuntur equi.* ——

The Gen'ral, Spoils, and *Mars* dire Shape precedes
Chariots and Chargers heap'd with Crests, and Steeds
Mourning are led

Ovid,
> *Scuta sed & galeæ gemmis radientûr & auro,*   De Ponto,
>   *Sténtque super victos trunca tropæa viros.*   Lib. iii.
>   Eleg. iv.

But Gems, and Gold their Shields, and Helms adorn,
The Trophies on the vanquish'd Shoulders born.

Next, the Images of the Cities, Towns, Castles, Mountains, and Rivers, taken. *Ovid*,   De Tristib.
Lib. iv.
Eleg. ii.

> *Cumque Ducum titulis oppida capta leget:*
> *Hic lacus, hi montes, hæc tot castella, tot urbes,*
>   *Plena feræ cædis, plena cruoris erant.*

There taken Towns, and Princes Titles read:
There Lakes, there Mountains, Forts, and Cities stood;
Full with dire Slaughter; full of Purple Blood.

> *Protinùs, argento veros imitantia muros,*
>   *Barbara cum victis oppida lata viris:*
> *Fluminàque in montes, & in altas proflua sylvas,*
>   *Armaque cum telis in strue juncta suis.*

Next, Barb'rous Cities with the Captives past
True Walls resembling in pure Silver cast:
And Rivers that 'mongst Woods and Mountains glide,
And Arms, and Weapons, rais'd like Trophies, ride.

Livy * says, that *Scipio Asiaticus* carried in Triumph the Images of an hundred and thirty four Towns. *Pliny* † reckons up twenty seven Ci-
    * Lib. xxxviii.
    † Nat. Hist. Lib. v. Cap. v.
ties,

ties, Towns, Nations, Mountains, &c. led before *Cornelius Balbus*. *Silius Italicus*, of the Triumph of *Scipio Africanus* over *Carthage*.

Mox victas tendens Carthago *ad sidera palmas*
Ibat, & effigies oræ jam lenis Iberæ,
Terrarum finis Gades, *ac laudibus olim*
Terminus Herculeis Calpe, *Bætisque lavare*
Solis equos dulci consuetus fluminis undâ,
Frondosumque apicem subigens ad sidera mater
Bellorum fera Pyrene, *nec mitis* Iberus,
Cùm simul illidit Ponto *quos attulit amnes.*

—— Next, lifting to
The Stars her Conquer'd hands, did *Carthage* go,
Then the Effigies of th' *Iberian* Land,
Now Peaceable; with *Gades*, that doth stand
The Period of the Earth; and *Calpe*, that,
Of old, *Alcides* praise did terminate:
With *Bætis*, which the Horses of the Sun
Is wont to bathe in Streams that gently run:
And high *Pyrene*, which gives Birth to Wars,
And lifts her heavy Head unto the Stars:
With rude *Iberus*, that with Fury flings
Against the Sea the Rivers, that he brings.

Mr. ROSS.

Then followed the Moneys of Silver, Vessels, Garments, &c. Plutarch, *After which, three thousand men carrying the Moneys of Silver in seven hundred and fifty Silver Vessels; each of them weighing three Talents, four men to a Vessel.*

Next the Trumpeters. Plutarch, *The next day betimes in the Morning went the Trumpeters sounding a Charge.* After whom were led the Oxen ordain'd for Sacrifice. Livy, *The Victimes, which go before, are not the least part of the Triumph.* These were white, taken out of the Medows of the River *Clitumnus*. Virgil,

Hinc

Hinc albi, Clitumne, greges, & maxima taurus
Victima, sæpe tuo perfusi fluviine sacro,
Romanos ad Templa Deûm duxêre Triumphos.

Georg. 1.

This snowy Flocks, and Bulls prime Off'rings yields,
Which bath'd, *Clitumnus*, in thy Sacred Floods,
Rome's Triumphs draw to Temples of the Gods.

Upon which place *Servius*, *Clitumnus is a River in* Menavia, *which is a part of* Umbria, *as* Umbria *is of* Tuscia, *whence whatsoever Beasts drink, they bring forth their young ones white.* Claudian,

Quin & Clitumni sacras victoribus undas,
Candida quæ Latiis præbent armenta Triumphis.

Panegyr. IV.

Clitumnus sacred Streams, whose Snow-white Breed
The conqu'ring *Romans* in their Triumphs need.

Ovid,

Candidáque adductâ collum percussa securi
Victima purpureo sanguine tingit humum.

De Tristibus, lib. IV. Eleg. II.

Struck with an Axe the pure white Sacrifice
Earth with a purple River dies.

Next the Gold and Golden Vessels, taken from the Enemy. Plutarch, *After the Sacrifices went those that carried the Gold, divided, as the Silver was, into Vessels, weighing each three Talents, the number of the Vessels, seventy seven: with those that carried the Sacred Cup, which Æmilius had caus'd to be made of ten Talents of Gold, adorn'd with several pretious Stones,* &c. Then followed the Arms of the Conquered Prince. *After which he sent the Chariot of* Perseus, *and his Arms, and his Crown plac'd upon his Arms.*

Next the Captives, richly clad, but laden with Chains; the Captive Prince with Chains of Gold, the rest according to their quality. Silius Italicus,

Ante Siphax feretro residens captiva premebat
Lumina, & auratæ servabant colla catenæ.
Hic Hanno, clarique genus Phœnissa juventa,
Et Macedum primi, atque incocti corpora Mauri,

Lib. ...

Tum Nomades, notusque sacro, cùm lustrat arenas,
Hammoni Garamas : &c.
Sed non ulla magis mentésque oculósque tenebat,
Quàm visa Hannibalis campis fugientis imago.

—Before him *Siphax*, Captivate,
Upon a Beere, his Eyes dejected, sate,
His Neck in Golden Chains preserv'd. And here
Hanno, and young *Phænician* Nobles were;
Then *Macedonian* Princes; next to these
The *Moors* with parched Skins; then *Nomades*
And *Garamantians* known to Horned *Jove*,
Where they the Sands survey, *&c.*
Yet nothing more delights their Mind, and Eyes,
Then *Hannibal*, as in the Field he flies.

Mr. ROSS.

Propertius,

Lib. xi.
Eleg. i.

Aut Regum auratis circumdata colla catenis,
Actiáque in Sacra currere rostra via.

Or else their Kings in Golden Fetters bound;
The Sacred way with *Actian* Wheels resound.

Ovid,

De arte Am.

Ibant antè duces onerati colla catenis.
Before, the Princes went in Golden Chains.

Trebellius, speaking of Queen *Zenobia*, *Jam primùm ornata gemmis ingentibus, ità ut ornamentorum onere laboraret: vincti erant pedes auro, manus etiam catenis aureis, nec collo aureum vinculum deerat.* She was now so deck'd with great Gems, that she was oppress'd with the weight of her Ornaments: her Feet, Hands, and Neck were bound with Chains. But this was not constant: for in a Triumph of *Pompey's Appian* mentions a great number of Captives, οὐδένα δεδεμένον, but *none bound*.

Next followed the Crowns, which the Cities, Friends of the Romans, had presented to the General. *Virgil*,

Ipse

Ipse sedens niveo candentis limine Phœbi
Dona recognoscit sociorum, aptátque superbis
Postibus. ———

He in bright Porches of great *Phœbus* sits,
And gifts of Nations to proud Pillars fits.

Plutarch, *After which were carried* 400. *Golden Crown's, which the Cities had sent to* Paulus Æmilius *by their Ambassadours, as a reward of his Victory.*

Next, he that rid in Triumph, in his Triumphal habit, elegantly described by *Juvenal*.

Quid si vidisset Prætorem in curribus altis
Exstantem, & medio sublimem in pulvere Circi
In tunica Jovis, *& pictæ Sarrana ferentem*
Ex humeris aulæa togæ, magnæque Coronæ
Tantum orbem quanto cervix non sufficit ulla?
Quippe tenet sudans hanc publicus, & sibi Consul
Nè placeat, curru servus portatur eodem.
Da nunc & volucrem sceptro quæ surgit eburno,
Illinc Cornicines, hinc præcedentia longi
Agminis officia, & niveos ad fræna Quirites,
Defossa in loculis quos sportula fecit amicos.

Had he the *Prætor* in his Chariot spi'd
Amidst the dusty *Circque* in Triumph ride,
In *Joves* bright Vest, in an imbroider'd Gown
Of *Tyrian* Purple, and a mighty Crown,
For any Head too weighty, and too large,
That is forsooth a sweating Servants charge:
Least that the *Consul* in such pomp should pride,
The Slave and he both in one Chariot ride.
On th' Ivory Scepter th' Eagle seen displai'd,
Here Cornets, there his friendly Cavalcade;
Romans in white march neer the Horses Reins,
Friends by the Basket and their Belly-gains.

The Army followed the Chariot of their General. Plutarch, *The whole Army was crown'd with Lawrel, following the Chariot of their General in their ranks, and orders.* Who usually sang Io Triumphe. Ovid, speaking of the Triumph of *Drusus Germanicus*;

Tempora Phœ: à lauro cingentur, Ioque
 Miles, Io magnâ voce Triumphe, *canet.*

Io the Army with fresh Lawrel Crown'd
Io Triumphe as they march resound.

De laud. Stilicon. Claudian,
Ipse albis veheretur equis, currumque secutus,
Laurigerum festo fremuisset carmine miles.

Drawn with white Steeds; with Wreaths his Chariot hung,
The Army follow'd with a joyfull song.

Lib. iv. od. iii. as by the Spectators also. *Horace*, of *Augustus*,

Tuque dum procedis, Io Triumphe,
Non semel dicemus, Io Triumphe.

Io Triumphe whilst you march in state,
Io Triumphe we reiterate.

Thus having briefly touched upon the Antiquity, and use of Triumphal Arches, we shall descend to the illustration of the Descriptions in particular.

THE

The first ARCH.

MUNDAY, *April* the two and twentieth, His MAJESTY went from the *Tower*, through the City, to *Whitehall*.

In his passage through *Crouched Fryers*, He was entertained with Musick, a Band of eight Waits, placed on a Stage.

Near *Algate*, another Band of six Waits entertain'd him in like manner with Musick, from a Balcony, built to that purpose.

In Leaden-Hall-Street, neer Lime-Street End, was erected the first *Triumphal Arch*, after the Dorick order. On the *North-side*, on a *Pedestal* before the *Arch*, was a *Woman personating* REBELLION, mounted on an Hydra, in a *Crimson Robe*, torn, Snakes crawling on her Habit, and begirt with Serpents, her Hair snaky, a Crown of Fire on her Head, a bloody Sword in one Hand, a charming Rod in the other. Her Attendant CONFUSION, in a deformed Shape, a Garment of severall ill-matched Colours, and put on the wrong way; on her Head, Ruines of Castles; torn Crowns, and broken Scepters in each Hand.

THere was no War in the *Roman*, or *Greek* Common-wealths call'd by any name properly answering to *Rebellion*, which comprehends only the violation of that Natural duty, which the Subject owes to the supreme Governour: for though we find *Rebellio* in *Tacitus*, of Subjects that rise against their Prince, and *Rebellis* too in *Claudian*, speaking of *Africk* a Subject to *Rome*, but then in Arms against the *Roman* Emperour under *Gildo*, as

> ———*segetes mirantur Iberas*
> *Horrea: nec Libyæ senserunt damna rebellis*
> *Jam Transalpinâ contenti meße Quirites.*

In Eutropium Lib. i.

> The Roman Grange *Iberian* Corn admires,
> Nor did rebellious *Libya*'s loss resent,
> But with *Transalpine* Harvests was content.

and in another place, speaking of the *Moors*;

De bello Gildonico.

Nonne

> *Nónne meam fugiet Maurus, cùm viderit, umbram?*
> *Quid dubitas? exsurge toris: invade rebellem:*
> *Captivum mihi redde meum———*

> Will not the *Moor* fly when he sees my Ghost?
> Why doubt'st Thou? rise: storm that Rebellious Coast;
> My Captive me restore.———

Yet we find that word attributed also to *Alarick*, and his Army, no Subjects of the *Roman* Empire, but only Confederates, by the same Authour,

De VI. Consulat. Honorii.

> *Oblatum Stilico violato fœdere Martem*
> *Omnibus arripuit votis, ubi Roma peric'lo*
> *Jam procul, & belli medius Padus arbiter ibat:*
> *Jámque opportunam motu strepuisse rebelli*
> *Gaudet perfidiam.*

> He freely undertook so just a War,
> The League being broke, and *Rome* from danger far,
> While the Armies *Poe* divides; *Stilico* Arms:
> Glad of th' occasion those Rebellious swarms
> In such a place conjoyn'd.

Wherefore we must look for its Description under Civil Discord, and Sedition, which *Petronius Arbiter*, in the Civil War betwixt *Cæsar* and *Pompey*, ha's very elegantly delivered.

> *Infremuere tubæ, ac scisso* Discordia *crine*
> *Extulit ad Superos* Stygium *caput. Hujus in ore*
> *Concretus sanguis, contusáque lumina flebant.*
> *Stabant atrati scabrâ rubigine dentes;*
> *Tabo lingua fluens; obsessa draconibus ora:*
> *Atque intertorto laceratam pectore vestem,*
> *Sanguineam tremulà quatiebat lampada dextrâ.*

> The Trumpets sound, and Discord, with torn hair,
> Her *Stygian* front advanceth to the air.

O're

O're her smear'd Visage clotted blood lies spread,
Her blubber'd Eyes are beat into her Head,
Her iron Teeth rough with a rusty scale,
Her Tongue drops gore, Serpents her Brows impale:
Rending her pleited Vest, and red Attire,
Her trembling Hand brandisheth bloody Fire.

But we cannot better take a view of Sedition, and Discord, then in the Description of the Authours of it, feign'd to be the Furies: as *Virgil*,

Tu potes unanimes armare in prælia fratres,
Atque odiis versare domos: tu verbera tectis,
Funereásque inferre faces: tibi nomina mille,
Mille nocendi artes: fœcundum concute pectus.
Disjice compositam pacem, sere crimina belli:
Arma velit, poscátque simul, rapiátque juventus.

Unanimous Brothers thou canst arm to fight,
And settled Courts destroy with deadly spight:
Storm Palaces with Steel, and Pitchy Flames,
Thou hast a thousand wicked Arts, and Names:
Thy Bosom disembogue, with Mischief full,
And Articles concluding Peace annull.
Then raise a War, and with bewitching Charms
Make the mad People rage to take up Arms.

Statius gives a Description of one of them very correspondent to ours,

Thebaid. Lib. 1.

Centum illi stantes umbrabant ora Cerastæ:
Turba minor diri capitis; Sedet intus abactis
Ferrea lux oculis, qualis per nubila Phœbes
Atraciâ rubet arte labor: Suffusa veneno
Tenditur, ac sanie gliscit cutis, igneus atro
Ore vapor, quo longa sitis, morbíque, famésque,
Et populis mors una venit, riget horrida tergo
Palla, & cærulei redeunt in pectora nodi.

Tum

Tum geminas quatit illa manus: hæc igne rogali
Fulminat, hæc vivo manus aëra verberat hydro.

An hundred Snakes up in a Party made
From her dire Head, her horrid Temples shade,
Her fix'd Eyes sunk, their Brazen Gleamings shroud,
So charm'd bright *Phœbe* blusheth through a Cloud:
Poyson'd her swoln Skin shines with gore, her Breath
Ushers in Flame, Thirst, Famine, Plague, and Death:
Her dreadful Robes rough on her Shoulders sit,
Which on her Bosom Crimson Ribbans knit:
Then both her hands she shakes; with Fun'ral Fire
This thunders, that jerks Air with Serpents dire.

Of *Tisiphone* Virgil,

Æn. vi

Continuò sontes ultrix accincta flagello
Tisiphone quatit insultans, torvósque sinistrâ
Intentans angues, vocat agmina sæva sororum.

Cruel *Tisiphone* insulting shakes
Her dreadful Whip, and arm'd with twisted Snakes
In her left hand, straight on the guilty falls,
And Troops of unrelenting Furies calls.

Pindar calls Sedition ἐχθρὰ κουροτρόφον, *a bad Nurse for Children.* The reason may be taken from these Verses of *Homer* describing the consequents of it;

Iliad. xxii

Ὑῖάς τ' ὀλλυμένους, ἑλκυσθείσας τε θυγάτρας
Καὶ θαλάμους κεραϊζομένους, καὶ νήπια τέκνα
Βαλλόμενα ποτὶ γαίῃ, ἐν αἰνῇ δηϊοτῆτι,
Ἑλκομένας τε νυοὺς ὀλοῇς ὑπὸ χερσὶν Ἀχαιῶν.

My slaughter'd Sons, my Daughters ravish'd, see,
My Court destroy'd, and from the Nurses knee
Their tender Babes snatch'd by the cruel Foe,
And in one Sea their Bloods commixed flow.

The

The HYDRA, on which Rebellion is mounted, the Ancients have very variously represented. *Pausanias attributes but one Head to it, Pisander Camirensis † many, Alcæus nine, Simonides fifty, πεντηκοντακέφαλος, whom Virgil follows,

*In Corinthiacis.
† Ibid.

> Quinquaginta atris immanis hiatibus Hydra
> Sævior intus habet sedem ——

Æn. vi.

> Hydra with fifty ugly Jaws, one more
> Cruel then this by half,'s within the door.

"On the South Pedestal is a Representation of BRITTAIN'S MO-
"NARCHY, supported by LOYALTY, both Women; Monarchy, in a large
"Purple Robe, adorn'd with Diadems, and Scepters, over which a loose
"Mantle, edg'd with blue and silver Fringe, resembling Water, the
"Map of Great Britain drawn on it, on her Head London, in her
"right Hand, Edinburgh; in her left, Dublin: Loyalty all in White,
"three Scepters in her right Hand, three Crowns in her left.

Purple is call'd by Tertullian *Regiæ dignitatis insigne*, a Badg of Royal Dignity. Lactantius, *Et sicuti nunc Romanis indumentum Purpuræ insigne est Regiæ dignitatis assumptæ, sic illis*, &c. Claudian of Rufinus;

De Idololat.
Lib. iv. cap. vii.
In Rufinum, Lib. ii

> Imperii certus; tegeret ceu Purpura dudum
> Corpus, & ardentes ambirent tempora gemmæ.

> Certain of Empire, as if Purple now
> Had cloath'd his Limbs, and Gems impal'd his Brow.

So Strabo says, that the Posterity of Androclus, Son of Codrus King of Athens, had at Ephesus, besides many other Honours granted them, a Purple Robe in token of their Royal descent. According to which, we finde in Sidonius Apollinaris, *Purpuratus* to be equivalent with *Imperator*, Epist. lib. ii. *Qui videbatur in jugulum Purpurati jamjam ruiturus*; Who seem'd ready to murder the Emperour: and, *Serò cognoscunt, posse reum Majestatis pronunciari etiam eum, qui non adfectâsset habitum Purpuratorum*; They too late understand, that even he, that affected not the Habit of the Emperours, might be found guilty of Treason. From whence the Civilians observe, that it was Treason to assume the Royal Robes. And Ammianus Marcellinus speaks of a Woman, who had suborn'd several to accuse her Husband of High Treason, for having stoln the Emperour Diocletian's Purple Vest out of his Sepulchre, and hiding it. Eusebius;

Epist. xiii.

He (Diocletian) first beautified his Shoes with Gold, and Pearls, and pretious Stones. For the Kings before him were honoured in the same manner with the Consuls, having onely a Purple Vest for a badge of their Royalty. The same saith *Pæanius*, who translated *Eutropius*; *The Royal Robe before was distinguish'd only by its Purple colour.* Wherefore, when any resolv'd Tyrannically to sieze upon the Royal Dignity, they immediately usurp'd a Purple Robe; which they sometimes forc'd from a Standard, as *Trebellius* reports of *Saturninus*. The same *Authour*; *Gordianum Proconsulem reclamantem, & se terræ affligentem, opertum Purpurâ imperare coëgerunt & primò quidem invitus Gordianus Purpuram sumpserat: postea verò, quum vidit neque filio, neque familiæ id latam esse, volens suscepit Imperium*; *They forc'd Gordian the Proconsul, who denied, and cast himself upon the ground, to be vested in Purple, and receive the Title of Emperour: at first he was very unwilling to receive the Purple Robe, but, when he saw, that that was unsafe for his Son, and Family, he receiv'd the Empire willingly.* Where *Purpuram sumere*, and *sumere Imperium*, are the same. Sometimes they committed Sacrilege upon the Statues of the Gods. *Vopiscus*; *Depositâ Purpurâ ex simulachro Veneris, cum cyclade uxoria, à militibus circumstantibus amictus, & adoratus est*; *Taking a Purple Robe from the Statue of Venus, and his Wife's inner Vest of Gold, he was invested, and adored by the Souldiers as Emperour.* *Trebellius*; *Celsum Imperatorem appellaverunt peplo Deæ Cœlestis ornatum*; *They put on Celsus the Vest o' the Goddess of Heaven, and call'd him Emperour.* Wherefore, when we read of the *Consular Purple Robes* under the *Romane Emperours*, as in that of *Latinus Pacatus*, *Quorum alter, post amplissimos Magistratus, & purpuras Consulares*; and of *Sidonius*,

margin: In Gordianus.

margin: In Saturnino.

— — *Te pictâ Togatum*
Purpura plus capiat; quia res est semper ab ævo
Rara frequens Consul: — — —

Purple should rather thee affect, since we
One often made a *Consul* seldome see:

it must be understood either of the *Senatorian* Segments added to their *Consular* Robes, or of a *Purple* mix'd with some other Dye; which is mentioned in *Theodosius's Code*: as a Warp of Purple, the Woof of another colour, or the like. For the *Imperial Interdict* comprehends all of whatsoever degree; *Temperent universi, cujuscunque sint sexûs, dignitatis, artis, professionis, & generis, ab hujusmodi speciei possessione, quæ soli Principi, ejusque domui dedicatur*; *Let every one, of what Sex, Dignity, Art, Profession, and Birth they be, forbear the possession of this sort of Purple, which is appropriated to the Prince alone, and his house.*

passing to His Coronation.

The first Imperial Edict of this nature is conceived to be in the time of the Emperour *Nero*: which is to be understood *de holoveris*, of pure unmix'd Purple.

Neither was Purple peculiar to the Imperial Robes onely, but to their Pens too. The Emperur *Leo* forbad, that any Rescripts of his should bear other then a Purple Inscription. So *Nicetas*, in the Life of *Manuel* the Emperour, says, That, at his entrance upon the Empire, he sent Letters to *Constantinople*, written with Purple. *Constantinus Manasses* in his Annals, *The Emperour granted the request of his Sister, and taking a Pen in his hand confirm'd the Paper in Purple Letters.* And *Palæologus* the Emperour, swearing subjection to the *Roman* See in the Church of *Santo Spirito* at *Rome*, subscribed in Letters of Purple. *Epitome Chron. Werweronis.*

The art of making this Purple, both for Robes, and Ink, is still preserv'd, but we meet not with the materials; though we have left us both the place, and manner of taking, preparing, and whatsoever is necessary for that purpose. *L. Sacri, C. de diver. Rescr.*

Monarchy is said to be supported by *Loyalty*; because the Love of the Subject is the securest Guard of the Prince. *Seneca*, in a Discourse betwixt *Nero* and *Seneca* the Philosopher,

> Ne. *Ferrum tuetur Principem.* Se. *Melius Fides.*
> Ne. *Decet timeri* Cæsarem. Se. *At plus diligi.*

> Ne. Arms *Cæsar* guard. Se. But better Loyalty.
> Ne. Kings should be fear'd. Se. They rather lov'd should be.

We find not any name for *Loyalty* in the time of the *Roman* Emperours, except *Fides*, or *Fidelitas*: as in the Coyns of the Emperour *Philippus*, *Chml. Pag. XXXI.*

which was signified by the extension of the hand. *Lucan* speaking of the Army, promising Fealty to *Julius Cæsar*,

> —— *His cunctis simul assensere cohortes,*
> *Elatásque altè, quæcunque ad bella vocaret,*
> *Promisere manus* ——

> All rais'd their hands with joint consent, that they
> Would fight for him, and his Commands obey
> 'Gainst whomsoe're ——

Isidorus Hispal. *Mos erat Militaris, ut, quoties consentiret exercitus, quia voce non potest, manu promittat;* It was the *Military Custom,* that as often as the *Army* consented, because they could not with their voice, they should promise with their hand.

Which Posture is represented in these *Medaigles* of the Emperours *Trajan,* and *Hadrian,*

Crotiac.
Tab. xxxiii,
C. xxxviii.

Claudian, speaking of a Rebellion in the *Western* parts of the Empire,

> *Interea turbata FIDES, civilia rursus*
> *Bella tonant, dubiumque quatit Discordia mundam.*

> Mean while the Peace was broke, Ensigns unfurl'd,
> And Discord thundring shook the stagg'ring World.

Loyalty is cloathed in white, to signifie its purity, and innocency. *Color albus præcipuè decorus Deo est, tum in cæteris, tum maximè in textili,* Cicero. *Horace.*

Lib. i. Od.
xxxv.

> *Te Spes, & albo rara Fides colit*
> *Velata panno* ——
> Thee Hope, and Faith embrace
> Cloathed in white.

passing to His CORONATION.

"*The first Painting on the South-side is a Prospect of His Majestie's*
"*landing at Dover Castle, Ships at Sea, great Guns going off, one kneeling,*
"*and kissing the King's Hand, Souldiers, Horse, and Foot, and many*
"*People gazing: above,*

ADVENTUS AUG.

"*Beneath the Painting this Motto,*

IN SOLIDO RURSUS FORTUNA LOCAVIT.

This Inscription ADVENTUS AUGUSTI is often found among the Coyns of the *Roman* Emperours upon a peaceable return; which is signified by the extension of the right hand: for saith *Quintilian, Fit & ille habitus, qui esse in Statuis Pacificator solet, qui protenso brachio manum inflexo pollice extendit*; That Gesture is used too, which in Statues is a token of Peace, which extends the Arm, and Hand, inflecting the Thumb. In which Posture there is extant at *Rome* the Statue of the Emperour *M. Aurelius Antoninus*: and another before the *Laterane*, mention'd in the Additions to *Pierius*. The same we finde in the Coyns of *M. Julius Philippus*, and *Fl. Jovianus*, with the same Inscription, ADVENTUS AUGUSTI.

Institut. Lib. XI. cap. III.

Crojac Tab. lviii. Baron. Tom. iv. Annal.

"*The Painting on the North-side, opposite to this, is a Trophy with decol-*
"*lated Heads, having over it,*

ULTOR A TERGO DEUS.

"*Taken out of* Horace,

—— *sequitur Rebelles*

Ultor à tergo Deus ——

"God's Vengeance Rebels at the Heels pursues.

The Motto beneath,

AUSI IMMANE NEFAS, AUSOQUE POTITI.

His Majestie's Entertainments

A Trophy amongst the ancient *Romans* was ordinarily a Trunk of a Tree, fitted with the Arms of the Conquered Enemy, according to that of *Virgil*,

Æ: Lib: xi.

Ingentem quercum, decisis undique ramis,
Constituit tumulo, fulgentiáque induit arma,
Mezenti Ducis exuvias, tibi magne tropæum
Bellipotens : aptat rorantes sanguine cristas,
Teláque trunca viri, & bis sex thoraca petitum
Perfossumque locis, clypeumque ex ære sinistræ
Subligat, atque ensem collo suspendit eburnum.

A stately Oak on Rising-Ground he plac'd,
And Boughs disrob'd, with glorious Armour grac'd;
With King *Mezentius* Spoils the Trunks he loads,
Great *Mars*, thy Trophy, Warlik'st of the Gods;
His Breast-Plate, run twice six times thorow, rears,
And Plumes bedew'd with Blood, and broken Spears,
His Brazen Shield on the left Shoulder tied,
Hanging his Sword in Ivory by th' side.

And in the same Book,

Da nunc, Tybri pater, ferro, quod missile libro,
Fortunam, atque viam duri per pectus Halesi,
Hæc arma, exuviásque viri tua quercus habebit.

Grant, Father *Tyber*, Fortune to this Lance,
And that this Jav'lin, which I now advance,
May through *Halesus* Bosom passage make,
And let thy Oak his Spoils, and Armour take.

Statius,

T: Theb: Lib: ii.

Quercus erat, teneræ jamdudum oblita juventæ,
Huic laves galeas, perfossáque vulnere crebro

Inserit

*Inserit arma ferens, huic truncos ictibus enses
Subligat, & fractas membris spirantibus hastas.*

There was an aged Oak, on which he put
Bruis'd Casks, and Corslets, thrust-through, hack'd, and cut:
Next Swords in Battel broken guirds upon,
And splinter'd Spears from dying Bodies drawn.

The Trophie of *Jupiter* over the Giants is at large, and elegantly described by *Claudian*;

*—— Phlegræis sylva superbit
Exuviis, totúmque nemus victoria vestit.
Hìc patuli rictus, hic prodigiosâ Gigantum
Tergora dependent, & adhuc crudele minantur
Affixæ facies truncis : immaniáque ossa
Serpentum passim tumulis exsanguibus albent,
Et rigidæ multo suspirant fulmine pelles,
Nulláque non magni jactat se nominis arbor.
Hæc centum-gemini strictos Ægeonis enses
Curvatâ vix fronde levat ; liventibus illa
Exultat Cori spoliis : hæc arma Mimantis
Sustinet ; hos onerat ramos exutus Ophion.
Altior & cunctis abies, umbrosáque latè,
Ipsius Enceladi fumantia gestat opima
Summi Terrigenûm regis, cader*é*tque gravatâ
Pondere, ni lapsum fulciret proxima quercus.
Indè timor, numénque loco, nemorisque senectæ
Parcitur, æthereisque nefas nocuisse Tropæis.*

De rapt*u*
Pros*er*p.
Lib. iii.

—— The Woods in Spoils *Phlegræan* pride,
The whole Grove Vict'ry cloath'd. Here Gapings wide
Of horrid Jaws ; there Backs of hideous size
Hung, and stak'd faces threatning still the Skies:

Huge

>   Huge Serpents Skeletons in bloodless Piles
>   There bleaching white lay in voluminous Coyls,
>   Whose scaly Sloughs smell with Sulphureous Flame:
>   No Tree but boasts some mighty Giant's Name.
>   This, loaden, under stern *Ægæon* yields,
>   Who us'd an hundred Swords, as many Shields;
>   That brags bold *Corus* bloody Spoils: this bears
>   The Arms of *Mimas*; that *Ophion's* wears.
>   But higher then the rest, with spreading shade,
>   A Firr *Enceladus* Crest and Corslet lade,
>   The Giants King; which with its weight had broke,
>   If not supported by a neighb'ring Oak.
>   Hence a Religious Aw preserves the Woods,
>   And none dares wrong the Trophies of the Gods.

Lib. iii. cap. ii. But when the City of *Rome* grew greater in power, the Trophies were more magnificent. L. Florus, *How acceptable those two Victories were, may be conjectured from hence, that* Domitius Ahenobarbus, *and* Fabius Maximus *erected in the same place where the Battels were fought Turrets of Stone, upon which were Trophies, adorn'd with the Arms of the Enemy, a Custome not in use before amongst us. For the people of* Rome *never upbraided their Conquered Enemies with their Victories.*

Lib. ii. On these Trophies was inscribed both the Name of the Conquerour, and the People conquered. Tacitus, *Laudatis pro concione victoribus,* Cæsar *congeriem armorum struxit superbo cum titulo; debellatis inter* Rhenum Albimque *nationibus, exercitum* Tiberii Cæsaris *ea Monimenta* Marti, & Jovi, & Augusto *sacravisse:* Cæsar, *having commended the Victors, raised an heap of Arms with this proud Inscription, The Army of* Tiberius Cæsar, *having vanquish'd the People between the River* Rhene, *and the* Albe, *consecrates these Monuments to* Mars, Jupiter, *and* Augustus. And, to the same purpose, *Miles in loco prælii* Tiberium *Imperatorem salutavit* (absentem) *struxitque aggerem, & in modum Tropæorum arma, subscriptis victarum gentium nominibus, imposuit.* There are two Trophies of *Marius's* still remaining at *Rome*, one of which ha's a Breast-Plate with Military Ornaments, and Shields, before it a young man captive, with his hands bound behind him; on each side of it two Winged Victories. So *Pliny* tells us of a Trophie erected to the honour

TROPHEA MARII DE BELLO CYMB. PVTAT: AD ÆD: D: CVSEBR

PHEA MARII DE BELLO CIMBR: PVTAT. AD ÆD. D. CVS EBROM ROMÆ

nour of *Augustus* in the *Alps* with this Inscription, IMPERATORI CÆSARI DIVI F. AUG. PONTIF. MAX. IMPERATORI XIV. TRIBUNITIÆ POTESTATIS. S. P. Q. R. QUOD EIUS DUCTU AUSPICIISQVE GENTES ALPIUM OMNES, QVÆ A MARI SUPERO AD INFIMUM PERTINEBANT, SUB IMPERIUM P. R. SUNT REDACTÆ. *Stobæus* says, that *Othryades*, taking the Spoils of some of his Enemies, erected a Trophy, and writ this Title with the Blood of the wounded;

THE LACEDÆMONIANS OVER THE ARGIVES.

These Trophies were consecrated to the Gods, and therefore could not be demolish'd without Sacrilege. So *Dio* says of *Cæsar*, that, after his *Pontick* Victory, he durst not deface the Trophy of *Mithridates*, ὡς ᾗ τοῖς ἐμπολεμίοις Θεοῖς ἱερώμενον, *because sacred to the Gods of War.* So, when his Friends had given order, that a Sword, which hung up in a Temple of the *Arubeni*, as a Spoil from *Cæsar*, should be taken down, ἐκ εἴασεν, ἱερὸν ἡγούμενος, *he would not suffer it, accounting it sacred.* Vitruvius, *Posteà autem* Rhodii, *religione impediti, quòd nefas esset Tropæa dicata removere, circa locum eum ædificium struxerunt;* But afterwards the Rhodians, *out of a religious fear, because it was unlawful to remove the dedicated Trophies, erected a Building about the place.* The Gods, to whom the Romans consecrated their Trophies, we finde in *Livy*: *Omnis generis arma cumulata in ingentem acervum, precatus* Martem, Minervámque, Luámque Matrem, *& cæteros Deos, quibus spolia dicare jus fásque est.*

The Motto ULTOR A TERGO DEUS, over the *Trophie*, is in reference to the Coyn of the Emperour *Claudius*, which represents *Martem Ultorem* with a *Trophie* on his Shoulder,

but more particularly to that History of *Augustus*, who, after the War was ended, which he undertook for the revenge of his Father's blood,

murdered

Dio, lib.liv. murdered by some *Common-wealth's* men in the *Senate*-house, conse-
† *Suetonius.* crated a † *Temple* MARTI ULTORI, which he had vowed during the War. *Ovid,*

Fast. Lib. v.
>Mars *ades, & satia scelerato sanguine ferrum,*
>> *Stetque Favor causa pro meliore tuus:*
> *Templa feres; &, me Victore, vocaberis* ULTOR.
>> *Viverat, & fuso lætus ab hoste redit.*

> Glut Steel, O *Mars*, with impious Blood; incline
> To my just Cause, a Temple shall be thine:
> I Conqu'rour, Thou shalt be REVENGER stil'd.
> He vow'd, and glad return'd, his Enemy foil'd.

The Form of the *TEMPLE* we have in this Coyn of *Augustus,*

Chxnl, Pag. 225.

So when he had re-taken the Colours from the *Parthians*, which
Fast. ibid. *Crassus* had lost, he gave him the Title of BIS-ULTOR. *Ovid,*

> *Ritè Deo Templúmque datum, noménque* BIS-ULTOR,
>> *Emeritus voti debita solvit honor.*

> The God BIS-ULTOR stil'd, his Temple made,
>> So he his Vows devoutly paid.

We finde alſo mention of *MARS ULTOR* in an ancient Inſcription in *Gruter*.

Pag. cccxvii. 8.

      D.   M.
T. FLAVIO. AUG. LIB.
LIBERALI. ÆDITUO
MARTIS. ULTORIS
CLAUDIA. EXOCHE
CONJUGI
BENEMERENTI. ET.
SIBI. FECIT.
VIXIT. ANN. LVII.

The *Motto* beneath the *Trophy* is taken out of *Virgil*. who ſpoke it of thoſe, who were, for the like Crimes, condemn'd to the Pains of *Erebus*, as he cloſes the Deſcription of it in the Sixth of his *Æneis*,

Hic quibus inviſi fratres, dum vita manebat,
Pulſatúsve parens, & fraus innexa clienti;
Aut qui divitiis ſoli incubuêre repertis,
Nec partem poſuêre ſuis; (quæ maxima turba eſt;)
Quique ob adulterium cæſi, quique arma ſequuti
Impia, nec veriti dominorum fallere dextras;
Incluſi pœnam expectant: nè quære doceri,
Quam pœnam; aut quæ forma viros, fortunáve merſit.
Saxum ingens volvunt alii, radiisque rotarum
Diſtricti pendent: ſedet, æternúmque ſedebit
Infelix Theſeus: *Phlegyásque miſerrimus omnes*
Admonet, & magnâ teſtatur voce per umbras,
"Diſcite juſtitiam moniti, & non temnere Divos.
Vendidit hic auro patriam, dominúmque potentem
Impoſuit; fixit leges pretio, atque refixit;
Hic thalamum invaſit natæ, vetitósque Hymenæos:
Auſi omnes immane nefas, auſóque potiti.

Here Brother-haters are with Pains repai'd,
Who flew their Parents, or their Friends betrai'd;
Or brooding lay on Golden Heaps alone,
These thousands are, which did impart to none;
Those in Adult'ry slain; or those rebel,
And did their native Prince to Traitors sell,
Here meet their Dooms; seek not these Woes to sound,
Nor by what way Fate did their Souls confound:
These rowl huge Stones, and stretch'd on Wheels do lie;
There *Theseus* sits, and shall eternally;
Aloud, through Shades, sad *Phlegyas* mourning cries,
Admonish'd, Justice learn, nor Gods despise.
This to a potent Prince his Country sold,
And Laws enacted, and repeal'd for Gold;
That beds his Daughter, and no Incest spar'd:
All dar'd bold Crimes, and thriv'd in what they dar'd.

" *The Painting over the Middle Arch represents the King, mounted in
" calm Motion,* USURPATION *flying before him, a Figure
" with many ill-favoured Heads, some bigger, some lesser, and one parti-
" cularly shooting out of his Shoulder, like* CROMWEL'S;
" *Another Head upon his Rump, or Tayl; Two Harpies with a Crown,
" chased by an Angel; Hell's Jaws opening. Under the said Represen-
" tation of the King pursuing* Usurpation *is this* Motto,

VOLVENDA DIES EN ATTULIT ULTRO,

" *Taken out of the Ninth Book of the Æneis,*

Turne, *quod optanti Divûm promittere nemo*
Auderet, volvenda dies, en! attulit ultró.

" What none of all the Gods durst grant, implor'd,
" Succesive Time does of its own accord.

The *Harpies* were described by the Ancients with the Faces of Virgins. *Hesiod,*

Ἠυκόμȣ;

Ἠυκόμους θ' Ἁρπυίας, Ἀελλώ τ', Ὠκυπέτην τε,
Αἵ ῥ' ἀνέμων πνοιῆσι, καὶ οἰωνοῖς ἅμ' ἕπονται,
Ὠκείης πτερύγεσσι.

In Theogonia.

Aello, and *Ocupet*, *Harpyes*, who,
Fair-hair'd, the Winds, and nimble Birds pursue,
Born on swift Wings. ———

and *Virgil*,

Æneid. iii.

—————*Quas dira* Celæno,
*Harpyiæque colunt aliæ, Phineia postquàm
Clausa domus, mensásque metu liquêre priores.
Tristius haud illis monstrum, nec sævior ulla
Pestis, & ira Deûm, Stygiis sese extulit undis.
Virginei volucrum vultus, fædissima ventris
Proluvies, uncæque manus, & pallida semper
Ora fame.*

See *Rhodiginus*, lib. xvi, cap. xxvi.

Where dire *Celæno* other *Harpyies* led,
When frighted they from *Phineas* Table fled.
No Monster like to these, no Plague more fell,
Nor sharper Vengeance Heav'n e're call'd from Hell.
The Fowl have Virgin Faces, and hook'd Claws,
Still purging Bellies, always greedy Maws,
With Hunger pale.———

The Form of these *Harpyies* is to be seen in Sculpture in the Church of Saint *Martin* at *Venice*, frequented, as a *Master-Piece* to draw these Monsters by, both by *Carvers*, and *Painters*; says *Erythræus* on this place of *Virgil*. They were expressed also with crooked Claws, from whence they were called Γαμψώνυχοι.

Apollonius,

Ἀλλὰ διὰ νεφέων ἄφνω πέλας ἀΐσσουσαι
Ἁρπυίαι στόματος χειρῶν τ' ἄπο γαμψηλῆσι
Συνεχέως ἥρπαζον.———

Argonaut. Lib. ii.

But

But *Harpyies*, hurried swiftly through the Air,
From Mouth, and Hands, with griping Talons tear
Still all away. ———

Rutilius Numantianus, in his *Itinerary*,

Harpyiæ, quarum discerpitur unguibus Orbis,
Quæ pede glutineo quæ tetigêre trahunt.

Harpyies, who rend the World, whose Bird-lime Feet,
And Talons, bear away whate're they meet.

There is a Coyn yet extant of *L. Valerius*, where we have an *Harpye* thus represented,

In *Eumenid.* That they had Wings, we finde in *Æschylus*, who, mentioning the *Furies* asleep about *Orestes*, doubting what they should be, says, they could not be *Harpyies* (for he had seen them often painted robbing *Phineus's* Table) because they had no Wings.

" *Above the Arch, on two Pedestals,* South-ward, *and* North-ward,
" *stand the Statues of* King JAMES, *and* King CHARLES *the*
" *First. In the middle somewhat higher, just over the Arch, the Statue of*
" *His Sacred Majesty. Under that of* King JAMES,

DIVO JACOBO.

" *Under that of* King CHARLES *the First,*

DIVO CAROLO.

" *Under*

" Under that of His Majesty this following Inscription;

D. N.

CAROLO II.

D. G. BRITANNIARUM IMP.

OPT. MAX.

UBIQVE VENERANDO,

SEMPER AUG.

BEATISSIMO AC PIISSIMO,

BONO REIP. NATO,

DE AVITA BRITANNIA,

DE OMNIUM HOMINUM GENERE

MERITISSIMO,

P. P.

EXTINCTORI TYRANNIDIS,

RESTITUTORI LIBERTATIS,

FUNDATORI QUIETIS,

OB FELICEM REDITUM,

EX VOTO L. M.

P.

S. P. Q. L.

The Title of *DIVUS* was constantly attributed by the *Romans* to their *Emperours* after their Consecration, or Ἀποθέωσις. *Ovid*, of *Julius Cæsar*,

> *Hanc animam intereà, cæso de corpore raptam,*
> *Fac Jubar, ut semper* Capitolia *nostra,* Forúmque,
> D ɪ v u s *ab excelsa prospectet* Julius *æde.*

> Mean while from his slain Corps his Soul convay
> Up to the Stars, and give it a clear Ray :
> That he, now *DIVUS*, may with influence
> Shine on our *Capitol*, and *Court* from thence.

Ælius Spartianus; Hadrianus, *rogante* Antonino, *DIVUS à Senatu appellatus est* : *Hadrian, at the request of* Antoninus *his Successour, had the Title of* D ɪ v u s *granted him by the Senate.* So *Claudian* feigns the Emperour *Theodosius* to assume that Title immediately upon his death,

> ——— *Cùm* D ɪ v u s *abirem,*
> *Res incompositas, fateor, tumidásque reliqui.*

> When I a G o d went hence, I left, 'tis true,
> The bus'ness hard, and much unsettled too.

After which *Consecration* they had *Temples* dedicated to them, (which *Augustus* admitted, while he was yet alive) *Flamens*, and *Under-Priests*. *Seneca* of *Augustus*,

<small>In *Octavia*.</small>
> *Pietate gnati factus eximià Deus,*
> *Post fata consecratus, & Templis datus.*

> Made by his Son's great Piety a God,
> Temples he built for him, and Altars had.

<small>*Ibid.*</small>
> *Sic ille patriæ primus* Augustus *parens*
> *Complexus astra est, colitur & Templis Deus.*

> Thus the first Father of his Countrey had
> In Heav'n a place, and worship'd as a God.

Spartian,

passing to His CORONATION.

Spartian, *Qui Templum ei pro Sepulchro apud Puteolos constituit, & Quinquennale certamen, & Flamen, & Sodales, & multa alia, quæ ad honorem quasi Numinis pertinerent.* The Senate erected him (Hadrian) *a Temple for a Sepulchre at* Puzzolo, *with a Quinquennial Game, a Flamen, and* Sodales, *and many other things belonging to the Honour of a God.* The *Flamen,* and *Sodales* of the deceased *Emperour,* we often meet with in ancient Inscriptions, as of *Cæsar's Flamen,*

M. PUBLICIO
M. F. SAB. SEXTIO
CALPURNIANO
EQVO. PUBLICO
FLAM. DIVI. JULI
PRÆF. ÆDIL. POT
QUÆSTOR. ÆRAR
SACERD. JUVEN. BRIX
COLLEGIA
CENTON. ET. FABROR.

and of *Hadrian's Sodales,*

L. FABIO. M. F. GAL. CILONI
SEPTIMINO. COS. PRAEF. URB
LEGG. AUGG. PR. PR. PANNON
SUPER DUCI. VEXILL. LEG. PRO
PR. PROVINCIAR. MOESIAE SUPER
PONTI ET BITHYNIÆ
COMITI. AUG. LEG. AUGG. PRO
PR. PROV. GALATIAE PRAEF.
AER. MILITARIS. PROV.
COS. ITEM. Q. LEG. PROV. NARBONENS
LEG. LEG. XVI. FL. F. SAMOSATE
SODAL. HADRIANAL
PR. URB. TRIB. PLEB. Q. PROV
CRETAE. TRIB. LEG. XI. CL.
X. VIR STLITIB. JUDICANDIS
MEDIOLANENSIS
PATRONO.

The manner, and solemnity of their *Confecrations* is at large delivered by [†] *Herodian*. There was a four-square Pile built of several Stories, fill'd with combustible matter; in the second was laid the Body of the deceased Emperour: *in the uppermost, and least of the Stories was held an Eagle. As soon as the Pile was set on fire, the Eagle was let fly: which the* Romans *think carries the* Emperour's *Soul from Earth to Heaven. From which time he is worship'd with the rest of the Gods.* The Form of the *Funeral Pile*, and the manner of their Translation into Heaven, we finde in many Coyns of the *Emperours*: as in these of *Antoninus Pius*, and *L. Verus*,

[† Lib. iv.]

Claudian ha's presumed to tell us the way they went thither, speaking of the Death of **Theodosius**,

[De iii. Consulatu Honorii.]

    ————— *nec plura loquutus,*
Sicut erat, liquido signavit tramite nubes,
Ingrediturque globum Lunæ, *luménque reliquit*
Arcadis, *&* Veneris *clementes pervolat auras.*
Hinc Phœbi *permensus iter, flammámque nocentem*
Gradivi, *placidúmque* Jovem, *stetit arce supremâ,*
Algenti quo zona riget Saturnia *tractu.*
Machina laxatur cœli, rutilæque patescunt
Sponte fores. Arctöa *parat convexa* Boötes,
Australes *reserat portas succinctus* Orion,
Invitántque novum sidus, pendéntque vicissim,
Quas partes velit ille sequi, quibus esse sodalis
Dignetur stellis, aut quâ regione moveri.

——— nor

######### nor more he said,
But through the yielding Clouds his passage made,
And reach'd the *Moon*, then *Mercury* forsakes,
And to the milder Sphere of *Venus* makes :
Thence to the *Sun*, and *Mars* malignant fire,
And milder *Jove*; then mounts the highest Sphere,
Where in a colder Circle *Saturn* lords.
Heaven's Purple Gates ope of their own accords.
Him to his *Northern* Car *Boötes* courts,
Orion girt unlocks the *Southern* Ports,
And the new Star invite: both him intreat
He would vouchsafe to nominate his Seat;
What Stars for his Associates he approv'd,
And in which Constellation would be mov'd.

They questioned not the Ἀποθέωσις even of the worst of their *Emperours*; as we see in these Verses of *Lucan* on *Nero*, that Prodigie of Nature,

######### *Te, cùm, statione peractâ,*
Astra petes serus, prælati regia cœli
Excipiet gaudente polo : seu sceptra tenere,
Seu te flammiferos Phœbi transcendere currus,
Tellurémque, nihil mutato Sole timentem,
Igne vago lustrare juvat: tibi Numine ab omni
(Cedetur, jurique tuo Natura relinquet,
Quis Deus esse velis, ubi regnum ponere mundi.
Sed neque in Arctos sedem tibi legeris orbe;
Nec polus adversi calidus quà vergitur Austri;
Unde tuam videas obliquo sidere Romam.
Ætheris immensi partem si presseris unam,
Sentiet axis onus : librati pondera cœli
Orbe tene medio: pars ætheris illa sereni
Tota vacet, nullæque obstent à Cæsare nubes.

— — Thee, ah! when, late, thou us shalt leave,
Courts pav'd with Stars shall joyfully receive,
Inviting thee to govern, or to sway
In *Phœbus* Chariot, and command the day:
Earth will not fear to see a newer Sun
With brighter Raies through th'old Eclipticks run.
Thee those, whom Heav'n's Apartments enclose,
And Nature leaves unto thy own dispose,
To be what God thou wilt, and where to raign:
But not thy Palace near the *Northern* Wain;
Nor *Southern* Stars intemperate Heat, erect,
Rome to behold with an oblique Aspect:
Sit in the middle, lest the Pole should crack
Under thy weight; poise the bright Zodiack,
Clear a Celestial House, where never Cloud
Shall *Cæsar*'s Star with duskie Vapours shroud.

We finde like expressions to those in the Inscription under His present Majesty, in several of the old ones collected by *Gruter*; as *Page* CLII. 8.

DN. GLORIOSISS. ADQ. IN
CLUTUS. REX. THEODORICUS. VICT.
AC. TRIF. SEMPER. AUG. BONO REIP.
NATUS. CUSTOS. LIBERTATIS. ET
PROPAGATOR. ROMANI. NOMINIS.
DOMITOR. GENTIUM.

And *Page* CCXLVII. 3.

IMP. CAES. NER. TRAIANO
AUG. GERM. DAC. PARTH. PON
MAX. TR. P. XV. COS. VI. P. P. DE
ROM. IMPERIO. DE. PATERNA
ET. AVITA. HISP. PATRIA. ET. DE
OMNI. HOMIN. GEN. MERITISS
POPULARES. PROVINC
AREVATUM
OPTIMO. PRINC.

Behind

"Behind the said Figure of CHARLES the Second, in a large Table
"is deciphered the ROYAL OAK bearing Crowns, and Scepters,
"instead of Acorns; amongst the Leaves, in a Label,

MIRATURQVE NOVAS FRONDES ET NON SUA POMA.

———————— "Leaves unknown
"Admiring, and strange Apples not her Own.

"As designing its Reward for the Shelter afforded His Majesty after the
"Fight at Worcester: an expression of Virgil's, speaking of the
"Advancement of Fruits by the Art of Graffing.

"The upper Paintings on the East-side are Ruinous, representing the
"Disorder the Kingdom was in, during His Majestie's Absence; with
"this Motto,

EN QVO DISCORDIA CIVES!

"But on the West-side they are finished, to represent the Restauration
"of our Happiness by His Majestie's Arrival; the Motto,

FELIX TEMPORUM REPARATIO.

"On the Royal Oak in a Label,

ROBUR BRITANNICUM.

In allusion to His Majestie's Royal Navy, those Floating Garrisons made of Oak. For *Themistocles* ha's observ'd, that [†] *Whosoever desires a secure Dominion by Land, must first get the Dominion of the Sea.* And therefore, when the Oracle, in the *Median* War, wish'd the *Athenians* to provide a *Wall of Wood* for their Defence, he [*] interpreted it a *Navy*.

[†] *Tull.* ad *Attic.* Lib. i Ep. vii.

[*] *Plutarch.* in vita *Themistoclis,* and *De vitando are alieno*

"Over the Great Table,

REDEUNT SATURNIA REGNA.

Which are at large described by [†] *Ovid*,

Aurea prima sata est ætas; quæ, vindice nullo,
Sponte suâ, sine lege, fidem, rectúmque colebat, &c.

[†] *Metam.* Lib. i.

The

The Golden Age *was first; which, uncompel'd,*
And without rule, in Faith, and Truth excel'd.
As then, there was nor Punishment, nor Fear,
Nor threatning Laws in Brass prescribed were.
Nor suppliant crouching Pris'ners shook to see
Their angry Judge : but all was safe, and free.
To visit other Worlds no wounded Pine
Did yet from Hills to faithless Seas decline.
Then unambitious Mortals knew no more,
But their own Countrie's Nature-bounded Shore.
Nor Swords, nor Arms were yet : no Trenches round
Besieged Towns, nor strifeful Trumpet's sound.
The Souldier of no use. In firm content,
And harmless ease, their happy days were spent.
The yet-free Earth did of her own accord
(Untorn with Ploughs) all sorts of Fruit afford.
'Twas always Spring : warm Zephyrus sweetly blew
On smiling Flowers, which without setting grew.
Forthwith the Earth Corn, unmanured, bears;
And ev'ry year renews her Golden Ears.
With Milk, and Nectar, were the Rivers fill'd,
And Honey from green Holly-Oaks distill'd.

Mr. SANDYS.

" *Under King* CHARLES the Second,

RESTITUTOR URBIS.

" *The Painting on the South-west side represents the Lord Mayor; deli-*
" *vering to the King the Keys of the City.*
" *In the Niches are four Figures. The first on the South-side, a Woman*
" *in pleasant Colours; the Emblem on her Shield, a Terrestrial Globe;*
" *the Sun rising, Bats, and Owls flying to the Shadow : the Word,*

EXCOECAT CANDOR.

" *The*

" *The Second hath on her Escutcheon a Swarm of Bees, whetting their*
" *Stings: the Word,*

PRO REGE EXACUUNT.

Pliny ha's observed, that of Animals none, but a Bee, ha's a *King*. Their Loyalty to him he ha's at large described. *The Obedience of the Communalty is to be admired. Whensoever the* KING *goes forth, the whole Hive accompanie him, gather round about him, encompass him, protect him, and suffer him not to be seen. Whensoever the Communalty is at work, he oversees them, and is alone free from the labour. About him there is constantly a certain Guard, the daily preservers of his authority. When they go forth, every one desires to be next the King, and rejoyces to be seen in his duty. When he is weary, they ease him with their shoulders: when he is altogether tired, they carry him.*

Nat.Hist. lib. xi. cap. xvii.

Claudian says, that they reverence their *Prince* at his Birth;

———— *sic mollibus olim*
Stridula ducturum pratis examina Regem
Nascentem venerantur apes. ————

So for their new-born King the Bees take Arms,
Who's through the Meads to lead their humming swarms.

From whence the *Ægyptians* made a BEE the *Hieroglyphick* of a *Loyal* People.

" *The Third, on the* North *side, hath on her Shield a Mountain burn-*
" *ing, Cities, and Vine-yards destroyed, and ruined: the Word,*

IMPIA FOEDERA.

The Covenant: in abhorrence of which villainous Combination, according to this Order of both Houses, it was burnt by the Common Hangman.

Die

Die Lunæ 20. Maii 1661.

THE Lords in Parliament assembled, having considered of a Paper sent unto them from the House of Commons, for burning of the Instrument, or Writing, called The Solemn League, or Covenant, by the hands of the Common Hangman; Do Order, that the said Instrument, or Writing, called The Solemn League, and Covenant, be burned by the Hand of the Common Hangman in the New-Palace at Westminster, in Cheapside, and before the Old-Exchange on Wednesday the Twenty second of this instant May. And that the said Covenant be forthwith taken off the Record in the House of Peers, and in all other Courts, and Places, where the same is recorded: And that all Copies thereof be taken down out of all Churches, Chapels, and other publick places in England, and Wales, and in the Town of Barwick upon Twede, where the same are set up.

Jo. Brown

Cleric. Parliamentorum.

" *The Fourth hath on her Escutcheon an Arm, as it were out of the*
" *Clouds; in the Hand a naked Sword: the Motto,*

Discite Justitiam Moniti.

Eight Mutes above, on Pedestals; four in White, four in Crimson.
The Musick of this Fabrick is ten Drummers, flanking Rebellion; twelve Trumpets flanking Monarchy.
Aloft under the two Devastations, twelve Trumpets, four Drums.
Within the Arch, on two Balconies, six Trumpets, four Drums.
While the Train passeth along, the Drums beat the Marches of several Countries, and the Trumpets sound several *Levets*. At which Time His Majesty drawing near, the Drums turn their March to a Battel, the Trumpets sound a Charge, and on a sudden Rebellion rowseth up her Self, at which, Drums, and Trumpets ceasing, Rebellion addresses to His Majesty the following Speech.

Stand!

Stand! Stand! who 'ere You are! this Stage is Ours,
The Names of Princes are inscrib'd on Flow'rs,
And wither with them! Stand! You must Me know,
To Kings, and Monarchy a deadly Fo;
Me, who dare bid You 'midst Your Triumphs stand,
In the great City of Your Native Land:
I am Hell's Daughter, Satan's *Eldest Child,*
When I first cry'd, the Powers of Darkness smil'd,
And my Glad Father, Thund'ring at my Birth,
Unhing'd the Poles, and shook the fixed Earth.
My dear Rebellion *(that shall be thy Name,*
Said He) Thou Emperours, and Kings shalt tame,
No Right so good, Succession none so long,
But thou shalt vanquish by thy Popular Throng,
Those Legions, which t'enlarge our Pow'r we send
Throughout the World, shall Thee (my Dear) attend.
Our mighty Champions, the Sev'n Deadly Sins,
By Malice, Profit, Pleasure, all their Gins,
Bring to our Kingdom some few spotted Souls;
Thou shalt by Treason *hurry them in Shoals.*

   Would You now know what Int'rest I have here?
Hydra I ride: great Cities are my Sphear:
I Sorc'ry use, and hang Men in their Beds,
With Common-wealths, and Rotas fill their Heads,
Making the Vulgar in Fanatique Swarms
Court Civil War, and dote on Horrid Arms;
'Twas I, who, in the late unnatural Broils,
Engag'd three Kingdoms, and two Wealthy Isles:
I hope, at last, to march with Flags unfurl'd,
And tread down Monarchy through all the World.

H   At

His MAJESTIE's Entertainments

At which Words, *Monarchy*, and *Loyalty*, unveiling themselves, *Rebellion* starts as affrighted, but, recollecting her self, concludes her Speech thus.

Ah! Britain, Ah! stand'st thou Triumphant there,
Monarchick Isle? I shake with horrid Fear.
Are thy Wounds whole? Upon thy Cheek fresh Smiles?
Is Joy restor'd to these late mournful Isles?
Ah! must He enter, and a King be Crown'd?
Then, as He riseth, sink we under Ground.

Rebellion having ended her Speech, *Monarchy* entertains His Majesty with the following.

To Hell, foul Fiend, shrink from this glorious Light,
And hide thy Head in everlasting Night.
Enter in Safety, Royal Sir, this Arch,
And through your joyful Streets in Triumph march;
Enter our Sun, our Comfort, and our Life.
No more these Walls shall breed Intestine Strife:
Henceforth Your People onely shall contend
In Loyalty each other to transcend.
May Your Great Actions, and immortal Name,
Be the whole Business, and Delight of Fame.
May You, and Yours, in a Perpetual Calm
Be Crown'd with Laurel, and Triumphant Palm,
And all Confess, whilst they in You are Blest,
I, MONARCHY, of Governments am Best.

Monarchy having ended her Speech, the Trumpets sound pleasant *Levets*, and the Drums beat a lofty *English* March, whilst His Majesty, the Nobility, and the Rear-Guard pass on.

The next Entertainment is at *Corn-hill*-Conduit, on the top of which stand eight *Nymphs* clad in White, each having an Escutcheon in one Hand, and a Pendent, or Banner in the other. On the Tower of the said Conduit, a Noise of seven Trumpets.

THE

THE SECOND ARCH.

NEAR the *Exchange*, in *Corn-hill*, is erected the Second *Arch*, which is *Naval*.

"On the East-side were two Stages erected; on each side of the
"Street, one. In that on the South-side was a *Person* representing the
"*River* Thames; his *Garment Loose, and Flowing, Colour Blew and*
"*White, waved like Water, a Mantle over, like a Sail; his Head*
"crown'd with London *Bridg, Flags, and Ozier, like long Hair, falling*
"o'ver his *Shoulders, his Beard long, Sea-green, and White, curl'd; an*
"*Oar in his right Hand, the Model of a Ship in his left, an Urn beside*
"him, *out of which issued Water; four Attendants in White, represent-*
"ing the four fresh *Streams, which fall into the River* Thames, viz.
"Charwel, Lea, Coln, *and* Medway.

The Antients did very much differ in the Description of their Rivers, as Ælian * relates. *Those, that worship Rivers, and those, that make their Images, some form them in the likeness of Men, others in the likeness of Oxen.* The Stymphalians *liken the Rivers* Erasinus *and* Metope, *the* Lacedæmonians Eurotas, *the* Sicyonians *and* Phliasians Asopus, *the* Argives Cephissus, *unto Oxen.* The Psophidians *liken* Erymanthus, *the* Heræans Alphæus, *the* Cherronesians, *that came from* Cnidus, *the River* Cnidus, *to Men.* The Athenians *worship the River* Cephissus *under the form of a Man, but wearing Horns.* In Sicily *the* Syracusians *liken* Anapus *to a Man, but the Fountain* Cyane *to a Woman.* Virgil * *describes* Eridanus *in the Form of an Ox.*

*Var. Hist. lib. ii. cap. xxxiii.

* Georg. iv.

> *Et gemina auratus taurino cornua vultu*
> Eridanus, *quo non alius per pinguia culta*
> *In mare purpureum violentior influit amnis.*

Golden *Eridanus*, with a double Horn,
Fac'd like a Bull, through fertile Fields of Corn,
Then whom, none swifter, of the *Ocean*'s Sons,
Down to the Purple *Adriatick* runs.

On which place says *Probus*; *It's feign'd like a Bull, either because its noise is like the lowing of a Bull, or because its Banks are crooked like Horns.* The same says *Cornutus*. The *Scholiast* on *Sophocles* renders other reasons, either *because they cut the ground like Oxen; or because Meadows, Pasture of Oxen, are always adjacent to them.* HORACE; *tauriformis Aufidus.* So we finde in *Pindar* that the Bull,[†] which *Perillus* gave to the Tyrant *Phalaris*, was the Image of the River *Gelon*. Very frequently we finde *Horns* attributed to them: as in *Virgil*[*],

[† *Pyth.*]
[* *Æn.* lib. viii.]

Corniger Hesperidum *fluvius regnator aquarum,*
Adsis ô tandem, propius tua numina firmes.

Horn'd Flood, of all th' *Hesperian* Rivers King,
Now shew thy power, and us assistance bring.

Ovid,

Cornibus hic fractis, viridi malè tectus ab ulva,
Decolor ipse suo sanguine Rhenus *erat.*

Here *Rhine* with Vine and Reeds ill cover'd stood,
His Horns being broke, distain'd with Native Blood.

Claudian,

[* *De laud. Etilicenis*, lib.i.]

—— Rhenúmque minacem
Cornibus infractis adeò mitescere cogis.

—— and threatning *Rhyne,*
His Horns being broke, thou did'st to Peace incline.

And again of *Eridanus*,

[*De vi. Con-sul. Honorii.*]

—— *ille caput placidis sublime fluentis*
Extulit, & totis lucem spargentia ripis.

Aurea

Aurea roranti micuerunt cornua vultu:
Non illi madidum vulgaris arundine crinem
Velat honos: rami caput umbravêre virentes
Heliadum, totisque fluunt electra capillis.
Palla tegit latos humeros; currùque paterno
Intextus Phaëthon *glaucos incendit amictus.*

Raising his Head above his Wat'ry Ranks,
His Golden Horns, reflecting, tip'd the Banks
With sprinkled light. Drops trickling from his Face:
He his moist Hair veil'd not with Oziers base,
And vulgar Reeds: fresh Pop'lars Shade his Brows,
And Amber from his curled Tresses flows.
A Robe his Shoulders hides; *Phaethon*'s wrought there,
His blew Vest burning in his Father's Chair.

So we finde them also in the form of a *Man*. As the River *Rhene*, as it is supposed: which Statue is still extant in *Rome* lying in a Rock, vulgarly call'd *Marforium* from *Mars*'s Temple in *foro Augusti*, his Hair and Beard long, as if dropping with Water; just as *Claudian* † describes the River *Tyber*,

† *De Prob. & Olyb.*

Illi glauca nitent hirsuto lumina vultu, &c.
Distillant per pectus aquæ, frons hispida manat
Imbribus, in liquidos fontes se barba resolvit.

His blew Eyes shine under his beetle Brows, &c.
His Fore-head swims, Water his Breast distills.
And his rough Beard dissolves in Crystal Rills.

And

And the River *Danubius* in the Coyns of the Emperours *Trajan*, and *Constantine*;

*Cevart.p.*18.
Crojac.Tab.
xxxv.

*Metam.*lib. xiii.

Their Heads were ordinarily environ'd with Reeds, Oziers, and the like. *Ovid*,* relating the Fable of *Acis* turn'd into a River,

——— *subitò mediâ tenùs extitit alvo*
Incinctus juvenis flexis nova cornua cannis.

From whence a Youth arose above the waste,
His horned Brows with quiv'ring Reeds imbrac't.

† *Æn.* lib. viii.

Virgil, † of *Tyber*, the King of Rivers,

Huic Deus ipse loci fluvio Tyberinus *amœno*
Populeas inter senior se attollere frondes
Visus. Eum tenuis glauco velabat amictu
Carbasus, & crines umbrosa tegebat arundo.

The Genius of the Place, old *Tyber*, here
Amongst the Pop'lar Branches did appear.
Of finest Linen were his Azure Weeds,
And his moist Tresses crown'd with shady Reeds.

where we may observe, that *Virgil* gives him a Sail for his Mantle.

* *De Prob.&*
Olyb.

Claudian *of *Tyber*,
——— *crispo densantur gramine colla:*
Vertice luxuriat toto crinalis arundo, &c.

——— *taurinâ*

passing to His CORONATION.

> ⸺⸺ *taurina levantur*
> *Cornua temporibus raucos sudantia rivos*, &c.
> *Palla graves humeros velat, quam neverat uxor*
> *Ilia, percurrens vitreas sub gurgite telas.*

> ⸺⸺ his Neck ripe Harvest bound ;
> An interwoven Reed his Temples crown'd, &c.
> ⸺ And from his rising Horns distils
> A Sweat, which swells to Crystal Rills, &c.
> A Vest he wore, which *Ilia*, his Spouse
> With Crystal Looms wove in her Wat'ry House.

OVID; *Metam.*

> ⸺ *capitis quoque fronde saligna*
> *Aut superimposita celatur arundine damnum.*

> ⸺ the damage of his Brows
> He shades with flaggie Wreaths, and sallow Boughs.

The *Statue* indeed of the River *Tyber*, now extant in *Rome*, ha's its Head inviron'd with several sorts of Leaves, and Fruits, to signifie the fertility of the places near it, caused by the same : yet it recedes not so far from the Fiction of the *Poets*, but that it holds a Reed in its Hand. And the reason is, because these thrive best in watry places.

They are ordinarily described too leaning on an *Urn*, out of which issues Water.

VIRGIL, describing the Shield of *Turnus*,

> *Cælatáque amnem fundens pater* Inachus *Urnâ.*

And *Inachus* powrs Water from his *Urn*.

CLAUDIAN † of *Eridanus*, † *De vi. Consul. Honorii.*

> *Fultáque sub gremio cælatis nobilis astris*
> *Æthereum probat urna decus.* ⸺

An Urn he bore, grav'd with Cœleſtial Signs
That prov'd his high deſcent. ─────

So is *Danubius* repreſented in the Coyns now mentioned. There is a little Image of *Nile* leaning on its right Hand, with its left Hand powring out Water from three Urns with one handle, about which play ſixteen little Children. Why *Nile* ſhould be figured with three Urns, this reaſon is given: becauſe the *Ægyptian* Prieſts attributed the encreaſe of it to three ſeveral cauſes eſpecially, rejecting all other opinions, which were innumerable. The ſixteen Children are the *Hieroglyphick* of ſixteen Cubits, the proper encreaſe of the River *Nile*: for, if it ſwelled higher, it cauſed dearth: for, by how much the more it ſwell'd, ſo much the longer it was before it return'd into its Channel, by which means the Seed-time was loſt: if much under fifteen, it irrigated not the whole Land, and ſo part was unfit to receive Seed. PLINY; *Juſtum incrementum eſt cubitorum ſedecim. Minores aquæ non omnia rigant; ampliores detinent, tardiùs recedendo. Hæ ſerendi tempora abſumunt, illæ non dant ſitiente. Utrumque reputat Provincia. In duodecim cubitis famem ſentit, in tredecim etiamnum eſurit, quatuordecim cubita hilaritatem afferunt, quindecim ſecuritatem, ſexdecim delicias.* There was alſo not long ſince a Marble *Coloſs* of the River *Nile* digg'd up at *Rome* with ſixteen Infants playing about it. And ſo doth *Philoſtratus* deſcribe it.

Of the falling of the *Mole,* and *Medway* into the *Thames*, *Draighton* ha's feigned a pleaſant Relation.

> *At length it came to paſs, that* Iſis, *and her* Tame,
> *Of* Medway *underſtood, a* Nymph *of wond'rous Fame.*
> *And much deſirous were their Princely* Tames *ſhould prove*
> *If, as a Wooer, he could win her Maiden-love.*
> *That of ſo great deſcent, and of ſo large a Dovver*
> *Might vvell allie their Houſe, and much encreaſe his Power:*
> *And ſtriving to prefer their Son the beſt they may,*
> *Set forth the luſty Flood in rich and brave Array;*
> *Bank'd vvith imbroidered Meads, of ſundry ſuits of Flovvrs,*
> *His* Breaſt *adorn'd vvith Swans, oft vvaſh'd vvith Silver Showrs:*

A

passing to His CORONATION.

A Train of gallant Floods, at such a costly rate,
As might beseem their care, and fitting his Estate.
   Attended, and attired magnificently, thus
They send him to the Court of great Oceanus,
The World's huge Wealth to see; yet with a full intent,
To woo the lovely Nymph, fair Medway, as he went.
Who to his Dame and Sire his duty scarce had done,
And whilst they sadly wept at parting of their Son,
See what the Tames befel, when 'twas suspected least.
   As still his goodly Train yet ev'ry hour encreast,
And from the Surrian Shores clear Wey came down to meet
His Greatness, whom the Tames so graciously doth greet,
That with the Fearn-crown'd Flood he, Minion-like, doth play;
Yet is not this the Brook enticeth him to stay:
But, as they thus in pomp came sporting on the shole,
'Gainst Hampton-Court he meets the soft and gentle Mole;
Whose eyes so pierc'd his Breast, that seeming to foreslow
The way, which he so long-intended was to go,
With trifling up and down he wandreth here and there,
And that he in her sight transparent might appear,
Applies himself to Fords, and setteth his delight
On that, which most might make him gracious in her sight.
   Then Isis and the Tame from their conjoyned Bed,
Desirous still to learn how Tames their Son had sped,
(For greatly they had hop'd, his time had so been spent,
That he e're this had won the goodly Heir of Kent)
And, sending to enquire, had News return'd again
(By such as they employ'd on purpose in his Train)
How this their onely Heir, the Isle's imperial Flood,
Had loiter'd thus in love, neglectful of his good.
   No mervail at the News, though Ouse and Tame were sad,
More comfort of their Son expecting to have had,

Nor blame them, in their looks much sorrow though they show'd,
Who, fearing lest he might thus meanly be bestow'd,
And knowing danger still increased by delay,
Employ their utmost pow'r to hasten him away.
But Tames would hardly on : oft turning back to show,
From his much-lov'd Mole how loth he was to go.

 The Mother of the Mole, old Homes-dale, likewise bears
The affection of her Childe, as ill as they do theirs :
Who, nobly though deriv'd, yet could have been content,
T'have match'd her with a Flood of far more mean descent.
But Mole respects her words, as vain and idle Dreams,
Compa'd with that high joy to be belov'd of Tames ;
And head-long holds her course his Company to win :
But Homes-dale raised Hills, to keep the stragler in ;
That of her Daughter's stay she need no more to doubt :
(Yet never was there help, but Love could finde it out.)
Mole digs her self a Path, by working Day and Night,
(According to her Name, to shew her Nature right)
And underneath the Earth for three miles space doth creep,
Till gotten out of sight, quite from her Mother's keep,
Her fore-intended course the wanton Nymph doth run,
As longing to embrace old Tame and Isis Son.

 When Tames now understood, what pains the Mole did take,
How far the loving Nymph adventur'd for his sake ;
Although with Medway match'd, yet never could remove
The often-quickning sparks of his more antient love.
So that it comes to pass, when by great Nature's guide
The Ocean doth return, and thrusteth-in the Tide,
Up, tow'rds the place, where first his much-lov'd Mole was seen,
He ever since doth flow, beyond delightful Sheen.

       Mr. DRAYTON in his *Poly-Olbion*.

"In

" *In the other* Stage *on the* North-side, *which is made like the upper Deck*
" *of a Ship, were three* Sea-men, *whereof one habited like a Boat-*
" Swain.

" *A* Shield, *or* Table, *in the Front of the Arch, bears this* Inscription,

NEPTUNO BRITANNICO,

CAROLO II,

CUJUS ARBITRIO

MARE

VEL LIBERUM, VEL CLAUSUM.

The Dominion of the Sea (signified here by this *Inscription*) ha's been in all Ages so remarkable, that, when the *Grecian Chronographers* could finde no Foot-step of Supreme Empire by Land, before the institution of their *Olympiads*, on whose Actions they could found their *Chronography*, they directed the Series of Time according to the succession of those Nations, who had the Empire of the Sea: which we see in † *Eusebius*; who reckons up nine several Nations, who successively held it, before the institution of the *Olympiads*, and distinctly enumerates the years they retain'd it. The same right the *Grecians* challenged in their League with *Artaxerxes*, King of a vast part of ASIA, after the overthrow of his Naval Forces by *Cimon* the *Athenian Admiral*; "Ἵππυ μὲν δρόμον ἀεὶ τ᾿ Ἑλληνικῆς ἀπέχειν θαλάσσης, ἐντὸς δὲ Κυανέων ϗ Χελιδονίων μακρᾷ νηὶ μὴ πλεῖν. *That he should not within a Horse Race approach the Greek Sea, nor sail within the* Cyanean, *and* Chelidonian *Islands with any Man of War.* The same Dominion of the Sea was afterwards assumed by the *Romans*, as we finde by the Commission granted to *Pompey*, "Ἄρχειν τ᾿ ἐντὸς Ἡρακλείων στηλῶν θαλάσσης, ἠπείρυ δὲ πάσης ἐπὶ σταδίυς τετρακοσίυς ὑπὸ θαλάσσης· *That he should have the Empire of the Sea within the* Streights, *and of the Continent for four hundred Stadia from the Sea.* And not long after *Dionysius Halicarnassæus* says, * *That* Rome *was Empress of the whole Sea, not onely of that within the*

† *Chronico.*

* *Orig. Rom. Lib. 1.*

Streights,

Streights, but of the Ocean it self, as far as it was Navigable. Whence *Augustus* had a *Dolphin* in his Coyns to signifie that Dominion,

* In Prolog. 8º.

† D. vi. Consul. Honorii.

And * *Valerius Maximus*, to *Tiberius* the Emperour, *The Consent both of Gods and Men ha's constituted you Governour of Sea, and Land.* Afterwards *Claudian* †,

———— *terræ dominos pelagique futuros,*
Immenso decuit rerum de Principe nasci.

Those, who must rule both Sea, and Land,
Ought to be Princes Sons of great Command.

And sure, if any Nation may plead Prescription for this Title, the King of ENGLAND may, having had a longer uninterrupted Succession in the Dominion of the BRITTISH *Seas,* then the ROMANS in the *Mediterranean*, or any other Nation, that *History* ha's acquainted us with. The Antiquity whereof being purposely, and at large declared by Mr. SELDEN, we shall onely take notice of two *Records* of it, the one taken out of the *Laws of Hoëlus Dha*, Prince of WALES, about the Year, 982. viz. *Quos cum Cunadio Rege Scotorum, Malcolmo Rege Cambrorum, & Maccusio Archipirata, ad civitatem Legionum sibi occurrentes, Rex Anglorum Eadgarus in Triumphi pompam deducebat. Unà enim impositos remigrare eos hanc coegit, dum in Prora ipse sedens Navis tennit gubernaculum : ut se hoc spectaculo Soli & Sali orbis Britannici Dominum prædicaret, & Monarcham.* The other is a Record in the Tower of *London*, entituled *De superioritate maris Angliæ*, &c. in which it evidently appears, that the Dominion of the *Brittish* Seas belong'd to the Kings of *England* time out of mind, even before *Edward* the First, and was so acknowledged by other Neighbouring Nations ; out of which

which we shall onely extract so much as may serve for our present purpose, viz. *That the Procuratours of the Admiral of the Sea of England, and of other places, as of the Sea Coasts, as of Genoa, Catalonia, Spain, Almain, Zealand, Holland, Freezland, Denmark, and Norway, do shew that the Kings of England, time out of mind, have been in peaceable possession of the Seas of England, in making, and establishing Laws, and Statutes, and Restraints of Arms, and of Ships, &c. and in taking Surety, &c. and in ordering all other things necessary for the maintaining of Peace, Right, and Equity, &c. and in doing Justice, Right, and Law, according to the said Laws, Ordinances, and Restraints, and in all other things, which may appertain to the exercise of Sovereign Dominion in the places aforesaid.*

"*The first Painting on the North side over the City-Arms, represents*
"N E P T U N E, *with his Trident advanced;* the Inscription,

NEPTUNO REDUCI.

NEPTUNE's Statue is seldom seen without a Trident in its hand. *Pausanias*[†], *Within the Temple there is an erect Brazen Statue (of* NEPTUNE) *with one foot upon a Dolphin, and on that side his Hand on his Thigh; in his other Hand a* Trident. And so he is every where described by the Poets.

[†] *In Phocicis.*

Perque tuum, pater Ægei Neptune, Tridentem.

But more of this hereafter.

The Motto NEPTUNO REDUCI we finde in two Medaigles, the one of the Emperour *Adrian*, the other of *Vespasian*, with these Letters on one side N E P T. R E D. and the image of one standing naked, a Mantle on his left Shoulder, in his right Hand a Whip with three Cords, in his left a Trident.

"*On the South-side, opposite,* M A R S, *with his Spear inverted, his Shield*
"*charged with a Gorgon; by his Knees, the Motto,*

MARTI PACIFERO.

So Homer describes the Shield of *Agamemnon*,

Τῇ δ' ἐπὶ μὲν Γοργὼ Βλοσυρῶπις ἐςεφάνωτο,
Δεινὸν δερχομένη, πεεὶ δὲ Δειμός τε φόβ&c; τε.

The Sable Field charg'd with a Gorgon's Head,
Mantled about with dismal Flight, and Dread:

and in another place the Armour of *Pallas*,

Ἐν δέ τε Γοργείη κεφαλὴ δεινοῖο πελώρου,
Δεινή τε σμερδνή τε, Διὸς τέρας αἰγιόχοιο.

Amidst, that horrid Monster Gorgon's Head,
Jove's direst Omen, fierce, and full of dread.

Pausanias; Under the Statue of Victory lies a Golden Shield, *with a Gorgon wrought upon it.* And it is observ'd by the *Scholiast* on * *Aristophanes*, that it was Customary among the *Grecians* to have a *Gorgon's Head on their Shields*, as he represents † *Lamachus's*. The Form of this *Gorgon's* Head is still to be seen at *Rome* on the Statues of the Emperours *Vespasian* and *Domitian*. It was feigned with Wings, to signifie the present death, that attended it: for whoever looked on it, immediatly was turn'd into Stone. The which at large, and very elegantly is declared by *Ovid*,

In Acharn.
† *In Pace.*

Metam. lib. v. Fab. i.

But when he saw his Valour oversway'd
By Multitude; I must, said he, seek aid
(Since you your selves compell me) from my Foe;
Friends turn your Backs: then Gorgon's Head doth show.
Some others seek, said Thessalus, *to fright*
With this thy Monster, and with all his might
A deadly Dart endeavour'd to have thrown:
But in that Posture became a Stone.
Next Amphix, full of spirit, forward prest,
And thrust his Sword at bold Lyncides Breast:

When in the Pass his Fingers stupid grow,
Nor had the pow'r of moving to or fro.
But Nileus *(he, who with a forged stile*
Vaunted to be the Son of sev'n-fold Nile,
And bare sev'n Silver Rivers in his Shield,
Distinctly waving through a Golden Field)
To Perseus *said; Behold, from whence we sprung!*
To ever-silent Shadows bear along
This comfort of thy Death, that thou did'st die
By such a brave, and high-born Enemy.
His utt'rance faulter'd in the latter Clause,
The yet unfinish'd Word stuck in his Jaws;
Who gaping stood, as he would something say,
And so had done, if words had found a way.
These Eryx *blames; 'Tis your faint Souls, that dead*
Your Pow'rs, said he, and not the Gorgon's *Head:*
Rush on with me, and prostrate with deep Wounds
This Youth, who thus with Magick Arms confounds.
Then rushing on, the ground his foot-steps stai'd
Now mutely fix'd, an armed Statue made.

   These suffer'd worthily. One, who did fight
For Perseus, *bold* Aconteus, *at the sight*
Of Gorgon's *Snakes abortive Marble grew,*
On whom Astyages *in fury flew,*
As if alive, with his two-handled Blade,
Which shrilly twang'd, but no incision made.
Who, whilst he wonders, the same Nature took,
And now his Statue ha's a wondring look.
It were too tedious for me to report
Their Names, who perish'd of the vulgar sort:

Two

*Two hundred scap'd the fury of the Fight;
Two hundred turn'd to stone at Gorgon's sight.*

Mr. SANDYS.

[† Epithal. P.l.] The Head is thus described † by SIDONIUS APOLLINARIS,

*Gorgo tenet pectus medium, factura videnti
Et truncata moras, nitet insidiosa superbùm
Effigies, vivitque animâ pereunte venustas.
Alta cerastarum spiris caput asperat atrum
Congeries, torquet maculosa volumina mordax
Crinis, & irati dant sibila tetra capilli.*

The *Gorgon*'s Head, which guards her Bosome, would
Change thee to Statue, should'st thou it behold.
The treach'rous Face shows proudly, and, though dead,
Life's beauty keeps. Snakes, matted round her Head,
In speckled Curls voluminously wreath,
And biting Tresses direly-hissing breath.

[* In *Arcad*.] PAUSANIAS * reports, that *Pallas* made a City impregnable, by communicating onely a little Hair cut off from her *Gorgon*'s Head.

The Title of PACIFER is attributed to *Mars* in the *Roman* Coyns; as in this of *Quintillus*,

[Hulsius.]

So we finde, that the *Romans* erected a Temple to *Mars Quirinus*, as well as *Mars Gradivus*. The first had his Temple within the City:
the

the other without in the *Appian*-way, not far from the Gate. The one, with a gentle, sedate Countenance, to preserve the tranquillity, and peace of the City: the other, to go out with them in their Wars abroad. *Gellius* * says, *That Herſila ſpeaking before* T. Tatius, *and deſiring Peace, prayed on this manner*, O Neria, Wife of Mars, I beſeech thee to grant us Peace, that we may enjoy a during, and proſperous Marriage. And therefore the Olive, the Symbole of Peace, was conſecrated to *Pallas*, the Goddeſs of War; becauſe War is therefore undertaken, that a ſecure Peace may be enjoyed. *Ideò arma inferri dicuntur, ut poſteà in pace vivatur*, ſays *Pliny*.

* *Noct. Att. Lib. xiii.*

" *Over the Arch, the Marriage of* Thame *and* Iſis.

The Marriage of Rivers is a frequent Fiction among the Poets: as of *Alpheus* and *Arethuſa*; therefore feign'd, becauſe *Alpheus*, a River of *Elis* in the *Morea*, paſſeth through the Ocean, unmix'd, to the River *Arethuſa* in the Iſland *Ortygia*, near *Syracuſe*, a City of *Sicily*. Which paſſage ha's been often tried, as by a Cup, ſays ⸸ *Strabo*, let fall in the River *Alpheus* in *Elis*, and found in *Arethuſa*: maintain'd alſo by an Oracle given to *Archias*, a *Corinthian*, that he ſhould thither deduce a Colony, where *Alpheus* is mingled with the Fountain of *Arethuſa*. The Marriage of theſe two we have deſcribed by * O v i d, where the Nymph *Arethuſa* ſpeaks, being ready to be turn'd into a River;

⸸ *Geogr. Lib. vi.*

* *Metam. Lib. v.*

> *Cold Sweats my then-beſieged Limbs poſſeſt:*
> *In thin thick-falling Drops my ſtrength decreaſt.*
> *Where e're I ſtep, Streams run; my Hair now fell*
> *In trickling Dew; and, ſooner then I tell*
> *My Deſtiny, into a Flood I grew.*
> *The River his beloved Waters knew;*
> *And, putting off th'aſſumed ſhape of Man,*
> *Reſumes his own, and in my Current ran.*
> *Chaſt* Delia *cleft the ground: then, through blind Caves,*
> *To lov'd* Ortygia *ſhe conducts my Waves,*
> *Affected for her Name: where firſt I take*
> *Review of day. This* Arethuſa *ſpake.*

Mr. S A N D Y S.

Thus *Anapus*, and *Cyane* are feign'd mutual Lovers; becaufe their Waters unite, and run together into the Sea. OVID,

> ——— *quòd ſi componere magnis*
> *Parva mihi fas eſt; & me dilexit* Anapus:
> *Exorata tamen, nec, ùt hæc, exterrita nupſi.*

If humble things I may compare with great,
Anapus lov'd me; yet did he intreat,
And me, not frighted thus, efpous'd.

The Marriage of *Tibur* and *Ilia* is frequently mention'd, OVID, fpeaking of both,

> *Atque ità ſe in rapidas perdita miſit aquas:*
> *Suppoſuiſse manus ad pectora lubricus amnis*
>   *Dicitur, & ſocii jura dediſſe thori.*

She leap'd amidſt the Stream with grief oppreſt:
The River puts his hand beneath her Breaſt,
And, as they fay, unloos'd her Virgin-Ceſt.

In another place,

> *Nec te prætereo, qui, per cava ſaxa volutus,*
>   *Tiburis Argæi ſpumifer arva rigas:*
> *Ilia cui placuit.* ————

Nor thee, roll'd through worn Rocks, do I pafs by,
Who on *Tyburtian* Grounds doſt foaming ly:
Whom *Ilia* pleas'd. ————

Lib. xii. SILIUS ITALICUS,

> *Ad genitorem Anio labens ſine murmure Tibrim.*
> *Hic, ùt ſigna ferox, dimenſáque caſtra locavit,*

Et

Et ripas tremefecit eques, perterrita pulsis
Ilia prima vadis sacro se conjugis antro
Condidit. ————

——— but on, like a rude Storm, he goes
To those low Banks, where *Anio* gently flows
With Sulph'rous Waters, and with Silence, to
Old *Tiber*'s Arms; when here the Line he drew
Of's Camp, and set his Standard up, and shook
His Banks with's Cavalry, first *Ilia*, strook
With Fear, flies to her Husband's sacred Cave,
And all the frighted *Nymphs* the Water leave.

Mr. Ross.

The Marriage of *Tame* and *Isis*, here mention'd, is pleasantly related by Mr. DRAYTON [†];

[†] *In his* Poly-Olbion, *Song* 15.

Now Fame had through this Ile divulg'd, in every ear,
The long-expected day of Marriage to be near,
That *Isis*, *Cotswold*'s Heir, long-woo'd, was lastly won,
And instantly should wed with *Tame*, old *Chiltern*'s Son.
 And now that Wood-man's Wife, the Mother of the Flood,
The rich and goodly Vale of *Alesbury*, that stood
So much upon her *Tame*, was busied in her Bow'rs,
Preparing for her Son as many Sutes of Flow'rs,
At *Cotswold* for the Bride, his *Isis*, lately made;
Who for the lovely *Tame*, her Bridegroom, onely staid.
 Whilst every Crystal Flood is to this business prest,
The cause of their great speed and many thus request;
O! whither go ye Floods? what suddain Winde doth blow,
Then other of your kind that you so fast should flow?

What bufinefs is in hand, that fpurs you thus away?
Fair *Windrufh*, let me hear, I pray thee, *Charwel* fay:
They fuddainly reply, What lets, you fhould not fee,
That for this Nuptial Feaft we all prepared be?
Therefore this idle chat our Ears doth but offend;
Our leifure ferves not now thefe Trifles to attend.

But, whilft things are in hand, old *Chiltern* (for his life)
From prodigal expenfe can no way keep his Wife;
Who feeds her *Tame* with Marl, in Cordial-wife prepar'd,
And thinks all idly fpent, that now fhe onely fpar'd
In fetting forth her Son: nor can fhe think it well,
Unlefs her lavifh charge do *Cotfwold*'s far excel.
For *Alesbury*'s a Vale, that walloweth in her Wealth,
And (by her wholefom Air continually in health)
Is lufty, frim, and fat, and holds her youthful ftrength.
Befides her fruitful Earth, her mighty breadth, and length,
Doth *Chiltern* fitly match: which mountainoufly high,
And being very long, fo likewife fhe doth lie;
From the *Bedfordian* Fields, where firft fhe doth begin,
To fafhion like a Vale, to th'place where *Tame* doth win
His *Ifis* wifhed Bed; her Soil throughout fo fure,
For goodnefs of her Glebe, and for her Pafture pure,
That as her Grain, and Grafs, fo fhe her Sheep doth breed,
For Burthen, and for Bone, all other that exceed:
And fhe, which thus in Wealth abundantly doth flow,
Now cares not on her Childe what coft fhe do beftow.
Which when wife *Chiltern* faw (the World who long had try'd,
And now at laft had laid all garifh Pomp afide;
Whofe hoar and chalky Head defcri'd him to be old,
His Beechen Woods bereft, that kept him from the Cold)
Would fain perfwade the Vale to hold a fteddy rate;
And with his curious Wife thus wifely doth debate:

Quoth

Quoth he, you might allow what needeth, to the most :
But where as less will serve, what means this idle Cost ?
Too much a Surfet breeds, and may our Childe annoy :
These fat and lushious Meats do but our Stomacks cloy.
The modest comely mean in all things likes the Wise,
Apparel often shews us Womanish precise.
And what will *Cotswold* think, when he shall hear of this ?
He'l rather blame your Waste, then praise your Cost, I wiss.

But, Women wilful be, and she her Will must have,
Nor cares how *Chiltern* chides, so that her *Tame* be brave.
Alone which tow'rds his Love she easily doth convay ;
For the *Oxonian Owse* was lately sent away
From *Buckingham,* where first he finds his nimbler Feet ;
Tow'rds *Whittlewood* then takes : where, past the noblest Street,
He to the Forest gives his farewel, and doth keep
His course directly down into the *German* Deep,
To publish that great day in mighty *Neptune*'s Hall,
That all the Sea-gods there might keep it Festival.

As we have told how *Tame* holds on his even course,
Return we to report, how *Isis* from her sourse
Comes tripping with delight, down from her daintier Springs ;
And in her Princely Train, t'attend her Marriage, brings
Clear *Churnet, Coln,* and *Leech,* which first she did retain,
With *Windrush* : and with her (all out-rage to restrain,
Which well might offered be to *Isis,* as she went)
Came *Yenload* with a Guard of *Satyres,* which were sent
From *Whichwood,* to await the bright and God-like Dame.
So *Bernwood* did bequeath his *Satyres* to the *Tame,*
For Sticklers in those stirs, that at the Feast should be.

These Preparations great when *Charwel* comes to see,
To *Oxford* got before, to entertain the Flood,
Apollo's Aid he begs, with all his sacred Brood,

To

To that most learned place to welcome her repair,
Who in her coming on was wax'd so wond'rous fair,
That, meeting, strife arose betwixt them, whether they
Her Beauty should extol, or she admire their Bay.
On whom their sev'ral gifts (to amplifie her Dower)
The *Muses* there bestow; which ever have the power
Immortal her to make. And, as she past along,
Those modest *Thespian* Maids thus to their *Isis* song,

    Ye Daughters of the Hills, come down from every side,
And due attendance give upon the lovely Bride:
Go strew the Paths with Flowers, by which she is to pass:
For be ye thus assur'd, in *Albion* never was
A Beauty (yet) like hers: where have ye ever seen
So absolute a *Nymph* in all things, for a Queen?
Give instantly in charge the day be wond'rous fair,
That no disorder'd Blast attempt her braided Hair.
Go, see her State prepar'd, and every thing be fit,
The Bride-Chamber adorn'd with all beseeming it.
And for the Princely Groom, who ever yet could name
A Flood, that is so fit for *Isis*, as the *Tame?*
Ye both so lovely are, that knowledge scarce can tell,
For Feature whether he, or Beauty she excel:
That, ravished with joy each other to behold,
When as your Crystal Wasts you closely do enfold,
Betwixt your beauteous selves you shall beget a Son,
That when your lives shall end, in him shall be begun.
The pleasant *Surrian* Shores shall in that Flood delight,
And *Kent* esteem her self most happy in his sight.
The Shire that *London* loves, shall onely him prefer,
And give full many a gift to hold him near to her.
The *Skeld*, the goodly *Mose*, the rich and Viny *Rhein*,
Shall come to meet the *Thames* in *Neptune's* watry Plain.

                                         And

And all the *Belgian* Streams, and neighb'ring Floods of *Gaul*,
Of him shall stand in aw, his Tributaries all.

   As of fair *Isis* thus the learned Virgins spake,
A shrill and suddain Bruit this *Prothalamion* brake;
That *White-horse*, for the love she bare to her Ally,
And honoured Sister-Vale, the bounteous *Alesbury*,
Sent Presents to the *Tame*, by *Ock* her onely Flood,
Which for his Mother-Vale so much on greatness stood.

   From *Oxford Isis* hasts more speedily, to see
That River, like his Birth, might entertained be:
For that ambitious Vale, still striving to command,
And using for her place continually to stand,
Proud *White-horse* to perswade much business there hath been,
T'acknowledge that great Vale of *Eusham* for her Queen.
And but that *Eusham* is so opulent, and great,
That thereby she her self holds in the Sovereign Seat,
This *White-horse* all the Vales of *Britain* would or'ebear,
And absolutely sit in the Imperial Chair;
And boasts as goodly Heards, and num'rous Flocks to feed,
To have as soft a Glebe, as good increase of Seed;
As pure and fresh an Ayr upon her Face to flow,
As *Eusham* for her life: and from her Steed doth show,
Her lusty rising Downs as fair a Prospect take,
As that imperious *Wold*; which her great Queen doth make
So wond'rously admir'd, and her so far extend.
But to the Mariage, hence, industrious Muse descend.

   The *Naiads*, and the *Nymphs* extremely over-joy'd,
And on the winding Banks all busily imploy'd,
Upon this joyful day, some dainty Chaplets twine;
Some others chosen out, with fingers neat and fine,
Brave Anadems do make: some Bauldricks up do bind;
Some, Garlands: and to some the Nosegays were asign'd;

As

As beſt their Skill did ſerve. But, for that *Tame* ſhould be
Still man-like as himſelf, therefore they will, that he
Should not be dreſt with Flow'rs, to Gardens that belong,
(His Bride that better fit) but onely ſuch as ſprong
From the repleniſh'd Meads, and fruitful Paſtures near:
To ſort which Flow'rs ſome fit; ſome making Garlands were;
The Primroſe placing firſt, becauſe that in the Spring
It is the firſt appears, then onely flouriſhing;
The azur'd Hare-bell next with them they neatly mixt:
T'allay whoſe luſhious Smell they Woodbind plac'd betwixt.
Amongſt thoſe things of ſcent, there prick they in the Lilly;
And near to that again her Siſter Daffadilly.
To ſort theſe Flow'rs of ſhow with th'other that were ſweet,
The Cowſlip then they couch, and th'Oxſlip, for her meet:
The Columbine amongſt they ſparingly do ſet,
The Yellow King-cup, wrought in many a curious fret,
And now and then among, of Eglantine a ſpray,
By which again a courſe of Lady-ſmocks they lay:
The Crow-flower, and thereby the Clover-flower they ſtick,
The Dayſie over all thoſe ſundry ſweets ſo thick,
As Nature doth her ſelf; to imitate her right:
Who ſeems in that her Pearl ſo greatly to delight,
That ev'ry Plain therewith ſhe powd'reth to behold:
The crimſon Darnel Flow'r, the Blew-bottle, and Gold;
Which though eſteem'd but Weeds, yet for their dainty hews,
And for their ſcent not ill, they for their purpoſe chuſe.

    Thus having told you how the Bridegroom *Tame* was dreſt,
I'le ſhew you how the Bride, fair *Iſis*, they inveſt;
Sitting to be attir'd under her Bow'r of State,
Which ſcorns a meaner ſort, then fits a Princely rate.
In Anadems, for whom they curiouſly diſpoſe
The Red, the dainty White, the goodly Damask Roſe,

For the rich Ruby, Pearl, and Amatift, men place
In Kings Emperial Crowns, the Circle that enchafe.
The brave Carnation then, with fweet and foveraign power
(So of his colour call'd, although a July-flower)
With th'other of his kind, the fpeckled and the pale:
Then th'odoriferous Pink, that fends forth fuch a Gale
Of fweetnefs; yet in fcents, as various as in forts.
The Purple Violet then, the Panfie there fupports:
The Mary-gold above t'adorn the arched Bar;
The double Dayfie, Thrift, the Button-batcheler,
Sweet William, Sops in Wine, the Campion: and to thefe,
Some Lavander they put, with Rofemary and Bays:
Sweet Marjoram, with her like, fweet Bafil rare for fmell,
With many a Flower, whofe name were now too long to tell:
And rarely with the reft, the goodly Flower-delice.

 Thus for the nuptial hour, all fitted point-device,
Whilft fome ftill bufied are in decking of the Bride;
Some others were again as ferioufly imploy'd
In ftrewing of thofe Hearbs, at Bridals us'd that be:
Which every where they throw with bounteous hands and fr
The healthful Balm and Mint, from their full laps do fly,
The fcent-ful Camomil, the verdurous Coftmary.
They hot Mufcado oft with milder Maudlin caft:
Strong Tanfey, Fennel cool, they prodigally wafte:
Clear Ifop, and therewith the comfortable Thyme,
Germander with the reft, each thing then in her prime;
As well of wholefome Hearbs, as every pleafant Flower,
Which Nature here produc'd, to fit this happy hour.
Amongft thefe ftrewing kinds, fome other wilde that grow,
As Burnet, all abroad, and Meadow-wort they throw.

L   " The

" *The Painting on the* North-*side*, *over* Neptune, *represents the*
" Exchange; *the Motto,*

—— GENERIS LAPSI SARCIRE RUINAS.

" *An Expression of* Virgil's, *in the fourth of his* Georgicks, *speaking*
" *of the Industry of Bees, never discouraged by their Losses; his Descri-*
" *ption of it running thus,*

>   *Quò magis exhaustæ fuerint, hoc acriùs omnes*
>   *Incumbent generis lapsi sarcire ruinas,*
>   *Complebúntque Foros, & Floribus Horrea texent.*

>   How much by Fortune they exhausted are,
>   So much they strive the Ruins to repair
>   Of their fal'n Nation, and they fill th' *Exchange*,
>   Adorning with the choicest Flow'rs their Grange.

" *The Painting on the* South-*side*, *over* Mars, *shews the* Tower *of*
" London; *the* Inscription,

CLAUDUNTUR BELLI PORTÆ.

This is in reference to the *Temple* of Janus, never shut, but in the time of *Peace*; nor opened, but in time of *War*. Therefore, when King *Latinus* had refused to raise a War against *Æneas*, and his Followers, and to that purpose, to open the Gates of the *Temple* of Janus, *Juno*, resolving to have a War prosecuted against him, opened them her self: mention'd by Virgil[†],

>   *Hoc & tum Æneadis indicere bella Latinus*
>   *More jubebatur, tristésque* recludere portas.
>   *Abstinuit tactu Pater, aversúsque refugit*
>   *Fœda ministeria, & cæcis se condidit umbris.*
>   *Tum Regina Deûm, cælo delapsa, morantes*
>   *Impulit ipsa manu* Portas : *&, cardine verso,*
>   *Belli ferratos rupit Saturnia postes.*

The King was here required by the States
War to denounce, and OPEN JANUS GATES.
He flies th' Engagement, and so foul a Cause,
And straight himself to privacy withdraws.
Then from high Heav'n the Queen of Gods descends,
And the resisting Portals open rends.
She breaks the Hinges, tears down Iron Bars,
And makes a spacious way for impious Wars.

"The Pedestals, in the Upper Story, are adorned with eight living Fi-
"gures, representing EUROPE, ASIA, AFRICK, and AMERICA, with
"Escutcheons, and Pendents, bearing the Arms of the Companies trading
"into those parts.

"EUROPE, a Woman arm'd a l'antique; on her Shield a Woman ri-
"ding on a Bull; at her foot a Coney.

The Effigies of *Europe* in Armour relates to the Warlike disposition of that part of the World, evidently seen in the *Greek*, and *Roman* Monarchies. We shall not need to describe her Armour in particular, but leave it to be taken from this Description of *Rome*, the Mistress of *Europe*, in *Claudian*,

> *Ipsa, triumphatis quæ possidet æthera regnis,*
> *Assilit, innuptæ ritus imitata* Minervæ:
> *Nam neque cæsariem crinali stringere cultu*
> *Colla, nec ornatu patitur mollire retorto;*
> *Dextrum nuda latus, niveos exserta lacertos,*
> *Audacem retegit mammam, laxûmque coërcens*
> *Mordet gemma sinum: nodus, qui sublevat ensem,*
> *Album puniceo pectus discriminat ostro.*
> *Miscetur decori virtus, pulchérque severo*
> *Armatur terrore pudor, galeæque minaci*
> *Flava cruentarum prætenditur umbra jubarum.*
> *Et formidato clypeus* Titana *lacessit*
> *Lumine, quem totâ variârat* Mulciber *arte.*

She who by conquering Realms the Sky possest,
Starts from her Seat, like Virgin-*Pallas* drest:
Her Hair no Fillet bound, nor was her Head
Drest up, Tresses hung o're her Shoulders spread,
Her right side nak'd, with stretch'd out Arms, her Breast
Boldly she bares, a Jemme claspt up her Vest,
Her Faulchion in a Purple Belt, more bright
Her Bosom rendred, setting off the white:
Valour with Beauty mix'd, a modest Blush
With terrour arm'd, her threatning Cask and Bush
Of Bloody Plumage cast a dreadful shade:
And *Gorgon*-Shield, that *Titan* so dismai'd,
Which *Vulcan* with such art and labour made.

Whom *Sidonius Apollinaris* followed so nearly, that there will need no other Translation then the precedent.

Paneg. Majorian.

Sederat exerto bellatrix pectore Roma
Cristatum turrita caput, cui ponè capaci
Casside prolapsus perfundit terga capillus.
Lætitia censura manet, terrorque pudore
Crescit, & invitâ superat virtute venustas.
Ostricolor pepli textus, quem fibula torto
Mordax dente vorat, tum quicquid mamma refundit
Tegminis, hoc patulo conclusit gemma recessu.
Hinc fulcit rutilus spacioso circite lævum
Umbo latus, videas hic crasso fusa metallo
Antra Rheæ, fœtamq; lupam, quam fauce retecta
Blandiri quoq; terror erat, quanquam illa vorare
Martigenas & picta timet, pars proxima Tybrin
Exprimit; hic scabri fusus sub pumice tophi
Proflabat madidum per guttura glauca soporem.

Her

passing to His Coronation.

Her Shield comprehends the Story from whence *Europe* had her name, agreeably to the Custome of the Ancients: as we finde by this description of the Shield of *Rome* in the same Authour.

Ibid.

> *Hic patrius Mavortis amor, fœtusq; notantur*
> *Romulei; post amnis inest, & bellua nutrix.*
> *Electro Tyberis, Pueri formantur in Auro.*
> *Tingunt æra lupam, Mavors adamante coruscat.*

> Here *Mars* escapes, and there the Twins he drew,
> And next the River, and the Shee-wolfe too:
> *Tyber* in Amber, and the Boyes in Gold,
> The Wolf in Brass, *Mars* he in Steel did mould.

The first part of which seems to be taken from that of *Æneas* in *Virgil*,

> *Illic res Italas, Romanorumque triumphos,*
> *Haud vatum ignarus venturique inscius ævi,*
> *Fecerat Ignipotens, illic genus omne futuræ*
> *Stirpis ab Ascanio, pugnataque in ordine bello*
> *Fecerat, & viridi fœtam Mavortis in antro*
> *Procubuisse lupam; geminos huic ubera circum*
> *Ludere pendentes pueros, & lambere matrem*
> *Impavidos; illam tereti cervice reflexam*
> *Mulcere alternos, & corpora fingere linguâ.*
> *Nec procul hinc, Romam,* &c.

> Th' Ignipotent God, well skill'd in Fates to come,
> The *Roman* triumphs and affaires of *Rome*,
> There had engrav'd, *Ascanius* Off-spring wrought,
> And all their bloody battels must be fought.
> The pregnant Wolfe in *Mars* green Covert lay,
> And hanging at her breasts two Infants play:
> Bending her neck she licks the tender young,
> And quiet, shapes their bodies with her tongue.
> Not far from this, *Rome,* &c.

Or from these of *Silius Italicus*, describing the Shield of *Flaminius*, a *Roman* Consul;

> *Tum clypeum quatit, aspersum quem cædibus olim*
> *Celticus ornârat cruor : humentique sub antro,*
> *Ceu fœtum, lupa permulcens puerilia membra*
> *Ingentem* Assarici *cælo nutribat alumnum.*

> Next, he assumes his Shield, where they behold
> The stains of *Celtick* blood, which he before
> In Battel shed : and, in it carv'd, he bore
> A She-Wolf's Figure, in her gloomy Den,
> Licking a Child's soft Limbs, as it had been
> Her Whelp, and nurs'd of the *Assarick* Line
> A Stem, that afterwards was made Divine.

Mr. Ross.

The other, from these Verses of *Moschus*, where he describes the Basket of *Europa*,

> Ἀργύρεος μὲν ἔην Νείλυ ῥόος· ἡ δ' ἄρα πόρτις
> Χαλκείη, χρυσοῦ δὲ τετυγμένος αὐτὸς ἔην Ζεύς.

> In Silver *Nilus* stood, the *Cow* in Brass,
> And *Jupiter* in Gold engraven was.

The *Fable* presented in the Shield of *Europe* is this. *Europa*, Daughter of *Agenor*, gathering Flowers near the Sea-side, was carryed away by *Jupiter*, in the Form of a Bull, into *Crete*, where she became his Spouse ; by whose Name he caused that part of the World to be called, according to this of *Manilius* [†],

† *Astronom. Lib. IV.*

> *Quod superest* Europa *tenet, quæ prima natantem*
> *Fluctibus excepitque* Jovem, *Taurumque resolvit.*
> *Ille puellari donavit nomine fluctus,*
> *Et monumenta sui titulo sacravit amoris.*

Europa last place held, whom *Jove* his Prize
Through Billows bearing, cast his Bull's disguise,
And gave that Sea, to her eternal Fame,
In memory of his Love, the Virgin's Name.

This Virgin was generally reputed a *Tyrian*. EURIPIDES,

Φοινικογενὴς παῖ ς̃ Τυρίας
Τέκνον Εὐρώπης ———

SENECA the *Tragedian*,

Tyriæ *per undas vector* Europæ *nitet* :

Through Waves *Tyrian Europa*'s bearer shone.

And *Herodotus*[†] conjectures this quarter of the World was named ב֑ן ς̃ Συρίης Εὐρώπης (which *Valla* renders, *ab* Europa *Tyria*) in his first Book, affirming, the *Cretans* sail'd to *Tyre*, and stole her from thence. The *Chronographers*, that follow *Eusebius*, rank this about the time of *Joshuah*, but the *Arundelian* Marbles (set forth by Mr. *Selden*) shew, that *Cadmus* came to *Thebes*, and built *Cadmea* at the same time, when *Amphictyon* reign'd in *Athens*, which was before the *Israelites* forsook *Egypt*. By this it is apparent, that *Europa* was not of *Tyre* ; for that was built long after, *viz.* according to *Josephus* [*], before the Temple of *Solomon*, which was begun in the 480. Year after the *Israelites* departure out of *Egypt*. It is supposed, that that part of the *Fable*, which feigns her carried away by a Bull, signifies no more, then that she was transported by Sea in a Ship called the *Bull*, from the Figure of a Bull on the Prow of it. So LYCOPHRON,

[†] *Lib.* iv.

[*] *Antiq. Jud. Lib.* viii. 2.

Ἐν ταυρομόρφῳ τραμπίδος μορφώματι

it being among the Ancients the usual Custom to nominate their Ships from the Ἐπίσημον, or *Insigne* on the Prow, as the *Tiger*, *Centaure*, and *Triton*, in the Navy of *Æneas*, mention'd by VIRGIL[†],

[†] *Æneid.* X.

Massicus *ærata princeps secat æquora* Tigri.

I'th' Brazen *Tigre Massicus* first stands.

Filius

Filius æquales comitatus classe catervas
Ingentem remis Centaurum *promovet.—*
Hunc vehit immanis Triton, *& cærula conchâ*
Exterrens freta.———

His Son attended with an equal Troop
Brings, with tuff Oars, the mighty *Centaure* up.
This mighty *Triton* bore, frighting the Tides
With his shrill Trump,——

We shall not need give any further account of this *Fab*
the further Relation of it to this Poem of *Moschus*,

Ἐυρώπῃ ποτὲ Κύπρις ἐπὶ γλυκὺν ἧκεν ὄνειρον,
Νυκτὸς ὅτε τρίτατον λάχος ἵσταται, ἐγγύθι δ᾽ ἠώς, &c.

A sweet Dream *Venus* once *Europa* lent,
In Nights third quarter, near the Morns ascent;
Whilst Slumber which her eye-lids sweetly crown'd,
Her Limbs unti'd, and her Eyes softly bound
(That time which doth all truer Dreams beget.)
Europa Phœnix-child, a Virgin yet,
Alone in a high Chamber taking rest,
Beholds two Countries that for her contest,
The *Asian*, and her opposite; both seem'd
Like Women; that a stranger, this esteem'd
A Native who (a Mother like) doth plead
That she of her was born, by her was bred;
The other violent hands upon her laid,
And drew by force the unresisting Maid;
Urging she was as prize to *Jove* design'd:
Out of the bed she starts with troubled mind:
And panting heart; the Dream to life's so near;
Long sate she silent; long both Women were

After

After she wak'd presented to her sense,
Till thus at length she breaks her deep suspence.

 Which of the Gods, as now I did repose,
Perplex'd my Fancy with delusive Shows?
My calmer Sleeps disquieting with fear:
What Stranger in my Slumber did appear?
Her love shot suddainly into my Breast
And kindness, like a Mother, she express'd.
The Gods vouchsafe this Dream a good event!

 She rose, and for her lov'd Companions sent,
In Years, and Friendship, equal, nobly born,
With them for Balls she us'd her self t'adorn;
Or in *Anaurus* current Bathes, with them,
She plucks the fragrant Lilly from her Stem
These straight come to her; each a Basket held
To gather Flowers; so walk they to a Field
Neighb'ring the Sea, whither they often went
Pleas'd with the Waters noise, and Roses scent.

 A Golden Basket fair *Europa* bare,
Rich, yet in *Vulcan*'s Workmanship more rare,
Which *Neptune* first to *Lybia* gave, when he
Obtain'd her Bed, to *Telephassa* she
Wife to her Son, from *Telephassa* last
This to unwed *Europe* her Daughter past
Which many Figures neatly wrought did hold.
Inachian Iö was here carv'd in Gold,
Not yet in Woman's shape, but like a Cow,
Who seem'd to swim, and force (enraged) through
The Briny Sea her way; the Sea was Blew;
Upon the highest point of Land to view
The Wave-dividing Heifer, two Men stand;
Jove strokes the wet Cow with his sacred hand;

Who, unto seven-mouth'd *Nilus* crossing over,
Did cast her Horns, and Woman's shape recover.
In Silver *Nilus* Flood, the Cow in Brass,
And *Jupiter* in Gold engraven was;
Mercury figur'd on the furthest round,
And next him lies distended on the ground
Argos, endu'd with many watchful Eyes,
Out of whose Purple Blood a Bird doth rise,
Proud of his various Flowry Plumes, his Tail
He spreadeth like a swift Ship under Sail,
And comprehends the Border with his Wings;
Such is the Basket fair *Europa* brings.

 All at the Painted Field arive, where these
With sev'ral Flow'rs their several Fancies please.
One sweet *Narcissus* plucks, another gets
Wilde Savory, Hyacinths, and Violets,
Many faln Spring-born Flow'rs the ground doth share,
Some strive which yellow *Crocus* fragrant Hair
Should faster pluck; i'th' midst the Queen doth stand
Gathering the Roses Beauty with her hand;
The Graces so by *Venus* are out-shind.
Nor must she long with Flowers divert her mind,
Nor long preserve unstain'd her Virgin Zone,
For *Jove*, upon the Meadow looking down,
By *Venus* subtle Darts was struck in love,
Venus hath power to captivate great *Jove*.
Who of frow'rd *Juno*'s jealousie afraid,
And that he might deceive the tender Maid,
In a *Bull*'s Shape his Deity doth vail,
Not such as are in Stables bred, or trail
The crooked Plough, the furrow'd Earth to wound,
Or run amongst the Heards in Pasture Ground,

Or

Or are to draw the laden Waggon us'd,
Yellow o're all his body is diffus'd,
Save a white Circle shines amidst his Brow,
His brighter Eyes with amorous Sparkles glow.
His Horns with equal length rise from his Head,
Like the Moon's Orb, to half a Circle spread.

  Into the Mead he comes, nor (seen) doth fright;
The Virgins to approach him all delight,
And stroke the lovely Bull, whose divine smell
Doth far the Meads perfumed Breath excel:
Before unblam'd *Europa*'s Feet he stood,
Licking her Neck, and the Maid kindly woo'd:
She stroak'd, and kiss'd him; and the Foam, that lay
Upon his Lip, wip'd with her hand away:
He softly bellow'd, such an humming sound
Forth breathing, as *Mygdonian* Pipes resound.
Down at her Feet he kneels, viewing the Maid
With writhed Neck, and his broad Back displai'd,
When she to th' fair-haird Virgins thus doth say;
Come hither dear Companions, let us play,
Securely with this Bull, and without fear;
Who, like a Ship, all on his Back will bear.
He tame appears to sight, and gently kind,
Diff'ring from others, a discursive mind
Bearing like Men, and onely Voice doth lack.

  This said, she smiling gets upon his Back;
Which the rest off'ring, the Bull leaps away,
And to the Sea bears his desired Prey;
She cals with stretch'd-out hands, she turns to view
Her Friends, alass unable to pursue;
Down leaps he, *Dolphin*-like glides through the Seas:
Up from the Deep rise the *Nereides*,

Mounted on Whales to meet her on the way:
Whilst hollow-sounding *Neptune* doth allay
The Waves, and is himself his Brothers guide
In this Sea-Voyage; *Tritons*, on each side,
(The Deep's inhabitants) about him throng,
And sound with their long shels a nuptial song;
She by transformed *Jupiter* thus born,
With one hand holding fast the Bull's large Horn
Her purple garment with the other saves
Unwet by the swoln Ocean's froathy waves:
Her mantle (flowing o're her shoulders, swell'd
Like a full sail, and the young maid upheld.
Now born away far from her native coast,
Her sight the wave-washt shore and mountains lost.
She sees the Heav'ns above, the Seas beneathe,
And, looking round about, these Cries doth breathe.

 O whither sacred Bull? who art thou, say?
That through undreaded floods canst break thy way:
The Seas are pervious to swift Ships alone,
But not to Bulls is their fear'd voyage known;
What food is here? or if some God thou be
Why dost, what misbeseems a Deity?
Upon the Land no Dolphins, no Bulls move
Upon the Sea; Thou Sea and Land dost prove
Alike; whose feet like Oares afsist thy hast;
Perhaps thou'lt soar through the bright Air at last
On high, and like the nimble Birds become.
Me most unhappy, who have left my home,
A Bull to follow, voyages unknown
To undertake, and wander all alone.
But *Neptune* thou, that rul'st the foaming Main
Be pleas'd to help me; sure I shall obtain

A sight of this great God, who is my guide,
Nor else could I these fluid paths have tride.
 The largely horned Bull thus answer'd; Maid
Be bold, nor of the swelling waves afraid,
For I am *Jove* who now a Bull appear,
And whatsoever shape I please can wear;
In this to measure the wide Sea constrain'd
For love of thee, thou shalt be entertain'd
By *Creet* my Nurse; our Nuptials shall be there
Perform'd, and thou of me great Sons shalt bear,
To whose imperious Scepters all shall bow.
 What he had said, event made good; *Creet* now
Appears in view; *Jove* his own form doth take,
And loos'd her Zone; the Hours their Bed did make,
She late a Virgin, Spouse to *Jove* became,
Brought him forth Sons, and gain'd a Mothers name.
Mr. STANLEY.

" ASIA, *On her Head a Glory, her Stole of Silk, with several Forms*
"*of Wild Beasts wrought on it.*

Among the Poets, we frequently find *Asia* called *Aurora*, from the rising of the Sun there: as in CLAUDIAN,

 Jam Princeps molitur iter, gentésque remotas
 Colligit Auroræ, *tumidus quascunque pererrat*
 Euphrates, *quos lustrat* Halys, *quos ditat* Orontes, *&c.*

 The Prince his Progress now designing calls
 Remotest Eastern Nations, they whose Walls
 Euphrates, Halys, and *Oront* improves,
 The *Arabs* leave their Incense-bearing Groves, *&c.*

 ―――― *Totam pater undique secum*
 Moverat Auroram: mistis hic Colchus Iberis,

Hic mitrâ velatus Arabs, *hic crine decoro*
Armenius.———

——— the Eastern World he rais'd:
There with *Iberians Colchians* mix'd, and there
Wilde *Arabs*, and fair-hair'd *Armenians* were.

And speaking of *Asia*, going to sollicite *Stilico* for Assistance,

Tendit ad Italiam *supplex* Aurora *potentem.*

To *Italy Aurora* supplyant bends.

From whence they represented her like the Rising Sun. *Claudian* implicitely delivers her ordinary Dress, though in regard of her calamity, at that time, in mourning,

Non radiis redimita comam, nec flammea vultum,
Nec croceum vestita diem ; stat livida luĉta.

No Raies, nor Glory dress'd her Brows, nor clad
In Purple day; but pale she look'd, and sad.

Her Mantle of Silk speaks her ancient Propriety in it : which came so late into *Europe*, that we finde no name for it in *Homer*, among his so frequent Descriptions of the Vestments both of Gods, and Men. Nay, not in the Poets of the Old, or Middle Comedy, some hundreds of Years after *Homer*. Whence we conjecture, it was first brought into *Europe* after the Conquest of *Alexander* the Great. After it was brought over, the *Europæans* seem to have had no certain knowledge how it was made. For, by what we can finde, they thought it to have grown naturally on the Trunk, or Leaves of some Trees in *Asia*. So *Virgil*,

Quid nemora Æthiopum *molli canentia lanâ,*
Velleráque ut foliis depeĉtant tenuia Seres?

Of Trees in *Æthiopia* white with Wool;
How from the Leaves the *Seres* Fleeces cull?

PLINY,

PLINY, *The Seres are the first, who are known to have a Woolly substance to grow on their Trees, which they comb off after they have sprinkled it with Water.* And *Julius Pollux*[*] speaks it as a report of some, that the *Seres* gathered their Silk from certain Worms, like unto the *Bombyces* of the Island *Coos*. Whence it appears, that in the time of *Commodus* the Emperour, in whose time *Pollux* wrote, it was generally believed to have been otherwise: and after that too, for *Claudian*, who flourish'd under the Emperour *Honorius*, agrees with *Pliny*;

[* *Onomastic.*]

——————— *& pollice docto*
Jam parat auratas trabeas, currúsque micantes
Stamine, quod molli tondent de stipite Seres,
Frondea lanigeræ carpentes vellera Sylvæ.

——————————— she rarely taught,
Rich Robes prepar'd, and Golden Chariots wrought,
With Thred, which from the Bark the *Seres* cull,
Shearing from spreading Boughs the Fleecy Wooll.

Servius indeed, who lived in the time of *Theodosius*, as appears by his being cotemporary with † *Macrobius*, had a right opinion of it, as appears from these words of his in the fore-cited place of *Virgil*,

[† *Macrob. Saturnal.*]

Amongst the Indians, *and* Seres, *are certain Worms upon the Trees, which are called* Bombyces; *which, like Spiders, spin a very fine Thred, from whence is made Silk.*

In the time of *Justinian*[*] the whole Mystery was disclos'd by some *Monks*, who brought from the *Indies* some of the Eggs of the Worms: Since which time that Manufacture ha's been constantly used in *Europe*.

[* *Zonaras.*]

That she ha's several Shapes, or Forms of strange Beasts wrought on her Vest, is agreeable to the ancient Customs of that Countrey. *Aristophanes*[†],

[† *Ranis.*]

Ὀυχ ἱππαλεκτρυόνας, ὀυδὲ τραγελάφυς, ἄπερ σύ,
Ἐν τοῖσι παραπετάσμασι τοῖς Μηδικοῖς γράφυσι·

Myne not like your Prodigious Monsters be,
Such as are wrought in Median Tapestry.

PETRONIUS

PETRONIUS ARBITER,

Tuo palato clausus pavo pascitur,
Plumato amictus auleo Babylonico.

A Peacock shall be cram'd for thee,
Adorn'd like *Median* Tapestry.

SIDONIUS,

Peregrina det supellex
Ctesiphontis ac Niphatis
Juga texta belluásque
Rapidas vacante panno
Acuit quibus furorem
Bene ficta plaga cocco
Jaculoque ceu forante
Cruor incruentus exit:
Ubi torvus, & per artem
Resupina flexus ora,
It equo reditque telo
Fugiens fugánsque Parthus.

From *Ctesiphont* straight get enough,
And *Niphates* fair Houshold stuff,
Wrought with Hills, and Wilde Beasts, which
The empty Prospect may enrich;
Who by well-feignd Wounds enrag'd,
Seem more desperately engag'd,
From *Javelins* fixed in their sides,
Blood in Bloodless Rivers glides;
Where the *Parthian* with such Art,
O're his Shoulder throws his Dart:
His Horse now charging, then retreats,
And flying, so his Foe defeats.

"AFRICA

"AFRICA, a Woman, in her Hand a Pomegranate; on her Head a
"Crown of Ivory, and Ears of Wheat; at her Feet two Ships laden
"with Corn.

Thus we finde the Statue of *Africk* at *Florence* leaning upon its left Hand, in which there is a Pomegranate; in her right Hand an *Umbrella*, to defend her from the heat of the Sun; for her Pillow, two great Waters, signifying the *Mediterranean*, and *Atlantick* Seas. So at *Mycenæ*, the Statue of *Juno* (Protectrice of *Carthage*, the Metropolis of *Africk*) made by *Polyclet*, holds in one Hand a Scepter; in the other, a Pomegranate. Therefore, when the Queen sacrificed to *Juno*, she wore a Rod of Pomegranate upon her Head, called by the Ancients *Inarculum*. FESTUS; *Inarculum virgulta erat ex malo Punico incurvata, quam Regina sacrificans in capite gestabat.*

She is crowned with Ears of Corn, to signifie the Fertility of the place. *Horace*,

> *Fulgentem imperio fertilis* Africæ
>   *Fallit sorte beatior.*

> Thou happier art, then he commands
>   Rich *Africk*'s fertile Strands.

Thus SIDONIUS introduces *Africa*,   *Paneg. Majoriani.*

> *Jam malè fœcundas in vertice fregit aristas,*
>   *Et sic orsa loqui est.*

> Her Wheat-ear'd Wreath now early full she broke,
>   And thus then spoke.

And CLAUDIAN,   *De Laud. Stilic. lib. ii.*

> *Tum spicis, & dente comas illustris eburno,*
>   *Et valido rubicunda die, sic* Africa *fatur.*

> With Iv'ry crown'd, and Wheat, red with the Sun,
>   And fainting Heats, thus *Africa* begun.

According to which Description of his, we finde her represented in a Coyn of *Antoninus Pius*,

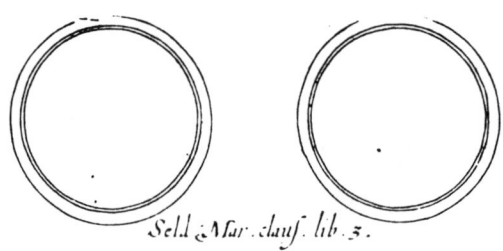

Seld. Mar. clauſ. lib. 3.

De Bello Gildonico.

The same Authour implicitely describes her, in the same manner, in another place,

— *mediis apparet in astris*
Africa, rescissæ vestes, & Spicea passim
Serta jacent, lacero crinales vertice dentes,
Et fractum pendebat ebur. —

Amidst the Stars next *Africa* appears
Her Garments torn, her Wreath of Wheaten Ears
Scatter'd about, Teeth braided on her Crown,
And broken Ivory hung. —

Plin. Nat. Hist. viii xi.

The Ivory on her Head, alludes to the great number of Elephants, bred in that part of the World; especially in that *part of* Africa *beyond the* Syrtick *Solitudes, and Desarts,* Æthiopia, Trogloditica, *and* Mauritania. *Petronius*,

Quæritur in silvis Mauri fera; & ultimus Ammon
Afrorum excutitur, ne desit bellua dente
Ad mortes pretiosa suas. —

The *Libyan* Wilds we seek, and th'utmost South,
To finde a Monster out, whose pretious Tooth
Proves its own bane. —

JUVENAL,

JUVENAL,

> *Dentibus ex illis quos mittit porta* Syenes;
> *Et* Mauri *celeres.* ——

<small>Sat. ii.</small>

> From whiter Teeth, which the *Syene* sends,
> And the swift *Moors.*——

Whence the *Romans*, in their Triumphs over *Africa*, usually had Elephants led before them, to denote the place of their Victory: as *L. Metellus*, in whose Coyns we finde either an Elephant, or his Triumphal Chariot drawn by two of them, or a Head of one of them under his Chariot.

<small>Plin. lib. viii. cap. vii.</small>

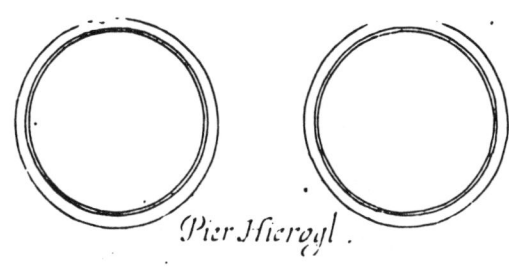

Pier. Hierogl.

Pliny says, that the Chariot of *Pompey* was drawn by four Elephants in his *African* Triumph. And we finde that the Fifth Legion bore the Effigies of an Elephant on their Colours, because they successfully manag'd a Battel against them, in the War betwixt *Cæsar*, and *L. Scipio*.

<small>Lib. eod. cap. vii.</small>

The two Ships at her Feet, relate to the *Classis Frumentaria*, which came yearly to *Rome* from *Africk*: frequently mention'd in the *Roman* Writers; which was instituted by *Commodus* the Emperour. Of whom *Lampridius*; *Classem Africanam instituit quæ subsidio esset, si forte* Alexandrina *frumenta cessassent.* He appointed an *African* Navy, which should furnish the City, in case the Corn from *Alexandria* should fail. Of which *Claudian*,

> *Tot mihi pro meritis* Libyam Nilumque *dedere,*
> *Ut dominam plebem bellatoremque Senatum*
> *Classibus æstivis alerent, geminóque vicissim*
> *Littore diversi complerent horrea venti.*

<small>De Bello Gildonico.</small>

Stabat

Stabat certa salus: Memphis si fortè negasset,
Pensabam Pharium Getulis messibus annum.
Frugiferas certare rates, latéque videbam
Punica Niliacis concurrere carbosa velis.

They gave me *Libya*, and the *Ægyptian* Shore
For my deserts, that they might with their Store
The People, and the Warlick Senate feed,
And with contrary Winds supply their need.
Famine farewel: if *Memphis* should deny,
Getulian Harvests will our Wants supply.
Freighted with Corn, I saw the *Punick* Fleet,
And Ships from *Nilus* in our Harbours meet.

And,

Laud. Stre-ax Rig.na.

——Phariæ *segetes &* Punica *messis*
Castro. um *devota cibo:* dat Gallia robur
Militis, &c. ———————

—— *Ægyptian Crops, and* Punick *Grain*
Our Camps with Bread, Gaul doth with Men maintain.

De Providentia Dei, Lib. vi.

Wherefore *Salvian*, after he had mention'd the Destruction of *Sardinia,* and *Sicily,* the Vital Veins, he calls *Africa* the Soul it self of the Common-Wealth of *Rome*. *Prudentius,*

In Symmachum.

Respice num Libyci *desistat raris arator*
Frumentis onerare rates, & ad Ostia Tibris
Mittere triticeos in pastum plebis acervos.

See if the *Libyan* Swain neglects to load
Our Ships with Corn, and to the *Ostian* Road
Sends Wheaten Mountains for the Peoples Food.

"AMERICA *Crown'd with Feathers of divers Colours, on her Stole a*
"*Golden River, in one Hand a Silver Mountain.*

So

So *Pompey*, in his Triumph over *Methridates*, among the rest of his Silver and Golden Representations carried *Montem aureum, quadratum, cum cervis & leonibus, & pomis omnis generis, circumdatâ vite aureâ*, A square Golden Mountain, encompassed with a Vine of Gold, with Harts and Lions upon it, and all manner of Fruit. The Mountain in her Hand is *Potosis* in *Peru*, whose Treasure ha's been accounted inexhaustible. *Josephus Acosta* relates, that in that Mountain there was found a Vein of Silver, about the height of a Spear above the Superficies of the Earth, three hundred Foot long, and thirteen broad. The same Authour witnesses, that the King of *Spain* receives yearly from thence a Million of Ducats; and that onely from the fifth part of the Silver. We have read of indeed of Silver Mountains in *Europe*; as that mention'd by *Strabo* in *Spain*; *Not far from* Costaon *is a Mountain, whence flows the River* Bætis, *call'd the* Silver Mountain, *in relation to the Silver Mines there*. And of a Golden Mountain in *Asia*, mention'd by *Menander*; Ἴνα ὁ Χαγάνος αὐτὸς ἦν, ἐν ᾗ τινὶ λεγομένω Ἐκτὰγ (presently after Ἐκτὲλ) ὡς ἂν εἴπω, χρυσοῦν ὄρος Ἕλλην ἀνήρ, *Where King* Chaganus *himself was, on a Mountain call'd* Ectag, *that is, the* Golden Mountain. And *Appian* before him; *Many Fountains bring down small Shavings of Gold from the Mountain* Caucasus; *the Inhabitants sinking Fleeces of Wooll very deep, take up what Shavings stick to them*: But these are all so considerable, in respect of the inestimable Treasure of this Mountain, that *America* may reasonably from hence, as all other Countries from what is most valuable, and appropriate to them, have its distinguishing Character.

The River on her Stole is the Golden River *Peru*. So *Claudian* represents *Brittain* with the Flux and Deflux of the Sea on her Vest;

> *Inde Caledonio velata* Britannia *monstro,*
> *Ferro pictâ genas, cujus vestigia verrit*
> *Cærulus, Oceanique æstum mentitus amictus.*

> *Britannia* then veil'd in a Boars rough Hide,
> Walk'd on the Sea, her Cheeks with Iron dy'd,
> Cloath'd with the changings of the Oceans Tide.

And SPAIN, with the Golden River *Tagus* on her Stole:

> ——— *glaucis tum prima* Minervæ
> *Nexa comam foliis, fulvâque intexta micantem*
> *Veste* Tagum, *tales profert* Hispania *voces.*

Then

> Then *Spain* with Olive-Branches crown'd, her Vest
> With Golden *Tagus* wrought, her self exprest
> In words like these. ———

<small>*M. x. clauf.*
L.b.ii.</small>

Which Leaves of *Minerva*, Mr. *Selden* mistook for a Palm. *Claudian*, in several places, describes the Olive in the same manner; as in his Epistle to *Hadrian*,

> *Hoc pro supplicibus ramis, pro fronde* Minervæ,
> *Hoc carmen pro thure damus.* ———

> This for *Minerva*'s supplicating Bough,
> This Verse for Incense we bestow.

And in another place,

<small>*In Europ-*
saum, Lib.ii.</small>

> ——— *pro fronde* Minervæ
> *Has tibi protendo lacrymas.* ——

> ——— for *Pallas* Boughs,
> These Tears we thee present,

LUCAN,

<small>*De Bell.*
Civ. lib.iii.</small>

> ——— *tamen ante furorem*
> *Indomitum, duramque viri deflectere mentem*
> *Pacifico Sermone parant, hostemque propinquum*
> *Orant Cecropiæ prælatâ fronde* Minervæ.

> ——— they to assuage
> His cruel Breast, accustomed to rage,
> *Minerva*'s Branches stretching forth, beseech
> The Neighb'ring Foe with a prepared Speech.

In which places 'tis evident, the Olive is signified, because carried in the Hands of Suppliants. *Statius*,

> ——— *ramúmque precantis Olivæ.*
> A supplicating Olive Branch.

Vittatâ

Vittatæ lauru͜s, & supplicis arbor Olivæ.

With Bays and supplicating Olives crown'd.

Whence *Virgil* makes *Æneas* send a hundred to King *Latinus*, all crown'd with Olive Branches, call'd there *Palladis rami*.

——— *ramis velatos Palladis omnes,*
Donaque ferre viro, pacemque exposcere Teucris.

And for the *Trojans* Terms of Peace propound,
With Royal Presents, all with Olive crown'd.

And *Statius* makes *Tydeus*, going in the name of *Polynices*, to demand the Kingdom of *Thebes*, carry a Branch of Olive in his Hand, as a token of Peace; and, his Demand being denied, to throw away the same, to signifie, and declare a War. So L I V Y, *Not far off was a Ship of the* Carthaginians, *covered with Mitres, and Branches of Olive; in which were ten Ambassadours, chief Princes of the City, sent to request Peace.*

C L A U D I A N gives the same Epithet too, to the Olive-leaves, in his Epistle to S E R E N A,

——— *glaucâ pinguis Oliva comâ.*

The unctuous Olive with a Silver Sprig.

And V A L E R I U S F L A C C U S,

——— *glaucásque comis prætexere frondes Imperat.*

Commands to braid their Hair with verdant Boughs.

The reason why *Claudian* so describes it, is, because that Tree was sacred to *Minerva*: which we finde attested by *Pliny*; *The Esculus (a Species of glandiferous Trees) is sacred to* Jupiter, *the Laurel to* Apollo, *the Olive to* Minerva, *the Myrtle to* Venus, *the Poplar to* Hercules; and is known from the Fable of the Contention of *Minerva*, and *Neptune*, concerning the Possession of *Athens*. And *Epopeus*, after a Victory, having erected and consecrated to her a Temple, and pray'd, that she would show some token of her acceptance of it, there presently sprung forth a Branch of Olive before it.

Argon n°.
Lib. III.

Nat. Hist.
lib. xii. c. i.

Pausan.
lib. ii.

This

This Errour of Mr. *Selden*'s produc'd another in his following words, when he gather'd from thence, that the River *Tagus*, and Palm-Trees were proper to *Spain*. *Hispaniæ Palmæ, & Tagus fluvius propria.* Indeed the Palm-Tree was the Symbol of *Judæa*, as we see in the Coyns of *Vespasian* and *Titus*,

from the abundance of them in that Countrey. STRABO; *Beside the common Palm, it (*Judæa*) brings forth the* Carupta, *not much inferiour to the* Babylonian. *Lucan*,

——*Et arbusto Palmarum dives* Idume.

And *Idumea* rich with Palm.

Lib. iii.   SILIUS ITALICUS,

Palmiferámque senex bello domitabit Idumen,

Palm-bearing *Idumæa* shall subdue.

But *Spain* was commended for the abundance, and excellency of its Olives. *Martial*,

Bætis, *Olivíferâ crinem redimite coronâ,*
Aurea qui nitidis vellera tingis aquis.

Bætis her Tresses crown'd with Olive Stems,
Dyes Golden Fleeces with her glitt'ring Streams.

Which Verses, compared with these of *Silius Italicus*, evidently evince, that *Palladis rami* signifie the Olive.

——*genuit quos ubere ripâ*
Palladio Bethes *umbratus cornua ramo.*

— both

passing to His Coronation.

—— both of equal age
Born upon *Bethes* Banks, whose horned Brows
Were overshadowed with fat Olive Boughs.

And in another place, of *Spain*,

Lib.1.

Nec Cereri *terra indocilis, nec inhospita* Baccho,
Nulláque Palladiâ *sese magis arbore tollit*.

A Land, where *Ceres*, and *Lyæus* too
Do dwell, and Olive-Trees in plenty grow.

Whence, in a Coyn of *Hadrian* the Emperour, we finde that Countrey signified by a Woman sitting, with her left hand leaning on the *Pyrenean* Mountains (Mr. *Selden* calls it a heap of Stones) in her right Hand holding a Branch of Olive; at her Feet a Coney:

Croyiac.
*Tab.*xxxix.

The Coney we finde too at the Feet of *Spain*, holding an Olive-Branch on her Shoulder, in a Coyn of the same Emperour.

Ibid.

The Coney at her Feet signifies either the incredible number of those Animals formerly in *Spain* (for *Varro* mentions a Town there

O undermin'd

undermin'd, and overthrown by them, as we finde in *Pliny*) or rather the abundance of Mines in that Countrey; the *Latine* word *Cuniculi*, from whence the allusion must be taken, being æquivocal, and answering to both. From one of which significations a part of *Spain* is call'd *Cuniculosa Celtiberia* by *Catullus*,

Tu præter omnes, une de capillatis,
Cuniculosæ Celtiberiæ fili.

The Mines are mentioned by *Claudian*, speaking of *Spain*,

Dives equis, frugum facilis, pretiosa metallis,
Principibus fœcunda piis. ———

With Steeds abounding, rich with Corn, and Ore,
And pious Princes store.———

And by SILIUS ITALICUS,

——— *hic omne metallum :*
Electri gemino pallent de semine venæ.
Atque atros chalybis fœtus humus horrida nutrit.
Sed scelerum causas aperit Deus. Astur avarus
Visceribus laceræ telluris mergitur imis,
Et redit infelix effosso concolor auro.

——— here Metals grow
Of matter mix'd: *Electrum*'s pallid Veins
Produc'd, and darker Steel the Earth contains:
But God those Springs of mischief deeply hides;
Yet *Astur*, covetous, the Earth divides,
And, in her mangled Entrails drown'd again,
Returns with Gold, and bears the pretious Stain.

But

passing to His CORONATION.

But to return. This River, says *Josephus Acosta*, gave the name to the whole Countrey of *Peru*. Of which *Levinus Apollonius* thus, under another name; where he describes the Rivers of the Mountainous PERU, *The chiefest far is the River* Argyreus (PERU) *from its abundance of Silver, which it casts up in glittering Sand, call'd in Spanish,* Plata: *it is equally liberal, and profuse of its Treasures unto all parts it passeth by, enriching its Inhabitants with an inexhaustible abundance both of Gold, and Silver.*

Hist. Nat. Ind. lib. i. cap. xiii. De Peruviæ regionis inventione.

"The uppermost great Table *in the fore-ground represents King* "Charles *the First, with the Prince,* now Charles *the Second, in His* "Hand, *viewing the Sovereign of the Sea, the Prince leaning on a Can-* "*non; the Inscription,*

> O NIMIUM DILECTE DEO, CUI MILITAT
> ÆQUOR,
> ET CONJURATI VENIUNT AD CLASSICA
> VENTI.

> For thee, O *Jove*'s Delight, the Seas engage,
> And mustr'ed Winds, drawn up in Battel, rage.

"*Above, over the Cornich, between the two Celestial* Hemi-spheres, "*an* Atlas, *bearing a* Terrestrial Globe, *and on it a Ship under Sail; the* "Word,

> UNUS NON SUFFICIT.

Thus we finde *Atlas* painted in an ancient Temple of *Jupiter's*. PAUSANIAS, *Amongst the rest, is the Picture of* Atlas, *bearing up Heaven, and Earth; by whom stands* Hercules, *as ready to assist him*: mention'd by *Claudian*,

In Eliacis.

> ————sic, Hercule quondam
> Sustentante polum, melius librata pependit
> Machina, nec dubiis titubavit Signifer astris.
> Perpetuâque senex subductus male parumper
> Obstupuit proprii spectator ponderis Atlas.

———————— so *Hercules* of old
Sustain'd the Pole, bore better on his Back
The poysed World, and fix'd the Zodiack:
Atlas a while, from his great Burthen free,
Admiring stood, the wond'rous Load to see.

Of whom thus Homer,

Ἀγαυῆ δ' θυγάτηρ ὀλοόφρον῀, ὅστε θαλάσσης
Πάσης βένθεα οἶδεν ἔχει δέ τε κίονας αὐτὸς
Μακράς, αἳ γαῖάν τε, καὶ οὐρανὸν ἀμφὶς ἔχουσιν.

Daughter of *Atlas*, who both Depth, and Sholes
Of th' Ocean plumbs, and holdeth two long Poles,
That mighty Heaven, and the Earth sustain.

In Προμ. Δεσμ.

Æschylus,

——————— ὃς πρὸς ἑσπέρους τόπους
Ἕστηκε κίον' οὐρανοῦ τε καὶ χθονὸς
Ὤμοις ἐρείδων, ἄχθος οὐκ εὐάγκαλον.

——————— who near the Western Main
Bears on his Back that Pillar, doth sustain
Both Heaven, and Earth, not easie to support.

Virgil,

——————— *ubi cœlifer* Atlas
Axem humero torquet stellis ardentibus aptum.

——————— where great *Atlas* bears,
Laden with Golden Stars, the glittering Sphears.

He was thus described from his admirable knowledge in the motions of the Heavens, and the nature of things here below. Pausanias *, *In which there is a place of ground call'd* Polosus, *where they say* Atlas *studied the Heavens, and the Earth.* Diodorus Siculus †, *They say, he (*Atlas*) was excellently skill'd in Astrology, and was the first, that published the Sphe-*
rical

* *In Bœotic.*
† *Lib. iii.*

rical *Figure of the Heavens: from whence he was said to bear the Heavens on his Shoulders; the Fable signifying the Invention, and Description of the Sphere.* Which seems not be understood of a solid Sphere, but a Sphere described on a Plane: the other Invention, by most of the Ancients, being attributed to *Archimedes*, who liv'd many Centuries of Years after him.

" *The great Painting on the* West-*side represents the Duke of* YORK,
" *habited* à l'antique, *like* Neptune, *standing on a Shell drawn by Sea-*
" *Horses, before which a* Triton *sounding, in one Hand a* Trident, *the*
" Reins *in the other; his* Motto,

   SPES ALTERA.

We generally finde *Neptune* among the Poets drawn by Sea-Horses. STATIUS,   *Theb. Lib. ii.*

> *Illic Ægeo Neptunus gurgite fessos*
> *In portum deducit equos, prior haurit habenas*
> *Ungula, postremi solvuntur in æquora pisces.*

> Here *Neptune* entring left th'*Ægean* Flood,
> Landing his Steeds, their formost Feet well shod:
> The hindmost cut the Waves with Finny Tails.

VIRGIL,   *Æneid. v.*

> *His ubi læta Deæ permulsit pectora dictis,*
> *Jungit equos curru genitor, spumantiáque addit*
> *Fræna feris, manibúsque omnes effundit habenas,*
> *Cæruleo per summa levis volat æquora curru.*

> When thus her troubled Breast he had asswag'd,
> He joyns his Chariot-Horse, and curbs th'enrag'd
> With Fomy Bits, then gives them lib'ral Rein,
> With blew Wheels flying o're the Azure Main.

They were called *Hippocampæ*. NONIUS; Hippocampæ, *equi marini, à flexu caudarum, quæ piscosæ sunt.* Hippocampæ are Sea-Horses, *so called from the flexion of their Tails, which are like Fishes.* FESTUS; *Campas marinos equos Græci à flexione posteriorum partium appellant,* "The "*Greeks* call Sea-Horses *Campæ,* from the bending of their posteriour "parts: from χάμπτω *to bend.*

In the Medaigles of *Caius Marius,* and *Quintus Creperius,* is represented *Neptune* riding upon these *Hippocampæ,* or Sea-Horses.

Carol Goltz. in Fastis ad 646.

And the Form of a Sea-Horse we have in the Coyn of the Emperour *Gallienus,*

Ibid.

As he holds the Reins of his Horses in one hand, so we finde him constantly with a Trident in the other. From whence he is call'd by the *Greeks,* † Τριαινοῦχος, ‡ Εὐτρίαινης *, Τριαινοκράτωρ, by *Pindar* Ἀγλαοτρίαινα· by the *Latines, Tridentifer,* and *Tridentiger.* OVID †,

† Proclus in Crat. Platonis.
‡ Epigr. Gr.
† Metam. lib. viii.

—————— ô proxima terræ
Regna vagæ, dixi, sortite Tridentifer undæ.

And,

Cumque Tridentigero tumidi genitore profundi.

VIRGIL,

—— *Túque, O, cui prima frementem*
Fudit equum magno tellus percussa Tridenti,
Neptune.——

———and

―――― and *Neptune*, thou, to whom
The Earth first *Trident* struck brought forth a Steed.

HOMER, *Iliad. μ´.*

Ἀυτὸς δ᾽ ἐνοσίγαι©- ἔχων χείρεσσι τρίαιναν
Ἡγεῖτ᾽· ἐκ δ᾽ ἄρα πάντα θεμείλια κύμασι πέμπε
Φιτρῶν, ἢ λάων.――――

Arm'd with his Trident, Neptune, leading on
Impetuous Waves, left neither Pile, nor Stone.

Callimachus, singularly, says, that his Trident was made by the *Telchines*, smiths in *Creet*. *Hymno in Delum.*

―――― ὄρεα θείνων
Ἄοει τριγλώχιν, τὸ οἱ Τελχῖνες ἔτευξαν.

―――― *Neptune* the Mountain struck
With's *Trident*, which the *Telechines* made.

Plutarch tells, that the *Trœzenians* mark their Moneys with a Trident, as a Testimony of their Devotion to *Neptune*.

Amongst the rest of *Neptune*'s Attendants was *Triton* his Trumpeter. OVID, *Metam.*

Cæruleum Tritona *vocat, conchâque sonanti*
Inspirare jubet, fluctúsque, & flumina signo
Jam revocare dato.――

Triton he calls, commanding him to sound
His hollow Shell, and call the Floods profound,
And Rivers back. ――――

VIRGIL, speaking of a Ship, *Æneid.*

―― *Immanis* Triton, *& cærula conchâ*
Exterrens freta. Cui laterum tenùs hispida nanti
Frons hominem præfert; in Pristin *desinit alvus:*
Spumea semifero sub pectore murmurat unda.

This

> This mighty *Triton* bore, frighting the Tides
> With his shrill Trump. His Face, and hairy sides
> Above presents a Man, a Whale the rest :
> And foamy Waves resound beneath his Breast.

Dionysiac.
XXXVI.
NONNUS,

> Τείων δ' ἐυρυγένει⊙ ἐβόμβεεν ἠθάδι κόχλῳ
> Ἀνδροφυὴς, ἀτέλεσ⊙, ἀπ' ἰξύ⊙ ἔγχλο⊙ ἰχθῦς.

> Broad-bearded *Triton* sounds his Trump at last,
> Half humane Shape, a Fish beneath the Waste.

Eidyll.
MOSCHUS,

> ——— τοὶ δ' ἀμφί μιν ἠχερέθονῖο
> Τείωνες, πόνῖοιο βαθυρρόου ἐναεῖῆρες,
> Κόχλοισι τὰ ἀεὶς γάμιν μέλ⊙ ἠπύονῖες·

> ——— *Tritons* on each side
> (The Deep's Inhabitants) about him throng,
> And sound with their long Shels a Nuptial Song.

"On the four Niches within the Arch were living Figures, with Escut-
"cheons, and Pendents, representing Arithmetick, Geometry, Astro-
"nomy, and Navigation.
"Arithmetick, a Woman habited à l'antique, with her Fingers erect:
"upon her Vestment Lines, with Musick Notes on them: in her Escut-
"cheon a Book opened, with a Hand pointing to the Figures, I. V. X. L. C. D. M.
"&c. Under,

PAR ET IMPAR.

The holding out of her Fingers erect points out to us that ancient manner of Supputation, known of old to most Countries in the World, but now out of use, by the Fingers of both Hands. This Supputation was divided into three parts; Digits, Decades, and Compound Numbers. The Digits comprehend all Numbers under ten, the Decads comprehend all tens, as 10, 20, 30, 40, 50, 60, 70, 80, 90. the Compound what was made of the other two, as 19, 27, &c. The Digits
first

were express'd by the three last Fingers, beginning with the little one. The Decads by the Thumb, either single, or in conjunction with the first Finger. Thus far reacheth the *Arithmetique* of the left Hand; so that, removing to the right, the first Number is an hundred: *Unius numerum, quo gestu significabantur in sinistra, translatum in dexteram centena conficere.* The Number of a Hundred, by the same gesture, is signified in the right Hand, that one in the left. And, *A numero nonagesimo, qui fuit in læva, per unius significationem, transferri in dexteram, & ibi centena constitui.* From which kind of *Arithmetique* we must understand that *Greek* Epigram of *Nicarchus,*

Irenæus
In *Valent.*
lib.i. cap.xiii.

Ἡ πολιὴ κροτάφοισι Κοτυτταρὶς ἡ πολύμυθος
  Γραῖα, δι᾽ ἣν Νέστωρ οὐκ ἔτι πρεσβύτατος·
Ἡ φάος ἀθρήσασ᾽ ἐλάφου πλέον, ἡ χερὶ λαιῇ
  Γήρας ἀριθμεῖσθαι δεύτερον ἀρξαμένη.
Ζώει, καὶ λεύσσει, καὶ ἁρπακτὸς οἷάτε Νύμφη,
  Ὥστε με διστάζειν μή τι πέπονθ᾽ ἀΐδης.

Grey-hair'd *Cotyttaris*, that infernal Scold,
Whom *Nestor* to compare with was not old;
Whose many Years the long-liv'd Harts surmount,
She on her left Hand twice begins to count.
Swift-footed as a *Nymph*, her sight not fails,
Sure, I believe, the Devil something ails.

And this of JUVENAL,

Rex Pylius, *magno si quidquam credis* Homero,
Exemplum vitæ fuit à Cornice secundæ.
Felix nimirum! qui tot per sæcula vitam
Distulit, atque suos jam dextrâ computat annos.

Nestor, if thou'lt great *Homer* credit give,
As long as did the long-liv'd Raven live;
Bless'd thou! who stood'st so many Lustres rage,
Till on thy right Hand thou did'st count thy Age.

So that as the Units were counted on the three Fingers of the left, so the first Nine Hundred were counted on the same three Fingers of the right; and as the Decads were counted on the Thumb, and

Fore-Finger of the left, so were the Thousands on the same of the right. Whence we may guess of the Figure of the Fingers, which *Pliny* * mentions in the Statue of *Janus*, dedicated by *Numa*, with his *Fingers so complicated, that the Note of* CCCLXV *Days, the signification of a Year, should demonstrate him the G t of Time.*

Of this manner of Supputation must be understood that Saying of *Orontes*, who, upon some distast taken by King *Artaxerxes*, had fallen into disgrace; "As the Fingers of Accountants now represent one, now "Myriads; so the Friends of Kings now are much in favour, now not at all. This manner of Supputation seems to have been ordinary among the *Romans*, used in their Pleadings before the Judge. QUINTILIAN†, *Si actor, non dico, si circa summas trepidat, sed se digitorum incerto solùm, aut indecoro gestu à computatione dissentit, judicatur indoctus.* " If the Pleader " not onely trembles about the Sums, but if by a doubtful onely, and un- " comely gesture, he differs from the Computation, he is esteemed un- " learned. *Apuleius* in his Apologetical Oration before ÆMILIANUS, *Si triginta annos pro decem dixisses, posses videri pro computationis gestu errâsse, quos circulare debueris, digitos aperuisse.* *If you had nam'd thirty Years for ten, you might seem to have mistaken in the gesture of your Computation, to have circl'd those Fingers, which you should have opened.* And therefore it is very strange, that, after so common an usage of this manner of Computation, it should be so far lost, that none can agree what it was.

The Authour of *Arithmetique*, according to *Æschylus*†, was *Prometheus*:

Καὶ μὴν ἀριθμὸν ἔξοχον σοφισμάτων
Ἐξεῦρον αὐτοῖς, γραμμάτων τε συνθέσεις.

The chief of Arts I Numbers found,
And first knew Letters to compound.

According to *Plato*, 'twas *Palamedes*: but *Pliny* * attributes the Invention of it to *Minerva*; *Eóque Minervæ Templo dicatam legem, quia numerus à Minerva inventus sit.*

The ancient Musick-Notes here mention'd, though for many hundred Years buried in obscurity, have been brought to light again out of some *Greek* Authours of Musick, lately publish'd by *Meibomius*. The Numbers are sufficiently known, though not so well as those we generally use, lately brought into *Europe* from the *Arabians*.

" Geometry

"Geometry, *a Woman in a pleasant* Green, *in her Shield a Com-*
"*pass, and a* Read; *the* Inscription,

DESCRIPSIT RADIO TOTUM QUÆ GENTIBUS
ORBEM.

Geometry is supposed by the Ancients to have had its original in *Ægypt*, where, after the yearly overflowings of the River *Nile*, they were forc'd continually to measure their ground out anew to distinguish Propriety. STRABO[†], Καθάπερ ἢ τ̄ Αἰγυπλίων εὕρημα Γεωμελείαν φασί, ὑπὸ τ̄ χωρομελείας, ἣν Νεῖλ⊙ ἀπεργάζελαι, συγχέων τὰς ὅρως κατὰ τὰς ἀναβάσεις· And, [*]Ἔδεινοι δὲ τ̄ ἐπ᾿ ἀκριβὲς ἢ κατὰ λεπτὸν διαίρεσεως διὰ τὰς συνεχεῖς τ̄ ὅρων συγχύσεις, ἃς ὁ Νεῖλ⊙ ἀπεργάζελαι καλά τὰς αὐξήσεις, ἀφαιρῶν, ἢ προστιθείς, ἢ ἐναλλάτ]ων τὰ σχήματα, ἢ τἆλλα σημεῖα ἀποκρύπ]ων, οἷς διακεινελαι τό τε ἀλλόλειον, ἢ τὸ ἴδιον· ἀνάγκη δὲ ἀναμετρεῖοϑαι πάλιν ἢ πάλιν. Ἐντεῦϑεν δὲ ἢ τὴν Γεωμελείαν συςτῆναι φασίν. For which end, because they made use of a Read, it was amongst them ever after for a Symbol of *Geometry*. So in a Silver Coyn of *C. Mamilius*, in one side there is a *Mercury* with a Cap, and *Caduceus*, on the other *Mamilius*, with a Read by him, with this Inscription, L I. M E T A N. that is, *Limitibus metandis*, where we finde hs Office of measuring Land implyed by a Read.

[† *Geogr.* lib. xvi.]
[* Lib. xvii.]

The Compass in her other Hand we have described by OVID,

[*Metam.* lib. viii. *Fab.* iii.]

— *& ex uno duo ferrea brachia nodo*
Junxit, ut æquali spatio distantibus illis
Altera pars staret, pars altera duceret orbem.

He two-shank'd Compasses with Rivet bound,
The one to stand still, th'other turning round,
In equal distances. — —

The Authour of it, *Talus*, being envyed by his Uncle *Dædalus* for this, and other Inventions, was thrown down headlong by him from the top of *Minerva*'s Tower: but in the middle of his fall, being favour'd by *Minerva*, the Patroness of Wit, was turn'd into a Bird; which we have in the following Verses:

Dædalus *invidit : sacrâque ex arce* Minervæ
Præcipitem misit, lapsum mentitus : at illum,

Quæ favet ingeniis, excepit Pallas, avémque
Reddidit, & medio velavit in aëre pennis.

—————— *Dædalus* thus began,
Who from *Minerva*'s sacred Turret flung
The envi'd headlong; and his falling fains:
Him *Pallas*, fautor of good Wits, sustains.
Who straight the Figure of a Fowl assumes;
Clad in the midst of Ayr with freckled Plumes.

Mr. SANDYS.

" *Astronomy, a Woman in a loose Vestment,* Azure, *wrought with*
" *Stars o' Gold, looking up to Heaven: in her Shield a Table, wherein are*
" *divers Astronomical Figures;* the Inscription,

AURO CIRCUMSPICIT ORIONA.

ASTRONOMY holding a *Sphere* in her left Hand, in her right a *Radius.*

So she is described by *Martianus Capella.* The Sphere, which he gives her, is that of *Archimedes*, as we see by the Epigram, in which he describes it,

Ipsa etiam, lævâ, Sphærâ fulgebat honorâ;
    Assimilis mundo, sideribúsque fuit.
Nam globus, & circi, Zonæque, ac fulgida signa
    Nexa recurrebant, arte locata pari.
Tellus, quæ rapidum consistens suscipit orbem,
    Puncti instar medio hæserat una loco.

In her left Hand she a *Celestial* Sphear,
Like the great World, glitt'ring with Stars did bear:
On the vast Globe the circulating Signes
Connexed ran in equidistant Lines

To rapid Orbs; the Earth, the fixed Base,
Like a small Point, just in the midst took place.

"Navigation, *a Woman in Sea-green Habit; in her* Escutcheon *an*
"Anchor, *with a* Cable *about it; the* Inscription,

TUTUM TE LITTORE SISTAM.

While the *Nobility* passed the *Triumphal Arch,* the three Sea-men entertained them with this Song from the Stage on the *North*-side of the *Arch.*

I.

From Neptune's *Wat'ry Kingdoms, where*
   Storms, and Tempests rise so often,
As would the World in pieces tear,
   Should Providence their Rage not soften;
From that fluctuating Sphere,
   Where stout Ships, and smaller Barks
Are toss'd like Balls, or feather'd Corks,
   When briny Waves to Mountains swell,
Which dimming oft Heav'n's glitt'ring Sparks,
   Then descending low as Hell;
     Through this Crowd,
     In a Cloud,
By a strange, and unknown Spell,
   We, newly Landing,
   Got this Standing,
All Merry Boys, and Loyal,
   Our Pockets full of Pay,
   This Triumphal Day,
To make of our Skill a Tryal,
   Of our little little Skill:
   Let none then take it ill,
We must have no Denyal.

II.

II.

We, who have rais'd, and laid the Poles,
  Plough'd frozen Seas, and scalding Billows;
Now stiff with Cold, then scorch'd on Coals,
  Ships our Cradles, Decks our Pillows;
'Mongst threatning Rocks, and treach'rous Shoals,
  Through Gibraltar's *contracted Mouth,*
And Realms condemn'd to Heat, and Drowth,
  Or Baltick Waves bound up in Ice,
Or Magellane *as Cold, though South,*
  Our good Fortune, in a trice,
    Through this Crowd,
    In a Cloud,
  Brings us where, in Paradise,
    We, newly Landing,
    Got thus Standing,
  All Merry Boys, and Loyal,
    Our Pockets full of Pay,
    This Triumphal Day,
  To make of our Skill a Tryal,
    Of our little little Skill:
    Let none then take it ill,
  We must have no Denyal.

III.

We, who so often bang'd the Turk,
  Our Broad-sides speaking Thunder,
Made Belgium *strike, and proud* Dunkirk,
  Who liv'd by Prize, and Plunder,
And routed the Sebastian *Shirk;*
  We paid their Poops, and painted Beaks,
Cleans'd before and aft their Decks,

Till their Scuppers ran with Gore,
Whilst in as fast salt Water breaks;
But we are Friends of this no more:
Through this Crowd,
In a Cloud,
We have found a happy Shore,
And, newly Landing,
Got this Standing;
All Merry Boys, and Loyal,
Our Pockets full of Pay,
This Triumphal Day,
To make of our Skill a Tryal,
Of our little little Skill:
Let none then take it ill,
We must have no Denyal.

Besides the three before-named, who sang the precedent Song, there were in like-manner habited, like Sea-men, six other Persons, who made a Winde-Musick.

The Musick in the Stage consisted of three Drums, and six Trumpets.

On the *East*-side, Winde-Musick, consisting of six Persons.

On two Balconies, within the *Arch*, Winde-Musick, consisting of twelve Persons.

On the *West*-Gallery were placed six Trumpets.

These, and all the other Musick, belonging to this Triumph, performed their Duty without Intermission, till such time, as His Majesty fronted the *Figure*, which represented *Thames*, and then ceased; upon which, *Thames* made the ensuing Speech,

Ten Moons, Great Sir, their Silver Crescents fill'd,
Since, mounted on a Billow, I beheld
You on the Bridg; but louder Joys there were,
That barr'd my Welcomes from Your Sacred Ear:

Now

Now I above my highest Bound have rear'd
My Head, to say what could not then be heard.
 Hail, Mighty *Monarch!* whose Imperial Hand
Quiets the Ocean, and secures the Land;
This City, whom I serve with Neighb'ring Floods,
Exporting Yours, importing Foreign Goods,
With anxious Grief did long Your Absence mourn;
Now with full Joy she welcomes Your Return;
Your blest Return! by which she is restor'd
To all the Wealth remotest Lands afford.
At Your Approach I hasten'd to the *Downs,*
To see Your moving Forts, Your Floating Towns,
Your *Sovereigns,* big with Thunder, plow the Main,
And swimming Armies in their Womb contain.
You are our *Neptune,* ev'ry Port, and Bay
Your Chambers: the whole Sea is Your High-way.
Though sev'ral Nations boast their Strength on Land,
Yet You alone the Wat'ry World command.
 Pardon, great Sir, fair *Cynthia* checks my stay;
But to Your Royal Palace, twice a day,
I will repair; there my proud Waves shall wait,
To bear our *Cæsar,* and His conqu'ring Fate.

We finde the Speech of the River *Tyber* on the like Solemnity, the Procession of the Senate, &c. attending on the two Brothers *Probinus,* and *Olybrius,* newly elected Consuls, in CLAUDIAN;

Est in Romuleo *procumbens Insula* Tybri,
Quà medius geminas interfluit alveus urbes
Discretas subeunte freto, paritérque minantes
Ardua turrigeræ surgunt in culmina ripæ.
Hìc stetit, & subitum prospexit ab aggere votum;
Unanimes fratres junctos, stipante Senatu,

Ire

Ire forum, strictásque procul radiare secures,
Atque uno bijuges tolli de limine fasces.
Obstupuit visu, suspensáque gaudia vocem
Oppressam tenuêre diu, mox inchoat ore.

 Respice, si tales jactas aluisse fluentis,
Eurota Spartane, tuis. Quid protulit æquum
Falsus olor, valido quamvis decernere cæstu
Nôrint, & ratibus sævas arcere procellas?
En nova Ledæis soboles fulgentior astris!
Ecce mei cives! quorum jam Signifer optat
Adventum, stellísque parat convexa futuris.
Jam per noctivagos dominetur Olybrius *axes*
Pro Polluce *rubens, pro* Castore *flamma* Probini.
Ipsi vela regent: ipsis donantibus auras,
Navita tranquillo moderabitur æquore pinum.
Nunc pateras libare Deis, nunc solvere multo
Nectare corda libet: niveos jam pandite cœtus
Naiades, & totum violis prætexite fontem:
Mella ferent sylvæ: jam profluat ebrius amnis,
Mutatis in vina vadis: jam sponte per agros
Sudent irriguæ spirantia balsama venæ.
Currat, qui sociæ roget in convivia mensæ
Indigenas fluvios, Italis *quicunque suberrant*
Montibus, Alpinásque *bibunt de more pruinas:*
Vulturnúsque rapax, & Nar *vitiatus odoro*
Sulfure, tardatúsque suis erroribus Ufens:
Et Phaëtonteæ *perpessus damna ruinæ*
Eridanus, *flavæque terens querceta* Maricæ
Liris, *&,* Oebaliæ *qui temperat arva,* Galesus.
Semper honoratus nostris celebrabitur undis
Iste dies; semper dapibus recoletur optimis.
 Sic ait, & Nymphæ, *patris præcepta sequutæ,*

Q   *Tecta*

Tecta parant peplis; ostróque infecta corusco,
Humida gemmiferis illuxit regia mensis.

An Isle 'midst *Tyber*, with her spreading sides,
The City, and his Silver Waves divides :
Banks on each Hand, and Tow'r-crown'd Margents rise,
Threatning with their approach the lofty Skies;
Here standing on a Summit, he survai'd
The loving Brothers, and the Cavalcade,
As on they march'd, bright Axes born before,
And double Rods brought from one single Floor.
Amaz'd he stood, long e're his joy could make
Way for his strugling Voice, at last he spake.
   Spartan Eurota, see, if thou could'st e're
Such Brothers boast : compar'd to these, what were
The Swan's fair Race, though well they knew the Cest,
And how to steer a Fleet with Storms distrest.
New Stars, behold ! out-shine *Ledæan* Fires.
Behold my People, whom the Sky desires:
For future Flames a place Heav'n ready makes.
Olybrius shall rule Night's duskie Ax
For *Pollux*, *Probine* shine for *Castor*'s Star,
They Sails shall swell, and gently move the Air,
That Sailors through calm Seas may steer the Pine.
Now pay Libations, now drink freely Wine.
You, *Naiades*, draw forth your beautious Ranks,
And strew with Violets your Fountain Banks:
Inebriated Streams, now overflow
Your Banks, turn'd Wine ; in Woods let Honey grow ;
The Meads sweat healing Balm ; let one strait all
The Neighb'ring Rivers to a Banquet call.

All

All those, who wash th' *Ausonian* Mountain's Feet,
And drink cold *Alpine* Snow; *Vulturnus* fleet;
Strong-sented *Nar*; and *Ufens* Streams, that grow,
By wand'ring through their own *Mæanders*, flow;
Eridanus too, who makes such pityous moan
For loss of his lamented *Phaëthon*;
And *Liris* feaking off *Marica's* Groves;
Galesus, who *Oebalian* Fields improves.
This day our Waves shall always keep in State,
This we with annual Feasts will celebrate.
This said, the *Nymphs*, obeying, thither throng,
The Walls, and Roof, with stately Arras hung:
His Wat'ry Court with Royal Purple shone,
And Boards enchac'd with Pearl, and pretious Stone.

The River *Thames* having ended his *Speech*, the three Sea-men, who entertain'd the Nobility with the former Song, addressed the following to His Majesty.

I.

King CHARLES, King CHARLES, *great* Neptune *of the Main!*
Thy Royal Navy rig,
And We'll not care a Fig
For France, *for* France, *the* Netherlands, *nor* Spain.
The Turk, who looks so big,
We'll whip him like a Gig
About the Mediterrane;
His Gallies all sunk, or ta'ne.
We'll seize on their Goods, and their Monies,
Those Algier *Sharks,*
That Plunder Ships, and Barks,
Algier, Sally, *and* Tunis,

We'll give them such Tosts
To the Barbary Coasts,
Shall drive them to Harbour, like Conies.
Tan tara ran tan tan
Tan tara ran tan tara,
Not all the World we fear-a;
The great Fish-Pond
Shall be thine-a
Both here, and beyond,
From Strand to Strand,
And underneath the Line-a.

II.

A Sail, a Sail, I to the Offin see,
She seems a lusty Ship;
Hoise all your Sails a-trip:
We'll weather, weather her, whate're she be.
Your Helm then steady keep,
And thunder up the Deep,
A Man of War, no Merchant She;
We'll Jet her on her Crupper;
Give Fire, Bounce, Bounce,
Pickeering Villains trounce,
Till Blood run in Streams at the Scupper.
Such a Break-fast them we shall,
Give with Powder, and Ball,
They shall need neither Dinner, nor Supper.
Tan tara ran tan tan
Tan tara ran tan tara,
Pickeering Rogues ne're spare-a;

With

With Bullets pink
Their Quarters;
   Until they stink,
   They sink, they sink,
Farewel the Devil's Martyrs.

III.

They yield, they yield; shall we the poor Rogues spare?
   Their ill-gotten Goods,
   Preserv'd from the Floods,
That King CHARLES, *and we may share?*
   With Wine then chear our Bloods,
   And, putting off our Hoods,
Drink to His MAJESTY *bare,*
The King of all Compassion:
   On our Knees next fall
   T' our Royal Admiral,
A Health for His Preservation,
   Dear JAMES *the Duke of* YORK;
Till our Heels grow light as Cork,
The second Glory of our Nation.
    Tantara ran tan tan
    Tantara ran tan tara
   To the Royal Pair-a,
Let every man
Full of Wine-a
    Take off his Can,
    Though wan, though wan,
To make his Red Nose shine-a.

His Majestie's Entertainments

The Sea-men having ended their Song, the several sorts of Musick performed their Duty, whilest His *Majesty* passed on towards *Cheap-side*.

At the *Stocks* the Entertainment was a Body of Military Musick, placed on a Balcony; consisting of six Trumpets, and three Drums: the Fountain there being after the *Thuscan* Order, venting Wine, and Water.

In like manner, on the Top of the great *Conduit*, at the Entrance of *Cheap-side*, was another Fountain, out of which issued both Wine, and Water, as in a Representation of *Temperance*; and on the several Towers of that Conduit were eight Figures, habited like *Nymphs*, with Escutcheons in one Hand, and Pendents, or Banners in the other: and between each of them Winde-Musick; the number, eight.

On the Standard also in *Cheap-side* there was a Band of Waits placed, consisting of six Persons.

THE

THE THIRD ARCH.

THE third Triumphal *Arch* stands near *Wood-street* end, not far from the place where the *Cross* sometimes stood.

"*It represents an Artificial Building of two Stories, one
"after the* Corinthian *way of Architecture, the other
"after the* Composite, *representing the* TEMPLE *of* CONCORD;
"*with this Inscription on a Shield,*

ÆDEM
CONCORDIÆ
IN HONOREM OPTIMI PRINCIPIS,
CUJUS ADVENTU
BRITANNIA TERRA MARIQ. PACATA,
ET PRISCIS LEGIBUS REFORMATA EST,
AMPLIOREM SPLENDIDIOREMQ.
RESTITUIT
S. P. Q. L.

CONCORD was reputed by the *Romans* in the number of their Goddesses, as we finde in JUVENAL,
  Cui colitur Pax, atque Fides, Concordia, Virtus;
and had several Temples, upon various occasions, vowed, and dedicated to her. There arose a dangerous Feud, which continued for some Years, between the Senate, and People of *Rome*: whereupon *Furius Camillus**, turning himself to the Capitol, desired of the Gods, that he might speak, and act that, which might tend to the benefit of the Commonwealth, and reconciliation of the two dissenting
  Parties;

*Anno U.C. CCCXXCVI.

Parties; and to that end vowed a Temple to CONCORD. Wherefore having called the Senate, after a long, and various Debate, upon certain Conditions, brought the Senate, and People to an Agreement. Which Temple, according to his Vow, by a Decree of the Senate, was erected, and dedicated to CONCORD. This is mention'd, though obscurely, *in tabulis Capitolinis*; but plainly, by OVID*:

* *Fastor. lib. 1.*

> *Nunc bene prospicies Latiam* CONCORDIA *turbam,*
>   *Nunc te sacratæ constituêre manus.*
> Furius, *antiquus populi superator* Etrusci,
>   *Voverat, & voti solverat ille fidem.*
> *Caussa, quòd à Patribus sumptis secesserat armis*
>   *Vulgus, & ipsa suas* Roma *timebat opes.*

> Now maist thou CONCORD, *Rome* with kindness see,
> Now sacred Hands a Fane erect for thee.
> *Furius*, who conquer'd the *Etrurian*, made
> A solemn Vow, which solemnly he paid.
> Because the People did their Princes beard,
> Taking up Arms; and *Rome* her own Wealth fear'd.

The like Vow was made by *L. Manlius* †, upon a Mutiny of the Army under his Command, and the Year after the Temple was erected, and dedicated by *M.* and *C. Atilius Regulus*, elected for that purpose. So in the Sedition of *Gracchus* *, who encamped on the *Aventine*, and refused the Conditions offered him by *L. Opimius* Consul, the Consul immediately vowed a Temple to CONCORD; and after his Victory over those seditious Conspirators, dedicated it *in Foro*. Which did highly incense the Communalty, who thought that CONCORD could not be founded on the Slaughter of their Fellow-Citizens: and some of them adventured to add this Inscription to the Title of the Temple,

† *Anno U.C.* DXXXV.

* *Anno U.C.* DCXXXII.

VECORDIÆ. OPUS. ÆDEM. FACIT. CONCORDIÆ.

passing to His CORONATION.

We finde mention of the like Temples in several Inscriptions, collected by *Gruter*; as in this,

D. N. CONSTANTINO. MAXIMO. PIO. FELICI. AC.
TRIUMPHATORI. SEMPER AUGUSTO. OB. AMPLI
CATAM. TOTO. ORBE. REM. PUBLICAM. FACTIS. CON
SILIISQ:

S. P. Q. R.

DEDICANTE. ANICIO. PAULINO. JUNIORE. C. V. COS
ORD. PRÆT. URBI.

S. P. Q. R.

ÆDEM. CONCORDIÆ. VETUSTATE. COL-
LAPSAM. IN MELIOREM. FACIEM. OPERE
ET. CULTU. SPLENDIDIORE. RESTITUE
RUNT.

And in another not unlike the former,

ÆDEM. CONCORDIÆ. VETUSTATE. COLLAPSAM
AMPLIOREM. OPERE. CULTUQ: SPLENDIDIOREM
RESTITUIT.

S. P. Q. R.

"In the Spandrils of the Arch there are two Figures, in Female Habits,
"leaning: One representing PEACE, the other TRUTH. That of Peace
"hath her Shield charged with an Helmet, and Bees issuing forth, and
"going into it; the Word,

PAX BELLO POTIOR.

"TRUTH, on the other side, in a thin Habit, on her Shield TIME,
"bringing Truth out of a Cave; the Word,

TANDEM EMERSIT.

R

"Over

" *Over the great Painting upon the Arch of the Cupula is represented*
" *a large* GERYON *with three Heads crowned; in his three right-Hands,*
" *a Lance, a Sword, and a Scepter; in his three left-Hands the three*
" *Escutcheons of England, Scotland, and Ireland: before him the King's*
" *Arms with three Imperial Crowns; beneath, in great Letters,*

CONCORDIA INSUPERABILIS.

GERYON, Son of *Chrysaor*, and *Callirrhoe*, according to *Hesiod*, was feigned by the *Poëts* to have three Heads, and as many Bodies, who was subdued by *Hercules*. Of whom VIRGIL*,

————nam maximus ultor
Tergemini nece Geryonis spoliisque superbus,
Alcides aderat, taurósque hàc victor agebat
Ingentes, vallémque boves amnémque tenebant.

Here the Revenger great *Alcides* stood,
Proud with the triple *Geryon*'s Spoils, and Blood;
The Conqu'rour drave his Cattel to these Grounds,
Whose Head possess'd the Vale, and River's Bounds.

And more largely SILIUS ITALICUS†,

Qualis Atlantiaco *memoratur littore quondam*
Monstrum Geryones *immane tricorporis iræ:*
Cui tres in pugna dextræ varia arma gerebant;
Una ignes sævos, ast altera ponè sagittas
Fundebat, validam torquebat tertia cornum,
Atque uno diversa dabat tria vulnera nisu.

—— So (famous in a former Age)
That horrid Monster of a Triple rage,
Geryon, fought on the *Atlantick* Shore:
Whose three Right-Hands three sev'ral Weapons bore;
One cruel Flames, behind him th'other drew
His Bow, the third his trusty Jav'lin threw;
And dealt three sev'ral ways, at once, a Wound.

The

The Origination of this Fable, and its Significations, are variously related. *Palæphatus* supposed him to have been feigned by the *Poets* to have three Heads, because he had his Birth in a City on the *Euxine* Sea, called Τρικάρηνια, that is, of *three Heads*. Others, that it related to the three Brothers, who unanimously govern'd *Spain*. And indeed, that *Spain*, by reason of its Tripartite Division, was signified by the *Hieroglyphick* of *Geryon*, is not onely the Opinion of some Authours, but appears from a Coyn of the Emperour *Hadrian*, the third time *Consul*, in which there is a three-headed Image leaning on a Spear; either to signifie his Peragration of *Spain*, or his Origination from thence. Others have referr'd this to the Vices of Speech, Body, and Soul, which *Hercules* overcame; which is confirm'd from the three Apples ordinarily held in one Hand of *Hercules*, still to be seen in a Statue of his in the *Farnesie*'s Palace at *Rome*, which, *Suidas* says, alluded to the same.

" *On the top of the* Cupula CONCORD, *a Woman in her right-Hand holding her Mantle; in her left-Hand a* Caduceus; *under her Feet a Serpent strugling, which she seems to tread down.*

That a Serpent was a *Hieroglyphick* of Enmity, and *War*, (for which cause it is presented trampled under the Feet of CONCORD) appears from many Writers, Histories, and Medaigles. ARTEMIDORUS [*], *A Serpent signifies a Disease, and brings Enmity: according as that hurts any one in his Dream, so shall his Disease, and Enemy.* And ACHMET [†], *Serpents generally, according to their proportion, signifie Enemies.* NICEPHORUS, Patriarch of *Constantinople*,

[* *Oneirocrit.* lib. ii. cap. xiii.]
[† *Oneirocrit.* cap. cclxxiii.]

Ὄφεις ἀναιρῖν, τὸς Ἐχθρὸς ν̓εα.

Killing a Serpent, think your Enemy you kill.

So DIODORUS says, that, according to the *Ægyptians*, *A Serpent is the Symbol of Hatred.* VIRGIL, describing *Alecto*, endeavouring to raise a War betwixt *Turnus* and *Æneas*, feigns her with two Snakes erect upon her Head;

—————— *Flammea torquens*
Lumina, cunctantem, & quærentem dicere plura
Reppulit, & GEMINOS *erexit crinibus* ANGUES:
Verberáque insonuit, validóque hæc edidit ore.

Rowling her bloody Eyes, she drives him back,
Labouring Requests, and once again to speak:
Then with two Serpents from her Snaky Hair
She scourging him did thus her Rage declare.

ÆSCHYLUS, of a Dream of *Clytemnestra*,

Τεκεῖν δράκοντ᾽ ἔδοξεν, ὡς αὐτὴ λέγει.
Ἐν σπαργάνοισι παιδὸς ὁρμίσαι δίκην.
Τίνος βορᾶς χρῄζοντα νεογενὲς δάκος·
Αὐτὴ προσέσχε μαζὸν ἐν τ᾽ ὀνείρατι.
Ὥστ᾽ ἐν γάλακτι θρόμβον αἵματος σπάσαι.

As she reported, in her Dream she thought,
Forth to the World that she a Serpent brought,
Swath'd like a tender Infant wanting meat,
And, pitying, lays the Monster to her Teat.
Milk issued forth commix'd with clotted gore.

From whence *Orestes* immediately conjectured she was to die by his Hand.

Δεῖ τοί νιν, ὡς ἔθρεψεν ἔκπαγλον τέρας,
Θανεῖν βιαίως· ἐκδρακοντωθεὶς δ᾽ ἐγὼ
Κτείνω νιν, ὡς τοὔνειρον ἐννέπει τόδε.

So she, who gave the Monster life, and breath,
Should therefore suffer by a violent Death:
And I, like an enraged Serpent, should
Kill her my self, and her sad Dream unfold.

Plut. in Gracchis.

Which may further be illustrated from several events. TIBERIUS GRACCHUS, *in his Bed, was clasp'd about by two Serpents. Which Prodigie when the South-sayers had considered, they counselled, that he should neither kill both, nor let both escape: and further said, that, if he kill'd the* Male, *it would cost his own life; if the* Female, *his Wife* Cornelia's. TIBERIUS, *bearing affection to his Wife, and withall thinking it more agreeable, that he, being the elder, should die first, kill'd the* Male, *and let the* Female *escape: and*

not

not long after died. The same evil consequence we finde in the History of C. Hostilius Mancinus†; *who, as soon as he had gone aboard a Ship, in order to his Voyage to* Numantia, *on a suddain heard a Voice cry,* Stay, Mancinus. *Whereupon he return'd back, and, at* Genoa, *going aboard again, found a Serpent in the Ship, which escaped from him. He was overthrown, and delivered up to his Enemies.* And Valerius Maximus * says, that in the dissension of *M. Fulvius Flaccus* about making some Laws, *two black Serpents, sliding into the Cell of* Minerva, *portended intestine Murders.* Thus we finde them generally to portend sad Events, but particularly they were the *Hieroglyphick* of *War*, and *Devastation.* This appears from that known Story of *Homer*, where he tells us, that, while the *Grecians* were sacrificing at *Aulis*, they saw a Dragon devour eight young Sparrows, with the Damm, and makes the Prophet *Calchas*† interpret it the duration of the War for nine years.

† Obsequens De Prodigiis, cap. lxxxiii.

* Lib. i. cap. lxxxvii.

† Iliad. β´.

'Ως ὅ γε κατὰ τέκν᾽ ἔφαγε στρουθοῖο, καὶ αὐτὴν,
Ὀκτὼ, ἀτὰρ μήτηρ ἐνάτη ἦν, ἣ τέκε τέκνα·
Ὣς ἡμεῖς τοσαῦτ᾽ ἔτεα πτολεμίξομεν αὖθι,
Τῷ δεκάτῳ δὲ πόλιν αἱρήσομεν εὐρυάγυιαν.

For, as this Serpent, which from th'Altar sprung,
Devour'd the woful Mother, and her Young,
Which with her tender Issue make up nine :
So many Years the Destinies design
This War shall last, and we the Tenth destroy
The lofty Bulwarks of well-builded *Troy.*

Where the Dragon signified the War; the number of the Birds, the Continuation of it. So when *Hannibal*, in a Dream, saw a Serpent of vast magnitude throwing down Rocks, Woods, and Towns, and enquired of the Gods the meaning of it, they return'd this Answer †,

† Silius Ital. l.b. iii.

Bella *vides optata tibi;* te maxima Bella,
Te strages nemorum, te toto turbida cælo
Tempestas, cædésque virûm, magnæque ruinæ
Idæi generis, lachrymosáque fata sequuntur.
Quantus per campos populatis montibus actas
Contorquet sylvas squallenti tergore Serpens,

Et

Et latè humectat terras spumante veneno :
Tantas, perdomitis decurrens Alpibus, *atro*
Involves BELLO Italiam : *tantóque fragore*
Eruta convulsis pro ernes oppida muris.

——————Thou do'st see
The War so much desir'd, and sought by Thee.
Thee greatest Wars attend ; the dreadful Fall
Of Woods, and Forests, with high Storms, that all
The Face of Heav'n disturb ; the Slaughter Thee,
And Death of Men ; the great Calamity
Of the *Idæan* Race, and saddest Fate
Do follow, and upon thee daily wait.
As great, and terrible, as that dire Snake,
Which now the Mountains with his Scaly Back
Depopulates, and drives the Forests through
The Fields before him, and doth Earth imbrue
With frothy Poison : Such thou, having past,
And overcome the *Alps*, with War shalt wast
All *Italy* ; and, with a Noise as great,
The Cities, and their Walls, shalt ruinate.

Mr. Ross.

Which is evidently seen in some Medaigles of the *Roman* Emperours, as in this Reverse of *Augustus's*.

Golz. Cæs.
A g. pag. xli.

Where two Serpents, that is, the Hostility, and Dissension of the *Roman* Empire, divided into two Factions, that of *Augustus*, and *Antony*, are se-
parated

parated by an intervening Victory; that of *Augustus* at *Actium*, and *Alexandria*. That upon these Victories this Coyn was stamp'd, may be collected from the Inscription on the other side, CÆSAR IMP. VII. that is *annus* U. C. DCCXXIV. in which * Year he triumph'd for the two Victories before-mention'd. The same is to be seen in a Reverse of *M. Antony's*.

Dio, Lib. l.

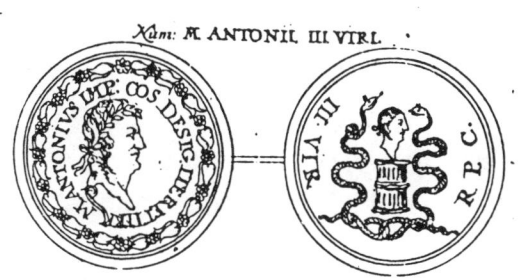

Goltz. *Jul. Cæs.* pag. xlviii.

Where a Woman (supposed to be CONCORD, with the Face of *Octavia*, Sister to *Augustus*, and Wife to *M. Antony*,) in a long Stole, holding in her left Hand a pure Spear, in her right a Pontifical Vessel, parts two Serpents, signifying the Armies of *Augustus*, and *Antony*. Which Interpretation of this Coyn is very much confirm'd from History. For this Pacification, obtain'd by the Prudence of *Octavia*, happened *anno* U. C. DCCXVI. *Agrippa*, and *Gallus*, being *Consuls*. That this Coyn was stamp'd after the Year DCCXIV. (the time of the Peace between *Sext. Pompey*, *C. Cæs. Octavianus*, and *Antony*,) appears from the Inscription on the other side, M. ANTONIUS IMP. COS. DESIG. ITER. ET. TERT. for *Appian* * says, that, after that Peace, the *Consulships* were appointed for the next four Years. For the first, *Antony*, and *Libo* (which *Antony* had been *Consul* before with *Julius Cæsar*;) next, *Cæsar*, and *Pompey*; after them *Ahenobarbus*, and *Sosius*; last, *Cæsar*, and *Antony*: τεῖτον δὲ τὴν μεγάλην ὑπατείαν, *then to become the third time* Consuls.

Vide Pighii Annal. ad *eum annum*.

* *De Civil. Bel.* Lib. v.

"On the West-side, the third great Figure, a Woman standing at the "Helm of a Ship; in her left Hand, a Cornu-copiæ; the Word,

FORTUNÆ REDUCI.

FORTUNE was not more various, and unconstant in her Motions, then those, that painted her, in their Descriptions. The first was *Bupalus*, who put a Celestial Orb (which *Pierius* unhappily chang'd, by the mistake of one Vowel, into a Foal) on her Head, and a *Cornu-copiæ* in her left Hand; as we finde her in a Reverse of a Coyn of the Emperour *Gallienus*, with this Inscription, ΕΦΕΣΙΩΝ ΤΥΧΗ Afterwards, some feigned her either standing upon a Stone, or the top of some Mountain exposed to the Winds, or upon a Wheel : others, upon the Prow of a Ship, holding a Sail with both her Hands; which is frequent in *Greek* Medaigles. PAUSANIAS makes mention of a Temple of *Fortune*, in which there was her Statue, holding a young *Plutus*, the God of Riches, in her Hand: as we finde her in ARISTOPHANES[*], to signifie, that she was the Mother, and Nurse of Wealth. Some attributed Wings to her, as EUSEBIUS mentions. HORACE[†],

[*] *In Pluto.*

[†] *lib. iii. Od. 29.*

——*si celeres quatit*
Pennas, resigno quæ dedit. ———

If she her nimble Pinions wave,
I straight resign whate're she gave.

The *Scythians*, both Wings, and Hands, but no Feet. When APELLES was asked, why he made *Fortune* sitting, he answered, *Because she never stood*. But we shall onely take notice of what is here before us. In the same manner we finde her described in a Stone, insculp'd on both sides, with this *Inscription* on one,

NUM. DOM. AUG. SACRUM. FORTUNÆ CONSERVATRICI HORRE OR. GALBANORUM. M. LORINUS FORTUNATUS MAGISTER S. P. B. D.

with the Image of *Fortune*, holding in her left Hand a *Cornu-copiæ*, in her right the Helm of a Ship : and so we finde her too in a *Reverse* of a Coyn of TRAJAN the *Emperour*, mention'd by Occo. The like says LACTANTIUS[*], *Effingebatur quidem* Fortuna *cum Cornu-copia, & Gubernaculo; tanquam opes tribuere putaretur, & humanarum rerum regimen obtinere :* Fortune *was made with a* Cornu-copiæ, *and the Helm of a Ship, as if she were reputed the Disposer of Wealth, and had the Government of Humane Affairs.* And PLUTARCH[†], after various instances on each side, at length concludes, that the *Roman* Empire ought more to *Fortune*, then to *Valour*, or *Prudence* : and therefore says, that, having left the *Persians*, and *Assyrians*, she lightly flew over

[*] *Lib. iii.*

[†] *De fortuna Romanorum.*

passing to His Coronation.

Macedonia, and presently she shaked off ALEXANDER; then passing through *Ægypt*, and *Syria*, often tryed the *Carthaginians*: but when she had once passed the *Tyber*, and entered the Palace, she laid aside her Wings, put off her *Talaria*, and forsook her unfaithful, and ever-mutable Sphere, as if she intended to stay there for ever. Indeed the *Romans* did confess as much; who, having dedicated sundry *Temples* to *Fortune*, with all variety of Honour, in the most eminent places of the City, never erected one to *Virtue*, or *Valour*, till the time of *Marcellus*, that took *Syracuse*; or of *Scipio Numantinus*, about the † five hundred sixty and third year after the building of the City. To *Prudence* never dedicated to any. Among the rest of *Fortune's* Titles none more frequent, then this of REDUX, to whom we read that DOMITIAN the *Emperour* built a *Temple*, mention'd by MARTIAL *,

† *Helvicus Chron. pag. 75. d.*

* *Lib. vii.*

Hìc ubi FORTUNÆ REDUCI *fulgentia latè*
Templa nitent.———

Here, where bright Fanes to RETURN'D FORTUNE shine.

Temples of the like nature are mention'd too by CLAUDIAN,

Aurea FORTUNÆ REDUCI *si Templa priores*
Ob reditum vovêre Ducum, non dignius unquam
Hæc Dea pro meritis amplas sibi posceret ædes, &c.

If they to FORTUNE REDUX vow'd of old,
Their Chiefs return'd with Conquest, Fanes of Gold;
The Goddess never more deserv'd then now,
That we should stately *Temples* her allow.

There are also many *Medaigles*, and those antient, of several *Emperours* with the same *Inscription*,

"*Above there are eight living Figures with Pennons, and Shields, repre-
"senting the four Cardinal Virtues, each with an Attendant.
"PRUDENCE, on her Shield Bellerophon on a Pegasus, running his
"Javelin into the Mouth of a Chimera; the Word,

CONSILIO ET VIRTUTE.

Bellerophon was the Son of *Glaucus* King of *Corinth*, renown'd both for Prudence, Courage, Beauty, and Modesty. Of whom thus HOMER[†],

† *Iliad.* vi.

Αὐτὰρ Γλαῦκος ἔτικτεν ἀμύμονα Βελλεροφόντην
Τῷ δὲ Θεοὶ κάλλος τε, ὴ ἠνορέην ἐρατεινὴν
Ὤπασαν ————

———— Glaucus Bellerophon,
In whom all Good concenter'd as in one:
And Heav'n this Prince a Pers'nage did afford,
Which all admir'd. ————

The *Poëts* feign many Stories of him. They say, he went to *Prætus*, King of the *Argivi*, by whom at first he was kindly entertain'd. But being afterwards falsly accused by *Antea*, the Wife of *Prætus*, for offering to tempt her Chastity, he sent him to *Iobates*, King of *Lycia*, with a Letter written purposely to have him kill'd. *Iobates*, to pleasure *Prætus*, sent *Bellerophon* against the *Chimæra*. But *Minerva*, the Goddess of *Prudence*, and *Valour*, protected his Innocence. Wherefore she bridled *Pegasus*, and delivered it to him. Upon whom being mounted, he slew the *Chimæra* with his Javelin. After which Victory he sent him against the *Solymi* (a Nation betwixt *Lycia*, and *Pamphylia*) and the *Amazons*. From whence he returned also Conquerour; *Iobates*, moved with his Prudence, and Valour, gave him to Wife his Daughter *Philonoë*, and afterwards dying, left him Successour in his Kingdom. Of which largely HOMER[*],

* *Ibid.*

Πρῶτον μέν ῥα Χίμαιραν ἀμαιμακέτην ἐκέλευσε
Πεφνέμεν· ἣ δ' ἄρ' ἔην θεῖον γένος, οὐδ' ἀνθρώπων.
Πρόσθε λέων, ὄπιθεν δὲ δράκων, μέσση δὲ Χίμαιρα,
Δεινὸν ἀποπνείουσα πυρὸς μένος αἰθομένοιο.

Καὶ

Καί τὼ μὲν κατέπεφνε, Θεῶν τεράεσσι πιθήσας.
Δεύτερον αὖ Σολύμοισι μαχέσσατο κυδαλίμοισι·
Καρτίστην δὴ τήν γε μάχην φάτο δύμεναι ἀνδρῶν.
Τὸ τρίτον αὖ κατέπεφνεν Ἀμαζόνας ἀντιανείρας.
  Τῷ δ' ἄρ ἀνερχομένῳ πυκινὸν δόλον ἄλλον ὕφαινε·
Κρίνας ἐκ Λυκίης εὐρείης φῶτας ἀρίστους
Εἶσε λόχον· τοὶ δ' οὔτι πάλιν οἶκόν δὲ νέοντο.
Πάντας γὰρ κατέπεφνεν ἀμύμων Βελλεροφόντης.
Ἀλλ' ὅτε δὴ γίγνωσκε Θεοῦ γόνον ἠΰν ἐόντα,
Αὐτοῦ μιν κατέρυκε, δίδου δ' ὅ γε θυγατέρα ἥν·
Δῶκε δέ οἱ τιμῆς βασιληΐδος ἥμισυ πάσης.

First he commands him stern *Chimæra* kill:
This hideous Monster, of no Mortal Race,
A Dragon's Tail had, and a Lion's Face,
Back'd like a shaggy Goat, still belching Flame:
This by Divine Assistance he o're-came.
Next he against renowned *Solym* fought;
This Victory, he said, was dearly bought.
He last against the *Amazons* prevail'd.
    But, when he saw all open Forces fail'd,
He fell to close contrivance, and did lay
An Ambuscade to kill him in his way;
Not one return'd of all, that were employ'd,
All were by bold *Bellerophon* destroy'd:
But when he knew he was of Heav'nly Blood,
His onely Daughter he on him bestow'd,
Investing straight with half his Regal Power.

The *Chimæra* is in the same manner described also by HESIOD*,

*In *Theogonia*, vers. 321.

Ἡ δὲ Χίμαιραν ἔτικτε, πνέουσαν ἀμαιμάκετον πῦρ,
Δεινήν τε, μεγάλην τε, ποδώκεά τε, κρατερήν τε.
Τῆς δ' ἦν τρεῖς κεφαλαί· μία μὲν χαροποῖο Λέοντος·
Ἡ δὲ Χιμαίρης· ἡ δ' ὄφιος κρατεροῖο Δράκοντος.

Πρόσθε Λέων, ὄπιθεν δὲ Δράκων, μέσση δὲ Χίμαιρα,
Δεινὸν ἀποπνείουσα πυρὸς μένος αἰθομένοιο.
Τὴν μὲν Πήγασος εἷλε, καὶ ἐσθλὸς Βελλεροφόντης.

She bore Chimæra *belching dreadful Fire,*
Mighty, and strong, extremely swift, and dire.
Three Heads the Monster had; a Lion's first,
And next a Goat's, a Serpent's last, and worst.
A Dragon's Tail she had, and Lion's Face,
Back'd like a Goat, belching out Flames apace;
Whom Pegasus *took, and stout* Bellerophon.

* Æneid. VII.

VIRGIL* also makes a *Chimæra* on the Helmet of *Turnus*, vomiting forth Fire;

Cui, triplici crinita jubâ, galea alta Chimæram
Sustinet, Ætnæos efflantem faucibus ignes.
Tam magis illa fremens, & tristibus effera flammis,
Quàm magis effuso crudescunt sanguine pugnæ.

On's Crest *Chimæra*, through a triple Tyre
Of bushy Horse-Mains, breath'd *Ætnæan* Fire.
Strangely it roars, and Flame more fiercely glows,
When in the Battel blood in Rivers flows.

† In Corinthiacis.

From that part of the History, wherein *Minerva* is said to bridle *Pegasus* for *Bellerophon*, there was built a Temple, and Statue of *Minerva* called Χαλινῖτις *Frænatrix*; as PAUSANIAS† relates.

That *Bellerophon* was the Son of *Glaucus*, King of *Corinth*, appears from a Medaigle of the *Corinthians* yet extant, on the Reverse of which is *Bellerophon* mounted on *Pegasus*, slaying the *Chimæra* with his Javelin: on the other side *VENUS*, with this Inscription ΚΟΡΙΝΘΙΩΝ, because at *Corinth VENUS* had a most splendid Temple. There is also a Coyn of *C. Cæsar*'s, in which *Bellerophon* kills the *Chimæra*, with this Inscription COL. JUL. COR. that is, *Corinth* the Colony of *Julius Cæsar*. Because *C. J. Cæsar* restored the City of *Corinth*,

rinth, utterly deſtroyed before by *Mummius*, as we finde in D I O, and in P A U S A N I A S in the beginning of his *Corinthiaca*.

What the Antients did denote by this Triple Form of *Chimæra*, is doubtful. N Y M P H O D O R U S the *Syracuſan* ſays, that *Chimæra* was a Mountain of *Lycia*, which perpetually vomited forth Fire, on the top of which lived Lions, in the middle (where were ſpatious pleaſant Medows) Goats, at the bottom Dragons. Which Mountain when *Bellephoron* had rendred habitable, he was ſaid to have ſlain *Chimæra*. But *Antigonus Cary*ſ*tius* ſays, it ſignified onely the People of three ſeveral Nations conquered by *Bellerophon*.

"J U S T I C E, *on her Shield a Woman holding a Sword in one Hand, a* "*Balance in the other* ; *the Word*,

QUOD DEXTERA LIBRAT.

Though this Deſcription of J U S T I C E, with a *Balance* in one Hand, hath been by late Writers accounted modern, yet it appears from *Occo* to have been antient, who thus found her repreſented in the Reverſe of a Coyn of *Trajan* the *Emperour*, with a *Caduceus* in the other Hand: if he miſtook her not for *Moneta Aug.* conſtantly ſo deſcribed; as may be ſeen in the Coyns of *Antoninus*, and other *Emperours*.

"TEMPERANCE, *a Viol in her left Hand, a Bridle in her right;*
"*the Word,*

FERRE LUPATA DOCET.

"FORTITUDE, *a Lyon having the Arms of* England, *in an*
"*Escutcheon; the Word,*

CUSTOS FIDISSIMUS.

"*The internal Part of this Triumph, or Temple, is Round, the upper*
"*part Dark, onely enlightened by Artificial Lights; the lower part divided*
"*into ten Parts by Pilasters with Pedestals.*

"*Within the* Temple *are twelve living Figures, three placed above the*
"*Rest.*

"*The First the* Goddess *of the* Temple *in rich Habit, with a* Cadu-
"ceus *in her Hand, and a* Serpent *at her Feet. Behind* the Goddess, *a*
"*Man in a Purple Gown, like a Citizen of* London, *presenting the* KING
"*with an* Oaken *Garland. Over the* KING's *Head,*

PATER PATRIÆ.

"*Over the Citizen's,*

S. P. Q. L.

OB CIVES SERVATOS.

There were several sorts of *Crowns* in use among the *Romans*, according to the variety of the Deserts of those, who were rewarded with them; *Obsidionales, Murales, Castrenses, Navales, Rostratæ, Civicæ.*

The *Obsidionalis* was given to him, who had rais'd a Siege; which was made of the Grass, that grew in the place besieged: and this was accounted more † honourable then any of the rest. The first among the *Romans*, that was rewarded with this sort of Crown, was *Q. Cincinnatus*; after him *P. Decius*, and *L. Sicinius Dentatus, Calpurnius Flamma*, and others.

† *Plin.* Lib. xvi. cap. iv.

The *Mural* Crown was the reward of him, that first scal'd the Walls, and entred the place assaulted; mention'd by SILIUS ITALICUS *,

* Lib. xii.

Fulvius *ut finem spoliandis ædibus, ære*
Belligero revocante, dedit; sublimis ab alto

Suggestu

Suggestu (magnis autor non futilis ausis)
Lavino generate, inquit, quem Sospita Juno
Dat nobis, Milo, *Gradivi cape victor honorem,*
Tempora Murali cinctus turrita coronâ.

But when, from Plunder of the Town, agen
The *Gen'ral*, by the Trumpet's sound, his Men
Had call'd (a Noble Cherisher of great
Attempts) to *Milo*, from his lofty Seat,
He thus began; *Lanuvian* Youth, whom we
From *Juno Sospita* receive, from me
This Martial Honour for thy Victory
Accept, and 'bout thy Tower'd Temples try
This Mural Crown.——————

Mr. Ross.

And in another place†,   † Lib. xv.

———*phaleris hic pectora fulget,*
Hic torque aurato circumdat bellica colla ;
Ille nitet celsus Muralis honore coronæ.

————here shining stood
One with rich Trappings on his Breast, and there
Another on his Warlick Neck did wear
A Golden Chain: this with a Mural Crown
Was honour'd,————

The *Castrensis* belong'd to him, that first entered the Tents of the Enemy: which, in the Infancy of the *Roman* Empire, was made of *Leaves*. With such an one *Romulus* rewarded *Hostus Hostilius*, Grand-Father to *Tulus Hostilius*, King of *Rome*: afterwards of *Gold*. This, without question, is the same with that, which otherwise is call'd *Vallaris*.

The *Corona Navalis*, or *Rostrata*, (for they seem not to be different, however *Lipsius* distinguisheth them) was the reward of him, that first boarded the Enemie's Ship, and took it: with this sort of Crown

POMPEY

POMPEY *the Great* honoured *M. Varro*; and AUGUSTUS *Agrippa.* The Form of it is still preserv'd in the Coyns of *Agrippa*,

Æn. viii. This is it, which VIRGIL * mentions,

Tempora Navali fulgent rostrata coronâ,

His Brows, deck'd with a Naval Garland, shone.

But that, which gave us occasion to mention these, is the *Corona Civica*, given to him, that in single Combat had rescued a Citizen, and slain the Enemy on the place: and this was made of *Oak*. Lucan,

—— *Emeritique gerens insignia doni*
Servati civis referentem præmia quercum.

—— Crown'd with an Oaken Wreath,
Rewards for such, a *Roman* sav'd from Death.

CLAUDIAN *,

Mos erat in veterum castris, ut tempora quercus
Velaret, validis fuso qui viribus hoste
Casurum potuit morti subducere civem.

'Twas th' ancient Guise in Camps, an Oaken Bough
Should wreath his Temples, who had slain a Fo,
And off a Citizen in danger brought.

And

And in another place [†], [† *De laude Serenæ.*]
> *Hunc cingit* Muralis *honos, hunc* Civica quercus
> *Nexuit, hunc domitis ambit* Rostrata *carinis.*

This *Mural* Honour crowns, that *Civick* Boughs,
This wreaths his Head with conquer'd Gallies *Prows.*

These were ordinarily prefix'd the Entrance of the *Emperour's* Palaces, as being *populi Servatores.* OVID[*], [* *Fast. Lib. 1.*]

> *Ante fores stabis, mediámque tuebere quercum,*
> *Protegat & nostras querna corona fores.*

Thou shalt protect the middle Oak before
The Gates; let Oaken Garlands save our Dore.

In another place,

> *En domus hæc, dixi,* Jovis *est; quod ut esse probarem,*
> *Augurium menti querna corona dabat.*

Behold, said I, this is *Jove's* House; I know
By th'Oaken Wreath, that needs it must be so.

Which seems to be derived from JULIUS CÆSAR: of whose Statues thus APPIAN, speaking of the Honours decreed to him; *There were several Figures inscribed on his Effigies: on some a Crown of Oak, as dedicated to the Saviour of his Countrey.* And DIO of *Augustus*; *When he denied the Monarchy, and discoursed of dividing the Provinces, it was decreed, that Laurels should be set up before his Palace, and a Crown of Oak hung over them, to signifie, that he was constantly overthrowing his Enemies, and saving his Fellow-Citizens.* The memory of which Honour conferred on him is preserved in several of his Coyns: in one there is a Crown of Oak betwixt two Branches of Laurel.

In another the same Crown betwixt two *CAPRICORNS* (he was born under that Sign) with a Globe, and the Helm of a Ship.

In one this *Inscription*, within the Crown of Oak, SALUS HUMANI GENERIS: to which PLINY*, without question, alluded in those words, *Dedit* AUGUSTUS *Rostratam coronam* AGRIPPÆ, *sea* CIVICAM *à genere humano recepit ipse.*

* *Nat. Hist. lib. xvi. cap. xii.*

There are several reasons propounded by PLUTARCH, and others after him, why this Crown should be made of this material; but none so probable as this, because the Oak was sacred to JUPITER and JUNO *Conservatoribus,* Σωτῆρσι, and Πολιούχοις.

The Habit of VENUS 'tis something difficult in particular to deliver; the antient *Artists* having been more willing to form her naked, as appears from the Statues of her still remaining in *Rome*, and from this *Poëm* of ANACREON upon VENUS engraved on a Basin,

Ἄγε τίς τόρευσε πόντον;
Ἄγε τίς μανεῖσα τέχνα, &c.

What bold Hand the Sea engraves,
Whilst its undermined Waves

In a Dishe's narrow round
Art's more pow'rful Rage doth bound?
See by some Promethean *mind*
Cytherea there design'd,
Mother of the Deities,
Expos'd naked to our Eyes
In all parts, save those alone,
Modesty will not have shown,
Which for Cov'ring onely have
The thin Mantle of a Wave:
On the Surface of the Main,
Which a smiling Calm lays plain,
She, like frothy Sedges, swims,
And displays her Snowy Limbs, &c.

Mr. STANLEY.

Yet, because there is something of it particular to her, we shall give some account of it from *CLAUDIAN*, who thus describes her Dress, when she was going to the Wedding of *HONORIUS* the *Emperour*:

> ———*natum gremio* Cytherea *removit:*
> *Et crines festina ligat, peplúmque fluentem*
> *Allevat, & blando spirantem numine ceston*
> *Cingitur, impulsos pluviis quo mitigat amnes,*
> *Quo mare, quo ventos, iratáque fulmina solvit.*

Venus the Boy lays from her Breast;
Binds up her Hair, and tucks her flowing Vest;
Girds on her *Cestus* breathing pow'rful love,
Which calms swoln Rivers by a Deluge drove,
The raging Seas, rough Winds, and thund'ring *Jove*.

What this *Cestos* is, may best be known from HOMER[†], who is the first, that mention'd it:

† Iliad. ξ´.

> Ἦ, ϰ̀ ὑπὸ στήθεσιν ἐλύσατο κεστὸν ἱμάντα,
> Ποικίλον· ἔνθα δέ οἱ θελκτήρια πάντα τέτυκτο.
> Ἔνθ᾽ ἔνι μὲν φιλότης, ἐν δ᾽ Ἵμερος, ἐν δ᾽ ὀαριστὺς,
> Πάρφασις, ἥτ᾽ ἔκλεψε νόον πύκα περ φρονεόντων.

This saying, off she takes her curious *Cest*,
Where all Allurements were of Love exprest,
Dalliance, Desire, Courtship, and Flatt'ries, which
The wisest with their Sorceries bewitch.

The *Roses*, and *Dolphin*, in the Hands of CUPID, signifie his Dominion on Land, and Sea: of which there is extant an *Epigram* of PALLADAS,

> Οὐδὲ μάτην παλάμαις κατέχει ΔΕΛΦΙΝΑ, ϰ̀ ΑΝΘΟΣ·
> Τῇ μὲν γὰρ Γαῖαν, τῇ δὲ Θάλατταν ἔχει.

The *Dolphin* he, nor *Roses* holds in vain:
In this Hand Earth, in that he holds the Main.

ANACREON,

> Ῥόδον ὦ φέριστον ἄνθος,
> Ῥόδον ἔαρος μέλημα, &c.

Roses, of all Flow'rs the King;
Roses, the fresh Pride o'th' Spring,
Joy of ev'ry Deity;
Love, when with the *Graces* he
For the Ball himself disposes,
Crowns his Golden Hair with Roses.

Of the *Dolphin* largely OPPIAN,

> Δελφῖνες δ᾽ ἀγέλησιν ἁλὸς μέγα κοιρανέουσιν,
> Ἔξοχον ἠνορέῃ τε, ϰ̀ ἀγλαΐῃ κομόωντες,

Ῥιπῇ τ' ὠκυάλῳ· διὰ γὰρ, βέλος ὥςε, θάλασσαν
Ἱπτανται, φλογόεν τε σέλας πέμπωσιν ὀπωπαῖς
Ὀξύταται, καὶ τὺ τὴν ὑποπτήσσονται χαράδρας,
Καὶ τὴν ὑπὸ ψαμάθοις εἰλυόμενον ἔδρακον ἰχθύν.
  Ὅσσοι γὰρ κύφοισι μετ' οἰωνοῖσιν ἄνακτες·
Αἰετοὶ, ἠ θήρεσσι μετ' ὠμηςῇσι Λέοντες·
Ὅσσον ἀειςεύωσιν ἐν ἑρπυςῆρσι Δράκοντες.
Τόσσον ᾗ ΔΕΛΦΙΝΕΣ ἐν ἰχθύσιν ἡγεμονῆς, &c.

The *Dolphin* rules the Scaly Flocks, endow'd
With Strength, and Swiftness; of his Beauty proud:
He, like a Lance discharg'd, through Billows flyes,
And dazling Flames darts from his glaring Eyes,
Finding out Fish, that frighted sculk in Holes,
Or Caves, and bed themselves in Sand like Moles.
  As Eagles monarch it 'mongst fearful Birds;
As Lions Tyrants act 'mongst subject Herds;
As much as cruel Serpents Worms excel:
So *Dolphins* Princes in the Ocean dwell.
No Fish dares them approach, nor be so bold
His Eyes, and dreadful Visage to behold.
Far from the Tyrant, fearing suddain Death,
Frighted they fly; fainting for want of Breath.
But when the *Dolphin*, hungry, hunts out Food,
The Silver Frie in Troops amazed scud,
Filling each way with fear: then Caves, and Holes,
Rocks, Bays, and Harbours fill with frighted Shoals.
From all parts driven he selects the best,
Choosing from Thousands out a plenteous Feast.

" *Of the nine lesser Figures; the first bears, on a Shield, the King of*
" *Bees flying alone; a Swarm following at some distance: the Word,*

REGE INCOLUMI MENS OMNIBUS UNA.

" *The*

"The Second, on his Shield, a Testudo advancing against a Wall; the "Word,

CONCORDIÆ CEDUNT.

"The Third, a Shield charged with Hearts; the Word,

HIC MURUS AHENEUS ESTO.

"The Fourth like a Spread-Eagle with two Heads, one of an Eagle, "the other of an Estrich; in the Mouth of the Estrich an Horse-shoe, in "the Talon of the Eagle a Thunderbolt; the Word,

PRÆSIDIA MAJESTATIS.

"The Fifth, a Bundle of Javelins; the Word,

UNITAS.

"The Sixth, two Hands joyned athwart the Escutcheon, as from the "Clouds, holding a Caduceus with a Crown; the Word,

FIDE ET CONSILIO.

"The Seventh, Arms laid down, Guns, Pikes, Ensigns, Swords; the "Word,

CONDUNTUR, NON CONTUNDUNTUR.

"The Eighth, a Caduceus, with a Winged Hat above, and Wings be- "neath, two Cornu-copiæs coming out at the middle, supported by a Gar- "land; the Word,

VIRTUTI FORTUNA COMES.

"The Ninth, a Bright Star striking a gleam through the midst of the "Escutcheon; the Word,

MONSTRANT REGIBUS ASTRA VIAM.

With these Figures is intermingled a Band of twenty four Violins.
The Bases, and Capitals within this *Triumph*, are as Brass, and the Pillars Steel.
The Triumph thus adorned, and the several Musick playing, all passed through, till such time as His Majesty came to the middle of the
Temple,

Temple, at which time the three principal living Figures, *viz.* CONCORD, LOVE, and TRUTH, who till then had not been seen, were, by the drawing of a Curtain, discovered, and entertained His Majesty with the following Song.

I.

Comes not here the King of Peace,
  Who, the Stars so long fore-told,
From all Woes should us release,
  Converting Iron-times to Gold?

II.

  Behold, behold!
Our Prince confirm'd by Heav'nly Signs,
      Brings healing Balm,
Brings healing Balm, and Anodynes,
To close our Wounds, and Pain asswage.

III.

He comes with conquering Bays, and Palm,
  Where swelling Billows us'd to rage,
Gliding on a silver Calm;
  Proud Interests now no more engage.

Chorus,

Let these arched Roofs resound,
  Joyning Instruments, and Voice,
Fright pale Spirits under Ground;
  But let Heav'n and Earth rejoyce,

We our Happiness have found.
He, thus marching to be Crown'd,
  Attended with this Glorious Train,
    From civil Broils
    Shall free these Isles,
Whilst He, and His Posterity shall reign.

I.

Who follow Trade, or study Arts,
Improving Pasture, or the Plow,
Or furrow Waves to Foreign Parts,
Use your whole Endeavours now.

II.

    His Brow, His Brow
Bids your Hearts, as well as Hands,
    Together joyn,
Together joyning bless these Lands;
Peace, and Concord, never poor,
Will make with Wealth these Streets to shine,
  Ships freight with Spice, and Golden Ore,
Your Fields with Honey, Milk, and Wine,
  To supply our Neighbours Store.

The first Song ended, CONCORD addressed her self to His Majesty, in these words,

Welcome, great Sir, to CONCORD'S *Fane;*
Which Your Return built up again;
You have her Fabrick rear'd so high,
That the proud Turrets kiss the Skie.
Tumult by You, and Civil War
In Janus *Gates imprison'd are.*

By

By You, the King of Truth, *and* Peace;
May all Divisions ever cease!
Your Sacred Brow the blushing Rose,
And Virgin Lily twin'd enclose!
The Caledonian *Thistle-Down*
Combine with these t'adorn Your Crown!
No Discord in th' Hibernian *Harp!*
Nought in our Duty flat, or sharp!
But all conspire, that You, as Best,
May 'bove all other Kings be Blest.

The Speech ended, His Majesty, at His going off, was entertained with the following Song,

With all our Wishes, Sir, go on,
    Our CHARLES, *three Nations Glory;*
That Worlds of Eyes may look upon,
    Behinde, Sir, and before Ye;
Go great Exemplar of our British *Story,*
    Paternal Crowns assume,
    That then Your Royal Name
    May, registred by Fame,
Smell like a sweet Perfume:
Not writ in Marble, Brass, or Gold,
    Nor sparkling Gems,
    Such as shine in Diadems,
But where all Nations may behold
    With brighter Characters enroll'd,
On th' Azure Vellum of configur'd Stars;
    Who fix'd, with gentle Smiles,
    Two fluctuating Isles,
And built well-grounded Peace on Civil Wars.

On the little Conduit, at the lower End of *Cheap-side*, were placed four Figures, or *Nymphs*, each of them having an Escutcheon in the one Hand, and a Pendent in the other.

In a Balcony, erected at the Entrance of *Pater-noster-*Row, were placed His Majestie's Drums, and Fife; the number of Persons, eight.

Between that and *Ludgate* there were two other Balconies erected: in one was placed a Band of six Waits; in the other, six Drums.

On the Top of *Ludgate* six Trumpets.

At *Fleet-*Bridge, a Band of six Waits.

On *Fleet-*Conduit were six Figures, or *Nymphs*, clad in White, each with an Escutcheon in one Hand, and a Pendent in the other; as also a Band of six Waits. And on the *Lanthorn* of the Conduit was the Figure of *Temperance*, mixing Water and Wine.

THE FOURTH ARCH.

IN *Fleet-street*, near *White-Friers*, stands the fourth Triumphal Arch, representing the *Garden* of PLENTY; it is of two Stories, one of the *Dorick* Order, the other of the *Ionick*. The Capitals have not their juſt Meaſure, but incline to the Modern *Architecture*.

" *Upon the great Shield over the Arch, in large Capitals, this Inſcri-*
" *ption,*

UBERITATI
AUG.
EXTINCTO BELLI CIVILIS INCENDIO,

CLUSOQVE JANI TEMPLO,

ARAM CELSISS.

CONSTRUXIT

S. P. Q. L.

To *Uberity*, or *Plenty*, there are frequent Dedications amongſt the

Reverses of the Coyns of the *Roman* Emperours; as of Augustus, and Galienus,

She is represented in a long Stole, or Mantle, the proper Habit of Women, holding in one Hand a *Patera*, or little Cup; in the other a *Cornucopia*. The latter is well known to be the Embleme of *Plenty*. Its original related by Ovid*: which, though unknown to few, the elegancy of the Relation will not give me leave to omit.

* Metam. l.b.ix. Fab. i.

> ——— *rigidum fera dextera cornu*
> *Dum tenet, infregit; truncáque à fronte revellit.*
> *Naiades hoc pomis, & odoro flore repletum*
> *Sacrârunt : divésque meo bona copia cornu est.*

> ——— my Brow he disadorns,
> By breaking one of my engaged Horns.
> The *Naiades* with Fruits, and Flow'rs this fill,
> Wherein abundant *Plenty* riots still.

The *Patera*, or little Cup, which she holdeth in the other Hand, is frequent in other Figures of Reverses; as

passing to His Coronation.

What is meant by EXTINCTO BELLI CIVILIS INCENDIO, *the extinction of the Flames of Civil War*, is fortunately known to us all, and may serve to explicate what follows, CLUSOQUE JANI TEMPLO, *the shutting of Janus's Temple*: a Rite instituted by NUMA, according to LIVY: *Numa Regno potitus Urbem novam, conditam vi & armis, Jure eam Legibúsque ac Moribus de integro condere parat: quibus cùm inter bella assuescere videret non posse (quippe efferatis militiâ animis) mitigandum ferocem populum armorum desuetudine ratus, Janum ad infimum Argiletum, indicem Pacis Bellíque fecit: APERTUS, ut in armis esse civitatem; CLAUSUS, pacatos circa omnes populos significaret.* NUMA, *being possess'd of the Kingdom, applyed himself to reform the new City, which was built by Force and Arms, and to build it anew by Rites, Laws, and Institutions: with which perceiving, that in the midst of War it was not possible to be effected, by reason that their minds were made rough and fierce by Arms; he conceiving that the fierce People might by their disaccustomance be made mild, he built a Temple to* Janus *at the bottom of* Argiletus, *the signifier of Peace, and War: which being* OPENED, *shewed that the City was in Arms*; SHUT, *that they were in peace with all Nations.* This VARRO* confirms, *The Janual Gate is so call'd from* Janus: *and therefore an Image of* Janus *is plac'd there, and a Rite instituted by* NUMA POMPILIUS (*as* LUCIUS PISO *in his Annals relates*) *that it should be always* SHUT *but in the time of War. We finde no where, that it was* OPENED *in the time of* POMPILIUS. PLUTARCH, in the Life of NUMA, *There is at* Rome *a Temple also of* JANUS, *with a two-leav'd Gate, which they call* Polemopyle, *the Gate of War. For it was decreed, that in the time of War that Temple should be* OPEN; *in Peace*, SHUT. But VIRGIL† *derives this Institution higher*,

* *De ling. Lat. lib.* iv.

† *Æneid.* vii.

> Mos erat Hesperio in Latio, quem protinus urbes
> Albanæ coluêre sacrum, nunc maxima rerum
> Roma colit, cùm prima movent in prælia Martem;
> Sive Getis inferre manu lachrymabile Bellum,
> Hyrcanísve Arabísve parant, seu tendere ad Indos
> Auroràmque sequi, Parthósque reposcere signa.
>   Sunt geminæ BELLI PORTÆ (sic nomine dicunt)
> Relligione sacræ, & sævi formidine Martis.

Centum ærei claudunt vectes, æternáque ferri
Robora, nec custos absistit limine Janus.
Has (ubi certa sedet Patribus sententia pugnæ)
Ipse, Quirinali *trabeâ, cinctúque* Gabino
Insignis, RESERAT *stridentia* LIMINA *Consul:*
Ipse vocat pugnas, sequitur tum cætera pubes,
Æreáque assensu conspirant cornua rauco.

There was an antient use in *Latium*,
Which *Alban* Towns held sacred, and now *Rome*,
Greatest in pow'r, observes; when they prepare
'Gainst *Arabs, Getes*, or fierce *Hyrcanians* War,
Or march to *India*, or the *Eastern* Main,
Or Ensign's from the *Parthians* to regain.
   Two Gates there be, are stil'd the PORTS OF WAR,
Sacred to *Mars* with reverential fear,
Shut with an hundred Iron, and Brazen Bands,
There in the Porch bifronted *Janus* stands.
Here, when the Senate have a War decreed,
The *Consul*, glorious in his Regal Weed,
And *Gabine* Robe, doth groaning Gates unbar,
In his own Person then proclaims the War.
The valiant Youth, attending, guard him round,
And doleful Trumpets *Diapasons* sound.

   This Temple was shut several times. First in the Reign of NUMA POMPILIUS, as PLUTARCH* testifies. Next, after the second PUNICK *War*, by T. MANLIUS *Consul*, says LIVY†. Thrice by AUGUSTUS: once after the Victory at *Actium*, about the time of the Nativity of our SAVIOUR; and then most justly, when there was an *UNIVERSAL PEACE* over the whole World.

* In *Vita Numæ*.
† *lib. i*.

Of which laſt there is a Monument extant at this day in *Spain*:

IMP. CÆS. DIVI F. AUGUSTUS PONT. MAX.
COS. XII. TRIBUNIC. POTEST. X. IMP. VIII.
ORBE MARI ET TERRA PACATO

TEMPLO JANI CLUSO

ET REP. P. R. OPTIMIS LEGIB. ET SANCTISS. INSTITUTIS REFORMATA
VIAM SUPERIORUM COSS. TEMPORE INCHOATAM
PRO DIGNITATE IMPERII LATIOREM LONGIOREMQUE
GADEIS USQUE PERDUXIT.

And at this time it may properly be ſaid to be ſhut at the fortunate arrival of our Sacred Sovereign into His Kingdoms, at what time there was a *GENERAL PEACE* throughout all *Chriſtendom*.

There is alſo a Coyn of AUGUSTUS, whoſe Reverſe is the Temple of JANUS ſhut; the *Inſcription*, JAN. CLU. not to mention that of NERO, PACE TERRA MARIQUE PARTA JANUM CLUSIT.

Goltz. Auguſt. pag. lviii.
Auguſtin. Dial. v.

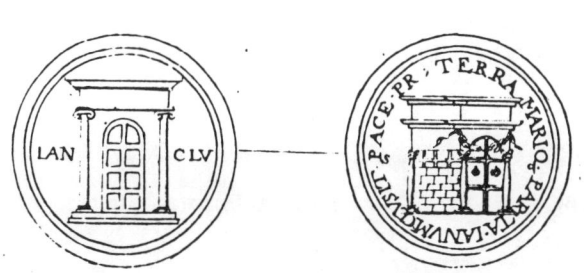

" *Over the* Poſtern, *on the* South-ſide *of the* Entrance *is* BACCHUS,
" *a* Youth *in a* Chariot *drawn by* Tigres; *the* Reins, Vine-Branches; *his*
" Mantle, *a* Panther's Skin; *his* Crown, *of* Grapes, *and* Ivy; *a* Thyrſus
" *in his left* Hand, *a* Cup *in his right*: *underneath,*

LIBER PATER.

" *The* Painting *over this repreſents* SILENUS *on his* Aſs, *Satyres*
" *dancing round about, in* Drunken *and* Antick *Poſtures: the* Proſpect, *a*
" Vine-yard.

The

The Statues of BACCHUS were of a very different form among the Antients. MACROBIUS*, *Liberi Patris simulacra partim puerili ætate, partim juvenili fingebantur; præterea barbata specie, senili quoque,* &c. *The Images of* BACCHUS *were partly like Boys, others like Youths, some with Beards, some like Old men.* ULPIAN†, *Chorus's of all Ages contended in the Feasts of* BACCHUS, *because they fram'd him of every Shape; for they paint him a Boy, an Old, and a Young man.* Of which MACROBIUS gives this Physical Reason, esteeming BACCHUS to be the same with the SUN; *Because the Sun in the Winter Solstice may seem a Boy, the days being then the shortest; but, by continual encreases in the Spring Æquinox, may seem a Youth; in the Summer Solstice, at his full age; afterwards in his diminution, an Old man.* In the form of an Old man we finde him worship'd by the *Græcians*, under the Name of *Bassareus*, and *Bryseus*; and at *Naples* under the Name of *Hebon*: MACROBIUS in the same place. Of *Hebon* there is still remaining this Monument,

* Saturnal. lib. 1. cap. xviii.

† Schol. in Midiam Demosth.

ΗΒΩΝΙ ΕΠΙΦΑΝΕΣΤΑΤΩΙ ΘΕΩΙ
ΙΟΥΝΙΟΣ ΑΚΥΛΑΣ ΝΕΩΤΕΡΟΣ
ΣΤΡΑΤΕΥΣΑΜΕΝΟΣ ΕΠΙΤΡΟΠΕΥΣΑΣ
ΔΗΜΑΡΧΗΣΑΣ.

So PAUSANIAS* tells us of a Bearded Statue of *Bacchus* holding a Golden Cup in his Hand. But most frequently he is represented in the form of a Boy, or Youth. TIBULLUS†,

* In Eliacis.

† Lib. iii.

Solis æterna est Phæbo Bacchoque juventus:
  Nam decet intonsus crinis utrumque Deum.

Phœbus, and *Bacchus* must be ever young :
For uncut Hair to either God belong.

OVID* of *Bacchus*,

* Metam. lib. iv. Fab. i.

——— *Tibi enim inconsumpta juventa,*
Tu puer æternus, tu formosissimus alto
Conspiceris cœlo.———

——— still do'st thou enjoy
Unwasted Youth, eternally a Boy.

The *Poëts* feign him riding in a Chariot drawn either by *Tigres*, *Leopards*, or *Lynces*. STATIUS[†],

[† Lib. iv.]

> *Liber pampineos materna ad mœnia currus*
> *Promovet, effrenæ dextrâ lævâque sequuntur*
> *Lynces, & uda mero lambunt retinacula* tigres.

   Thence to his Mother's City *Bacchus* rides,
   Rein'd *Lynxes* by his Viny Chariot sides,
   And *Tigres* lick'd the Harness moist with Wine.

HORACE,

[* Lib. iii. Od. iv.]

> *Hâc te merentem,* Bacche pater, *tuæ*
> *Vexêre* tigres, *indocili jugum*
>   *Collo trahentes.———*

   Blest *Bacchus* thee thy *Tigres* drew,
   Who Yoaks and Harness little knew.

OVID[†],

[† *Metam.* lib. iv. *Fab.*i.]

> ——— *tu bijugum pictis insignia frænis*
> *Colla premis* lyncum. ———

   ——————— thou hold'st in aw
   The spotted *Lynxes*, which thy Chariot draw.

These not onely drew his Chariot, but were his constant Companions; as we finde in the Ship of *Bacchus*, (taken from the Mariners, whom he had turn'd into *Dolphins*) described by OVID[*],

[* *Metam.* lib. iii.]

> *Quem circa* tigres, *simulacráque inania* lyncum,
> *Pictarúmque jacent fera corpora* pantherarum.

   Stern *Tigres*, *Lynxes* (such unto the eye)
   And spotted *Panthers* round about him lie.

His Ship is lively set forth by *Philostratus*[†]; which, or the like, is still to be seen in the Church of St. *Agnes* at *Rome*, formerly a Temple of *Bacchus*'s, in most exquisite *Mosaick* Work.

He was constantly crown'd either with Grapes, Ivy, or both. Ovid[*],

[† In *Imag.*]
[* *Metam.* lib. iii.]

> *Ipse racemiferis frontem circumdatus uvis*
> *Pampineis agitat velatam frondibus hastam.*

He, head-bound with a Wreath of clustred Vines,
A Jav'lin shook, clasp'd with their leavy twines.

> *Non crines, non serta loco, dextrámque reliquit*
> Thyrsus, *& intactæ ceciderunt cornibus uvæ.*

His Hair disorder'd now no Wreath adorns,
His *Thyrsus* fell, plump Grapes drop from his Horns.

Horace[†],

[† Lib. ii. Od. xix.]

> ——— *Deum*
> *Cingentem viridi tempora pampino.*

——— a virdant Vine
The God about his temples did entwine.

Tibullus,

> *Candide* Liber *ades, sic sit tibi mystica vitis,*
> *Sic hederâ semper tempora vincta feras.*

Bacchus assist, so may the sacred Vine,
So may fresh Ivy still thy Brows entwine.

So in *Achaia*, at the Feasts of *Bacchus*[*], the Children having wash'd themselves in the *River* Meilichus, they put on Crowns of Ivy, and so go to the Temple of Bacchus Æsymnetes.

[* *Pausanias* in *Achaicis*.]

Hence

passing to His CORONATION.

Hence *M. Antony**, having assumed the Title of Νέος Διόνυσος, *New Bacchus*, caused the Coyns, stamp'd with his Image, to bear a Crown of Ivy.

**Dio lib. xlviii.*

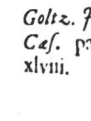
Goltz. Jul. Cæs. pag. xlviii.

And the Antients used this, as an Argument, to prove that *Bacchus* of the *Grecians*, and *Romans*, was the same with *Osiris* of the *Ægyptians*, because Ivy, which was sacred to *Bacchus*, was in *Ægypt* called Χενόσιρις, that is, *The Plant of* Osiris.

Why *Bacchus*, and those that drank, did wear a Crown of Ivy, *Athenæus* gives this Reason amongst the rest, because *there is great plenty of it, and it grows of it self, and is every where to be had, being not undelightful for sight, shading the Fore-head with its green Leaves, and Berries, and of a body fit for binding, besides that, cooling without any Carotique smell offensive to the Head.* The Wine-Bowls also were ordinarily adorn'd in the same manner. VIRGIL,

————— *pocula ponam*
Fagina, cœlatum divini opus Alcimedontis:
Lenta quibus torno facili superaddita vitis
Diffusos hederâ vestit pallente corymbos.

————— two Beechen Cups I'll stake,
Which the divine *Alcimedon* did make:
Whereon with a smooth turn soft Vines he shapes,
And with pale Ivy cloaths the spreading Grapes.

ANACREON,

Ποτήριον δὲ καλὸν,
Ὅσον δύω, βάθυνον, &c.

Ποίησον ἀμπέλους μοι,
Καὶ βότρυας κατ' αὐτό.

Vulcan come, thy Hammer take,
And of burnish'd Silver make
(Not a glitt'ring Armour, for
What have we to do with War?
But) a large deep Bowl, and on it
I would have thee carve no Planet,
Pleiades, Wains, nor Waggoners;
But to life exactly shape
Clusters of the Juicy Grape;
Whilst brisk *Love* their bleeding Heads
Hand in hand with *Bacchus* treads.

We finde him cloathed with the Skin of a *Tigre* (though that not the onely one Garment he used) in CLAUDIAN*:

* *De raptu Proserp. lib. i.*

—— *Lenisque simul procedit* Iacchus,
Crinali florens hederâ, quem Parthica *velat*
Tigris, & auratos in nodum colligit ungues.

—— So *Bacchus* march'd with Ivie crown'd,
Clad in a *Parthian* Tigre's spotted Hide,
And Golden Claws in neat composure ty'd.

A *Thyrsus* is a Spear adorn'd with Ivy at the upper end, which *Bacchus*, and his Attendants, made use of to sustain them in their drink. *Claudian*†, of *Bacchus*,

† *De raptu Proserp. lib. i.*

Ebria Mæoniis *fulcit vestigia Thyrsis.*

His *Lydian* Thyrse supports his reeling Limbs.

Pausanias*, *The Statue (of* Jupiter*) is like unto* Bacchus; *for it hath Buskins instead of Shoes, and it holds in one hand a Cup, in the other a Thyrsus.* This *Thyrsus*, with a *Cornu-copiæ*, is the *Hieroglyphick* of Mirth

* *In Arcadicis.*

in

in a Coyn of *Fauſtina's*; the Inſcription *HILARITAS.* In one hand ſhe holds a *Cornu-copiæ*, in the other a *Thyrſus*, on a Spear, covered from one end to the other with Leaves, and Coronets.

Silenus, and the *Satyres*, were the conſtant deboiſt Companions of *Bacchus*. Of whom *Pauſanias* * relates a Story told him by *Euphemus* a *Carian*, that, in a Voyage to *Italy*, by croſs Winds, their Ship was forced beyond the *Streights* into the *Atlantick* Ocean, and was driven by the Tempeſt upon the Iſlands, called, by the Mariners, *The Iſlands of Satyres.* Whoſe Inhabitants were of a yellowiſh colour, and had Tails not inferiour to thoſe of Horſes. Who, as ſoon as they ſaw the Ship arrived, preſently entered, and laid hold of the Women: ſo that the Mariners were forc'd, out of fear, to land them a Woman, whom the *Satyres* uſed not onely according to Nature, but abus'd all parts of her body: Nor were the young *Satyres* more devoted to *Venus*, then old *Silenus* to his Patron *Bacchus.* VIRGIL†,

* In *Aticis*.

† *Ecleg.* vi.

> ———— Chromis & Mnaſylus *in antro*
> Silenum *pueri ſomno vidêre jacentem,*
> Inflatum heſterno venas, ùt ſemper *,* Iaccho *;*
> Serta procul tantùm capiti delapſa jacebant,
> Et gravis attritâ pendebat cantharus ansâ.

> Say Muſe, how *Chromis* and *Mnaſylus* found
> In's Cave *Silenus* ſleeping on the ground,
> O'th' laſt nights *Bacchus* ſwell'd (his uſual guiſe)
> Far from his Head his fal'n off Garland lies.

So OVID*,

* *Metam.* lib. iv. fab. 1.

> ———— Bacchæ, Satyríque ſequuntur,
> Quique ſenex ferulâ titubantes ebrius artus
> Suſtinet, & pando non fortiter hæret aſello.

> Light *Bacchides*, and skipping *Satyres* follow,
> Whilſt old *Silenus*, reeling ſtill, doth hallow,
> Who weakly hangs upon his tardy Aſs.

Whence

_{*Pausanias.} Whence the *Eleans* *, in their Temple of *Silenus*, make *Drunkenness* delivering a Cup of Wine to him.

He was conceiv'd to be the Fosterer, and Educator of *Bacchus*; from _{† Eclog. iii.} whence AURELIUS NEMESIANUS† describes him with *Bacchus* in his Arms,

> *Cui Deus arridens horrendas pectore setas*
> *Vellicat, aut digitis aures adstringit acutas,*
> *Applauditve manu mutilum caput, aut breve mentum,*
> *Et simas tenero collidit pollice nares.*

> Smiling on him the God his bristly Hairs
> Plucks from his Breast, or nips his pricked Ears,
> His low Brow claps, and short'ned Chin, and grows
> Familiar, tweaking of his Saddle Nose.

_{* Antiq. Rom.} And thus we finde *Silenus* in an antient Statue at *Rome* *. The *Satyres* were painted with Goats Horns, and Feet, to signifie the insatiableness _{† Mythol. lib. iii.} of their Lust. FULGENTIUS† ; Satyri *cum caprinis cornibus depinguntur, quia nunquam novêre saturari libidine*; The Satyres are painted with _{* Carm. lib. ii. Od. xix.} Goats Horns, *because their Lust is unsatiable.* HORACE*,

> ————— aures
> *Capripedum* Satyrorum *acutas.*

The Goat-foot *Satyres* pricked Ears.

" On the North-*side opposite*, CERES, *drawn in a Chariot by winged*
" *Dragons, and crown'd with Ears of Corn : in her left Hand, Poppy* ; *in*
" *her right, a blazing Torch. The Painting over her is a Description of*
" *Harvest* ; *with*

CERES AUG.

That the Chariot of CERES was feigned to be drawn by *Dra*- _{† De raptu Proserp. lib. i.} *gons*, appears from several places in the *Poëts*. CLAUDIAN†,

> ——————*sinuosa* Draconum
> *Membra regens, volucri qui pervia nubila tractu*

Signant,

Signant, & placidis humectant fræna venenis.
Frontem crista tegit, pingunt maculosa virentes
Terga notæ, rutilum squamis intermicat aurum.

———— she sinewy *Dragons* guides,
Who at high speed cut yielding Clouds in twain,
Their Snaffles frothing with delightful bane,
Crested their Fronts, Backs mark'd with freckling green,
Their Scales, when brissell'd up, Gold shines between.

And immediatly after,

————*fulvis* SERPENTIBUS *attigit* Iden.

With yellow SERPENTS drawn she *Ida* reach'd.

OVID*, * *Fast.* lib. iv.

Dixit, & egrediens nubem trahit, inque DRACONES
Transit, & alifero tollitur axe Ceres.

Then going forth, a Cloud she draws, through Skies,
With *Dragons* drawn, her swift-wheel'd Chariot flies.

And a little before, of the same Goddess,

Quò simul ac venit frænatos curribus ANGUES
Junxit, & æquoreas sicca pererrat aquas.

Her harness'd Serpents in her Chariot puts,
And dry her way through swelling Billows cuts.

Where we see promiscuously used *angues*, and *dracones*. So the Rod of *Mercury*, which is perpetually represented with Serpents about it, by *Martial* is encompass'd by a *Dragon*:

Cyllenes *cælique decus, facunde minister,*
Aurea cui torto virga DRACONE *nitet.*

Heaven and *Cyllenes* Joy; Speaker divine,
A Golden Dragon on thy Wand doth shine.

And CLAUDIAN * speaking of the Golden Fleece kept by a Dragon,

* De Bello Get.co.

—— *insopitisque refusum*
Tractibus aurati custodem velleris ANGUEM.

The watchful *Dragon* kept the Golden Fleece.

The memory of *Ceres* her Chariot drawn by *Serpents* is preserv'd likewise in several old Marbles, and this *Medaigle*,

The reason why *Poppy* should be attributed to *Ceres*, and from thence be call'd by VIRGIL ¹ *Cereale papaver*, is variously rendered by SERVIUS: *Vel quod est esui sicut frumentum: vel quo Ceres usa est ad oblivionem doloris; nam, ob raptum Proserpinæ vigiliis fracta, gustato eo acta est in soporem: vel quia pani adspergatur.* Either because it is fit to eat, as Corn: or because Ceres used it to procure a forgetfulness of her grief; for, being wearied with continual watchings in pursuit of her Daughter Proserpina stoln from her, upon tasting of it, she fell asleep: or else because 'tis sprinkled upon Bread. But the *Mythologists*, who esteem *Ceres* to be the same with the *Earth*, make it onely a Symbol of the Fecundity of it; or, from its orbicular Figure, to signifie the rotundity of the Earth; from its inequality, the Vallies, and Mountains; from the multiplicity of its Grains, the vast multitude of Men, and Animals. For which reason the fertile Countrey of *Sicily* was sacred to her, which she contended for with *Vulcan*; and, in token of the Victory, the *Sicilians* dedicated her Statue with a little Image of Victory on her Hand. Which Statue
CICERO

Cicero[†] makes mention of. These *Poppies* are mention'd by several of the *Poëts*; as by

[† *Contra Verrem.*]

CALLIMACHUS,

———————— γέντο δὲ χερὶ
Στέμματα, ᾗ μάκωνας. ————

Poppies she took, and Garlands in her Hand.

THEOCRITUS,

———————— ἁ δὲ γελάσαι
Δράγματα, ᾗ μάκωνας ἐν ἀμφοτέρῃσιν ἔχοισα·

In either Hand she Corn, and Poppies had.

Porphyry, quoted by *Eusebius* [*], says, that *Ceres* was crown'd with Ears of Corn, about which were several Branches of *Poppy*, which were the Symbols of *Fertility*.

[* *De Præpar. lib. iii.*]

She was accounted by the Antients the Goddess, that first delivered to Mankind the Art of Tillage, whence they usually crown'd her with Ears of Corn. TIBULLUS,

Flava Ceres, *tibi sit nostro de rure corona*
   Spicea————

O yellow *Ceres*, round thy Golden Locks,
Place Garlands taken from our Countrey Shocks.

OVID,

Flava Ceres, *tenues spicis redimita capillos,*

Ceres, whose slender Hairs Corn-ears do bind.

Or put them in her Hand. So in the Reverse of a Coyn of *Julia Pia*, there

there is one leaning with her left Hand on a Spear, holding in her right Hand an Ear of Wheat, with this Inscription, *CEREREM*.

She is frequently described with a Torch in her Hand, from that known Story of her searching after her Daughter, stoln, and carried away by *Pluto* out of *Sicily*. Of which CLAUDIAN*,

* De raptu Proserp.

> *Accingor lustrare diem, per devia rerum*
> *Indefessa ferar: nullà cessabitur horâ.*
> *Non requies, non somnus erit, dum pignus ademptum*
> *Inveniam, gremio quamvis mergatur* Iberæ
> Tethyos, *& rubro jaceat vallata profundo.*
> *Non* Rheni *glacies, non me* Ripæa *tenebunt*
> *Frigora: non dubio Syrtis cunctabitur æstu,* &c.
> *Sic fatur, notæque jugis illabitur* Ætnæ,
> *Noctivago tedas inflammatura labori.*

> I'll search the day, no hour shall stop me hurl'd
> Unwearied through all Cranies of the World;
> No rest, no sleep, till my dear Pledge be found,
> Though she lie hidden in th' *Iberian* Sound,
> Or the Red-Sea. *Riphæan* Frosts, nor *Rhyne*,
> Crusted with Ice, shall hinder my Design:
> Nor yet the doubtful *Syrts* with wallowing Tides.
> This said, to *Ætna's* Top she makes a flight,
> Kindling her Torch for bus'ness of the Night.

So Pausanias* mentions a Statue of *Ceres,* holding in her right Hand a Torch, with her left Hand laid upon a Statue adjoyning, called *Despoina.* Statius†,

<small>* In *Arcadicis.*
† *Thebaid.* lib. xii.</small>

> *Qualis, ab Ætnæis accensâ lampade saxis,*
> *Orba Ceres magnæ variabat imagine flammæ*
> *Ausonium Siculûmque latus, vestigia nigri*
> *Raptoris, vastósque legens in pulvere sulcos.*

> Rob'd *Ceres* so at an *Ætnean* Stone
> Kindled her Torch, which blazing she drives on,
> Reprinting *Pluto*'s steps on either Coast,
> Plowing up dusty Clouds in Furrows vast.

Ovid*,

<small>* *Fastor.* lib. iv.</small>

> *Illic accendit geminas pro lampade pinus:*
>   *Hinc Cereris sacris nunc quoque teda datur.*

> There for a Torch two Pines the Goddess lights:
> Since, they with Tapers celebrate her Rites.

From whence she was call'd *Dea tedifera*:
  Et per tediferæ *mystica sacra* Deæ.

The like we meet with in the Collection of Gruter.

CERERI AUGUST.
MATRI. AGR.
L. BENNIUS. PRIMUS
MAG. PAGI.
BENNIA. PRIMIGENIA
MAGISTRA FECER.
GERMANICO. CÆSARE. II.
L. SEIO. TUBERONE. COSS.
DIES. SACRIFICI. XIII. K. MAI.

"On the West-side of the Arch, over the South Postern, the Goddess
"FLORA, in a various-coloured Habit; in one Hand, Red and White
"Roses; in the other, Lilies: on her head, a Garland of several Flowers.
"The Painting over this, a Garden with Walks, Statues, Fountains,
"Flowers, and Figures of Men and Women walking.

The Story of this Goddess FLORA is variously related: we shall onely take notice of the account *Lactantius* * gives of her. FLORA, having gain'd a great Estate by prostituting her Body, at her Death left the People of Rome her Heir, and allotted such a certain Sum of Money; the Yearly use of which should be expended in the Celebration of her Birth-Day with several Sports call'd FLORALIA. Which seeming a flagitious thing to the Senate, they took occasion, from the very name of the Sports FLORALIA, to add some Dignity to so shameful a business, to feign a Goddess FLORA, who had the care of Flowers, whom they shou'd Yearly appease for the greater plenty of their Corn, Vines, &c. Her various-colour'd Habit, with the reason of it, is mention'd by OVID †,

* Lib.ii. cap. xx.

† Fast. lib. v.

> *Cur tamen, ùt dantur vestes* Cerealibus *albæ,*
> *Sic est hæc cultu versicolore decens?*
> *An quia maturis albescit messis aristis?*
> *Et color, & species floribus omnis inest?*
> *Annuit.———*

> In white at *Ceres* Feasts why are they drest,
> While *Flora* wears a party-colour'd Vest?
> Is it because Corn looks in Harvest white,
> Whilst Flowers in various Colours take delight?

She was crown'd with Flowers, as we finde in these following Verses,

> *Annuit: & motis flores cecidêre capillis,*
> *Decidere in mensas ùt rosa missa solet.*

passing to His CORONATION.

She nods: and Flowers fell from her Head,
  Like Roses on a Table shed.

Answerable to the Life of the Authour were the Sports on her Festival; lascivious, and celebrated by lascivious Persons. OVID *,

Ibid.

Quærere conabar quare lascivia major
  His foret in ludis, liberiórque jocus, &c.
Turba quidem cur hos celebret meretricia ludos.

I did enquire why a more wanton way
These Sports are granted, and a freer Play:
Why Prostitutes should at these Rites attend.

Which *Cato* had no sooner entered, but his Gravity forc'd him to retire. MARTIAL,

Nôsses jocosæ dulce cùm sacrum Floræ,
Festósque lusus, & licentiam vulgi,
Cur in Theatrum Cato severe venisti?
An ideò tantùm veneras, ut exires?

Thou knew'st, that *Flora's* joyful Rites
Free Licence had, and all Delights;
Why cam'st thou *Cato* to the Play?
Cam'st onely thou to go away?

Which Story is more copiously related by *Valerius Maximus. Onuphrius Panvinius* mentions a Coyn, in which we have the first, that caused these Sports to be celebrated. *C. MEMMIUS FLORALIA PRIMUS FECIT.* She had her *Flamen*, mention'd by *Varro*†.

† *De ling. Lat.*

"Opposite to this, on the North-side, the Goddess POMONA
"crown'd with a Garland of several Fruits; in her right Hand, a Pru-
"ning Hook; in her left Hand, the Sun: at her Feet, all sorts of Grassing,
"and Gardening-Tools.

OVID,

OVID * thus describes her at large,

Metam. lib. xv. Fab. 16.

> *Rege sub hoc Pomona fuit: quâ nulla Latinas*
> *Inter Hamadryadas coluit solertiùs hortos:*
> *Nec fuit arborei studiosior altera fœtûs;*
> *Unde tenet nomen. Non sylvas illa, nec amnes,*
> *Rus amat, & ramos felicia poma ferentes.*
> *Nec jaculo gravis est, sed aduncâ dextera falce:*
> *Quâ modò luxuriem premit, & spatiantia passim*
> *Brachia compescit: fisso modò cortice, lignum*
> *Inserit, & succos alieno præstat alumno.*
> *Nec sentire sitim patitur, bibulæque recurvas*
> *Radicis fibras labentibus irrigat undis.*

POMONA flourish'd in those times of ease:
Of all the *Latian Hamadryades*,
None fruitful Hort-yards held in more repute,
Or took more care to propagate their Fruit;
Thereof so nam'd. Nor Streams, nor shady Groves,
But Trees producing gen'rous Burdens loves.
Her Hand a Hook, and not an Jav'lin bare:
Now prunes luxurious Twigs, and Boughs, that dare
Transcend their Bounds: now slits the Bark, the Bud
Inserts, enforc'd to nurse anothers Brood.
Nor suffers them to suffer Thirst, but brings
To moisture-sucking Roots soft sliding Springs.

She had her *Flamen* too, though the last of the fifteen. SEXTUS POMPEIUS, *Maximæ dignationis* Flamen *Dialis est inter* XV. Flamines: *&, quum cæteri discrimina Majestatis suæ habeant, minimi habetur* Pomonalis; *quòd* Pomona *levissimo fructui agrorum præsidet*. The Flamen *of* Jupiter *is of the greatest Dignity amongst the fifteen* Flamens. *There is a distinction betwixt all of them, but the meanest is the* Flamen *of* Pomona, *because she presides over the meanest Fruit of the Grounds.*

"BOREAS,

passing to His Coronation.

"BOREAS, *instead of Feet, two Serpents Tails, his Wings covered
"with Snow: his Emblem, a rockie Mountainous Country, and the Pleiades
"rising over it; his Motto,*

———SCYTHIAM SEPTEMQUE TRIONES
HORRIFER INVADIT———

That the Antients described BOREAS with Serpents Tails, instead of Feet, appears out of PAUSANIAS*, Ἐς ἀριϛερὰ πεϱιόντι Βορέας ἐςὶν ἡρπακὼς Ὠρείθυιαν. Οὐραὶ δὲ ὀφέων ἀντὶ ποδῶν εἰσιν αὐτῷ. *If you compass it on the left Hand, there is* Boreas *forcibly taking away* Orithyia: *He hath Serpents Tails instead of Feet.*

* In *Eliacis*.

Thus OVID describes him stealing away *Orithyia*,

Hæc Boreas, *aut his non inferiora loquutus,*
Excussit pennas: quarum jactatibus omnis
Afflata est tellus, latúmque perhorruit æquor.
Pulvereámque trahens per summa cacumina pallam,
Verrit humum, pavidámque metu caligine tectus
Orithyiam *adamans fulvis complectitur alis.*

Thus *Boreas* chafes, or no less storming, shook
His horrid Wings; whose aiery motion strook
The Earth with Blasts, and made the Ocean roar,
Trailing his dusty Mantle on the Floor.
He hid himself in Clouds of Dust, and caught
Belov'd *Orithyia*, with her fear distraught.

VIRGIL[†],

† *Georg*. iii.

Qualis Hyperboreis *Aquilo cùm densus ab oris*
Incubuit, Scythiæque *hyemes, atque aridà differt*
Nubila.———

As when from *Hyperborean* Mountains fierce
Boreas doth Clouds, and *Scythian* Storms disperse.

CLAUDIAN,

Fire with their Blood; others ran over to the Romans, *who alone had the Water could save them; and those* Antoninus *sav'd.* The same Authour, who liv'd in the time of *Commodus*, Son to *Antoninus*, mentions, from a Report in his time, the Magick of *Arnuphis*, as a cause of it, as it is deliver'd by *Xiphiline*, Patriarch of *Constantinople*: *'Tis reported, that Arnuphis, an Ægyptian Magician, then in company of the Emperour Marcus Antoninus, had invoked with his Magick Art, among other Gods, the aerial* Mercury, *by whose assistance he obtain'd the Showr.* And thus the Story is told by SUIDAS *. Others mention *Julian* the Magician. The *Christians* had a fair Plea for what they pretended, an acknowledgment from the Emperour himself, by Letter to the Senate, had not that Letter, still remaining, upon examination prov'd counterfeit. The Picture, being rare, we have caused here to be publish'd.

* *In Ἀρνϕις.*

Baronius mistook it for *Jupiter Pluvius*, who is never represented with Wings. This Winde is excellently describ'd by OVID †,

† *Metam. lib. 1.*

——— *madidis* Notus *evolat alis,*
Terribilem piceâ tectus caligine vultum;

Barba

"Boreas, *instead of Feet, two Serpents Tails, his Wings covered
"*with Snow: his Emblem, a rockie Mountainous Country, and the* Pleiades
"*rising over it; his Motto,*

——SCYTHIAM SEMPTEMQUE TRIONES
HORRIFER INVADIT——

That the Antients described Boreas with Serpents Tails, instead of Feet, appears out of Pausanias[*], Ἐς ἀριςεράς περιιόν̕ι Βορέας ἐσ̓ιν ἡρπακὼς Ὠρείθυιαν. Οὐραὶ δὲ ὄφεων ἀν̓ὶ ποδῶν εἰσιν αὐτῷ. *If you compass it on the left Hand, there is* Boreas *forcibly taking away* Orithyia: *He hath Serpents Tails instead of Feet.*

[* In *Eliacis.*]

Thus Ovid describes him stealing away *Orithyia,*

Hæc Boreas, *aut his non inferiora loquutus,*
Excussit pennas : quarum jactatibus omnis
Afflata est tellus, latumque perhorruit æquor.
Pulveredmque trahens per summa cacumina pallam,
Verrit humum, pavidámque metu caligine tectus
Orithyiam *adamans fulvis complectitur alis.*

Thus *Boreas* chafes, or no less storming, shook
His horrid Wings; whose aiery motion strook
The Earth with Blasts, and made the Ocean roar,
Trailing his dusty Mantle on the Floor.
He hid himself in Clouds of Dust, and caught
Belov'd *Orithyia,* with her fear distraught.

Virgil[†],

[† *Georg.*iii.]

Qualis Hyperboreis *Aquilo cùm densus ab oris*
Incubuit, Scythiæque *hyemes, atque aridâ differt*
Nubila.——

As when from *Hyperborean* Mountains fierce
Boreas doth Clouds, and *Scythian* Storms disperse.

Claudian,

CLAUDIAN*,

> *— cum turbine rauco*
> *Cùm gravis armatur Boreas, glaciéque nivali*
> *Hispidus, & Geticà concretus grandine pennas,*
> *Bella cupit, pelagus, sylvas, campósque sonoro*
> *Flamine rapturus.—*

> As with a Whirl-Winde when rough *Boreas* arms
> Wings stiff with Ice, and Snow, and *Gothick* Storms,
> Desiring War, the Woods, and Deeps profound,
> And Plains breaks thorough with a dreadful sound.

Auster, in a dark-coloured Habit, with Wings like Clouds; his Embleme, a Cloudy Sky, and Showers: his Motto,

NUBIBUS ASSIDUIS PLUVIAQVE MADESCIT.

The Authours of Natural History do attribute a Thunder-Bolt to the *South*-Winde alone. From whence *Virgil*, describing *Vulcan's* Shop,

> *His informatum manibus, jam parte politâ*
> *Fulmen erat, toto Genitor quæ plurima cœlo*
> *Dejicit in terras: pars imperfecta manebat.*
> *Tres imbris torti radios, tres nubis aquosæ*
> *Addiderant, rutili tres ignis, & alitis* Austri.

> A Thunder-Bolt half finish'd now in hand,
> (Many of these by angry *Jove* are thrown
> From Heav'n to Earth) the rest as yet not done.
> Three parts of Hail, three of a Wat'ry Cloud,
> As much of Fire, and three of Winde allow'd.

Upon which place SERVIUS. *Nonnulli manubias Fulminis his Numinibus,* Jovi, Junoni, Marti, *& Austro vento asserunt attribui, quod ex hoc Maronis loco ostendunt.* Of this Winde we have the Picture

---

* De raptu Proserp. l.b. 1.

cture in *Antoninus*'s Pillar at *Rome*, remarkable for the History, in which is represented the Rain, that fell in the Tents of the *Romans*, ready to perish for Drouth, and the Thunder, and Lightning, which at the same time destroyed the Enemy: obtain'd by the Prayers of a *Christian Legion*, as the *Fathers* of those times relate it; by others attributed either to the Piety of the Emperour, or the Magick of *Arnuphis*: of which CLAUDIAN;

> *Laus ibi nulla Ducum; nam flammeus imber in hostem*
> *Decidit: hunc dorso trepidum flammante ferebat*
> *Ambustus sonipes; hic tabescente solutus*
> *Subsedit galeâ, liquefactáque pulvere cuspis*
> *Canduit, & subitis fluxère liquoribus enses.*
> *Tunc contenta polo, mortalis nescia teli,*
> *Pugna fuit.* *Chaldæa mago seu carmina ritu*
> *Armavêre Deos; seu, quod reor, omne Tonantis*
> *Obsequium Marci mores potuêre mereri.*

> The Chiefs no Fame got there; the Enemie's force
> A fiery Show'r dispers'd: a burning Horse
> Bore this on's flaming Back; this over-turn'd,
> His Cask did melt, in Dust his Jav'lin burn'd,
> And melting Swords in smoaking Rivers glide.
> Heaven's Arcenal did for this Fight provide
> Weapons destroying more then Mortal Arms.
> Either the Gods were arm'd by Magick Charms,
> Or *Jove* so much to *Marcus* merits ow'd,
> That all this kindness he on him bestow'd.

It is thus described by DIO, *You might see at the same time Rain and Fire fall from Heaven: some were wet, and drank; others were burnt, and died. The Fire touch'd not the* Romans; *if it fell among them, it was immediatly quench'd. The Rain did their Adversaries no good, but rather like Oil increased the flame. They sought for Water, while the Rain fell on them. Some of them wounded themselves, as if they meant to quench the*

Fire with their Blood; others ran over to the Romans, *who alone had the Water could save them; and those* Antoninus *sav'd.* The same Authour, who liv'd in the time of *Commodus,* Son to *Antoninus,* mentions, from a Report in his time, the Magick of *Arnuphis,* as a cause of it, as it is delivered by *Xiphiline,* Patriarch of *Constantinople:* '*Tis reported, that* Arnuphis, *an Ægyptian Magician,* then in company of the Emperour Marcus Antoninus, *had invoked with his Magick Art, among other Gods, the aerial* Mercury, *by whose assistance he obtain'd the Showr.* And thus the Story is told by SUIDAS *. Others mention *Julian* the Magician. The *Christians* had a fair Plea for what they pretended, an acknowledgment from the Emperour himself, by Letter to the Senate, had not that Letter, still remaining, upon examination prov'd counterfeit. The Picture, being rare, we have caused here to be publish'd.

* In Ἀρνέφις.

Baronius mistook it for *Jupiter Pluvius,* who is never represented with Wings. This Winde is excellently describ'd by OVID †,

† *Metam. lib.* 1.

—————— *madidis* Notus *evolat alis,*
Terribilem piceâ tectus caligine vultum;

Barba

Barba gravis nimbis, canis fluit unda capillis,
Fronte sedent nebulæ, rorant pennæque sinusque.

With moist Wings *Notus* flies in sable Bags
His sowre Face hid, his Beard with Tempest sags,
His Hair sheds Crystal Drops, dark Clouds encamp
Upon his Brows, his Wings and Bosom damp.

His Thunder-Bolt is mention'd too by *Lucretius*;

Altitonans Volturnus, *&* Auster *ulmine pollens.*

"ZEPHYRUS, *like an* Adonis *with Wings*; *the Emblem, a Flow-*
"*ery Plain*; *the Word,*

—— TEPENTIBUS AURIS
DEMULCET——

So CLAUDIAN describes*, *De raptu Proserp. lib. ii.*

—— *Pater ô gratissime Veris,*
Qui mea lascivo regnas per prata volatu
Semper, & assiduis irroras flatibus annum, &c.
—— *ille novo madidantes nectare pennas*
Concutit, & glebas fœcundo rore maritat,
Quáque volat, vernus sequitur color: omnis in herbas
Turget humus, medióque patent convexa sereno.
Sanguineo splendore rosas, vaccinia nigro
Induit, & dulci violas ferrugine pingit.

Bless'd Father of the Spring, all Hail,
Who rul'st my Meadows with a wanton Gale,
And dew'st the Season with a constant breeze,*&c.*
From his moist Wings he richest *Nectar* sheds,
And the hard Glebe with pregnant Moisture weds:
Colour the Spring attends, and every where
Earth swells with Herbage, Heav'n's high Fore-head clear.

Roses in Red, Berries in Black he dies,
And gives the Violets Purple Liveries.

LUCRETIUS calls it *the Messenger of* Venus:

*Et ver, & *Venus, *& *Veneris prænuntius antè
Pennatus graditur* Zephyrus *vestigia propter.*

The Spring, and *Venus,* warming *Zephyre* brings
Love's gentle Herbinger on painted Wings.

PHILOSTRATUS† represents it thus, *A Youth smooth-fac'd, with Wings on his Shoulders, and on his Head a Garland of several Flowers.*

† *Imag.*

The Seat of this Winde was feigned by the Antients to be in *Spain.* SENECA*,

* In *Hercule Oetæo.*

—— *quæ* Zephyro
*Subdita tellus, stupet aurato
Flumine clarum radiare* Tagum.

The Lands, where *Zephyre* dwells, behold
With wonder *Tagus* shine in Gold.

CLAUDIAN†,

† In laudibus *Serenæ.*

Deseritur jam ripa Tagi, Zephyríque *relictis
Sedibus, Auroræ famulas properatur ad urbes.*

He *Tagus* banks, and *Zephyr's* Court forsakes,
And haste to Conquer'd *Eastern* Cities makes.

Not so much from the Vernal temperature of the place, as that it was esteem'd the remotest place from whence *Italy* received these *Western* Gales.

" The great Figure on the top of all represents PLENTY, crowned, a
" Branch of Palm in her right Hand, a Cornu-copiæ in her left.

The

passing to His CORONATION.

The Musick aloft on both sides, and on the two Balconies within, were twelve Waits, six Trumpets, and three Drums.

At a convenient distance before this Structure, were two Stages erected, divided, planted, and adorned like Gardens, each of them eight Yards in length, five in breadth. Upon that on the *North*-side sate a Woman representing PLENTY, crowned with a Garland of divers Flowers, clad in a Green Vestment embroidered with Gold, holding a *Cornu-copiæ*: her Attendants, two Virgins.

At His Majestie's approach to the *Arch*, this Person representing PLENTY rose up, and made Address to him in these Words;

> *Great Sir, the Star, which at Your Happy Birth*
> *Joy'd with his Beams (at *N*oon) the wond'ring Earth,*
> *Did with auspicious lustre, then, presage*
> *The glitt'ring Plenty of this Golden Age;*
> *The Clouds blown o're, which long our joys o'recast,*
> *And the sad Winter of Your absence past,*
> *See! the three smiling Seasons of the Year*
> *Agree at once to bid You Welcome here;*
> *Her Homage Dutious* Flora *comes to pay;*
> *With Her Enamel'd Treasure strows Your Way:*
> Ceres, *and* Pales, *with a bounteous Hand,*
> *Diffuse their Plenty over all Your Land;*
> *And* Bacchus *is so lavish of his Store,*
> *That Wine flows now, where Water ran before.*
> *Thus Seasons, Men, and Gods their Joy express;*
> *To see Your Triumph, and our Happiness.*

His Majesty, having passed the four *Triumphal Arches*, was, at TEMPLE-Bar, entertained with the View of a delightful Boscage, full of several Beasts, both Tame, and Savage, as also several living Figures, and Musick of eight Waits. But this, being the Limit of the Citie's Liberty, must be so likewise of our Description.

A BRIEF NARRATIVE OF HIS MAJESTIES SOLEMN CORONATION:

WITH

His Magnificent PROCEEDING, and ROYAL FEAST in

WESTMINSTER-HALL.

A BRIEF NARRATIVE
Of
His Majestie's Solemn Coronation.

Upon the 23d of *April*, being Saint *George*'s Day, about seven in the Morning, the *King* took Water from the *Privy-Stairs* at *White-Hall*, and landed at the *Parliament-Stairs*: from whence He went up to the Room behind the *Lords-House*, called the *Prince's Lodgings*: where, after He had reposed Himself for a while, He was arayed in Royal Robes of Crimson Velvet, furr'd with Ermine: By which time the *Nobility*, being come together in the *Lords-House*, and *Painted-Chamber*, Robed themselves.

The *Judges* also, with those of the *Long-Robe*, the *Knights* of the *Bath* (then in their Robes of Purple Satin, lined with white Taffaty) and *Gentlemen* of the *Privy-Chamber*, met in the Court of *Requests*. And, after some space, being drawn down into *Westminster-Hall*, where this great Solemnity (ordered by the Officers at Arms) began; the *Nobility*, in their proper Robes, carrying their Coronets in their Hands, proceeded according to their several Dignities, and Degrees, before His *Majesty*, up to His Throne of State; which was raised at the *West*-end of that large and noble Room, and there placed themselves upon each side thereof.

The *King* being thus set in a rich Chair, under a glorious Cloth of State, Sir *Gilbert Talbot* K^t, *Master* of the *Jewel-House*, presented the *Sword* of *State*, as also the *Sword* called *Curtana*, and two other *Swords*, to the *Lord High-Constable*; who took and delivered them to the *Lord High-Chamberlain*, and he laid them upon the Table before the *King*.

Then did he also deliver the *Spurs* to the *Lord High-Constable*; and he the same to the *Lord High-Chamberlain*, who also placed them upon the Table.

Immediately after the *Dean* and *Prebends* of *Westminster*, (by whom the *Regalia* had been brought in Procession from the *Abbey-Church* unto *Westminster-Hall*) being vested in rich Copes, came up from the lower end thereof, in manner following.

1 The *Serjeant* of the *Vestry*, in a Scarlet Mantle.
2 Then the *Children* of the *King's Chapel*, in Scarlet Mantles.
3 Then the *Quire* of *Westminster*, in Surplices.
4 Then the *Gentlemen* of the *King's Chapel*, in Scarlet Mantles.
5 Next the *Pursuivants*, *Heralds*, and *Provincial* Kings of Arms.
6 Then the *Dean*, carrying Saint *Edward's Crown*.

And after him five of the *Prebends* of that Church; the first carrying the *Sceptre* with the *Cross*.

The second the *Sceptre* with the *Dove*.

The third the *Orb* with the *Cross*.

The fourth King *Edward's Staff*.

The fifth the *Chalice* and *Patena*.

Passing thus through the *Hall*, and making their due Reverences in three places thereof; the *Quires*, with the Officers at Arms falling off on each side, towards the upper end of the Room; the said *Dean* and *Prebends* ascended the Steps; at the top whereof *Garter*, *Principal King of Arms* standing, conducted them to the *Table* placed before the *Throne*, where they made their last Reverence.

Which being done, the *Dean* first presented the *Crown*, which was by the *Lord High-Constable*, and *Lord Great-Chamberlain*, set upon the Table; who likewise afterwards received from each of the *Prebends* that part of the *Regalia*, which they carried, and laid them also by the *Crown*: which done, they retired.

Then

His MAJESTIE's Coronation.

Then, the *Lord Great-Chamberlain* presenting the *Regalia* severally to the *King*, His *Majesty* thereupon disposed of them unto the *Noble-men* hereafter named, to be carried by them in the *Proceeding* to the *Abbey-Church*, viz.

Saint *Edward's Staff* to the *Earl* of *Sandwich*.
The *Spurs* to the *Earl* of *Penbroke* and *Montgomery*.
The *Sceptre* with the *Cross* to the *Earl* of *Bedford*.
The *Pointed Sword* (born on the left hand of *Curtana*) to the *Earl* of *Derby*.
The *Pointed Sword* (born on the right hand thereof) to the *Earl* of *Shrewsbury*.
The *Sword* called *Curtana* to the *Earl* of *Oxford*.
The *Sword* of *State* to the *Earl* of *Manchester*.
The *Sceptre* with the *Dove* to the *Duke* of *Albe-marle*.
The *Orb* with the *Cross* to the *Duke* of *Buckingham*.
Saint *Edward's Crown* to the *Duke* of *Ormond*.
The *Patena* to the *Bishop* of *Exeter*; and lastly,
The *Chalice* to the *Bishop* of *London*.

All things being thus prepared, (it being about ten a Clock,) the *Proceeding* began from the *Hall* into the *Palace-Yard*, through the *Gate-House*, and the end of *King's-street*; thence along the *Great Sanctuary*, and so to the *West-end* of the *Abbey-Church*, all upon Blew Cloth, which was spread upon the Ground, from the *Throne* in *Westminster-Hall* to the great Steps in the same *Abbey-Church*, by Sir *George Carteret* Knight, His *Majestie's* Vice-Chamberlain, as *Almoner* for that Day by special Appointment.

The

The PROCEEDING to the CORONATION was in this following Order.

THE *Drums* four.
The *Trumpets* sixteen, in four *Classis*.
The *Six Clerks* of the *Chancery*.
Ten of the KING's *Chaplains*, having Dignities.
The *Aldermen* of LONDON.
The KING's *Learned Council* at *Law*.
The KING's *Solicitour*.   The KING's *Attorney*.
The KING's eldest *Serjeant* at *Law*.
The *Esquires* of the *Body*.
The *Masters* of *Request*.
The *Gentlemen* of the *Privy-Chamber*.
The *Knights* of the *Bath*, in their *Purple Robes*.
The *Barons* of the *Exchequer*, and *Justices* of both *Benches*, two and two, in order, according to their Seniority.
The *Lord Chief-Baron*.   The *Lord Chief-Justice* of the *Common-Pleas*.
The *Master* of the *Rolls*. The *Lord Chief-Justice* of the *Kings-Bench*.
The *Serjeant-Porter*.   The *Serjeant* of the *Vestry*.
The *Children* of the *King's Chapel*.
The *Gentlemen* of the *King's Chapel*.
The *Prebends* of *Westminster*.
The *Master* of the *Jewel-House*.
The *Knights* of the *Privy-Council*.
Port-cullis, Pursuivant at Arms.
The *Barons* in their Robes, two and two, carrying their Caps of Crimson Velvet, turn'd up with Miniver, in their Hands.
The *Bishops*, two and two, according to their Dignities, and Consecrations.
   Rouge-Croix,   *Blew-Mantle*,   Pursuivants.
The *Viscounts*, two and two, in their Robes, with their Coronets in their Hands.
   Somerset,   *Chester*,   Heralds.
The *Earls*, two and two, in their Robes, holding their Coronets in their Hands.

Richmond,

His Majestie's Coronation.

Richmond,   Windsor,   Heralds.
The Marquess of Dorchester,   The Marquess of Worcester,
in their Robes, with their Coronets in their Hands.

Lancaster,   York,   Heralds.
Norroy,   Clarencieux,   Provincial Kings,
carrying their Crowns in their Hands.

The Lord High-Treasurer,   The Lord High Chancellour.

Saint *Edward's Staff*, born by the Earl of Sandwich,
The *Spurs*, born by the Earl of Penbroke, and Montgomery,
Saint *Edward's Sceptre*, born by the Earl of Bedford.

| The *third Sword*, drawn, and born by the Earl of Derby. | The *Sword* called *Curtana*, drawn, and born by the Earl of Oxford. | The *Pointed Sword*, drawn, and born by the Earl of Shrewsbury. |

| The Lord Maior of London. | Garter, Principal King of Arms. | The Gentleman-Usher of the Black-Rod. |

The Earl of Lindsey,
Lord Great-Chamberlain of ENGLAND.

| The Earl of Suffolk, Earl Marshal for this present occasion. | The *Sword of State* in the Scabbard, born by the Earl of Manchester, Lord Chamberlain of the Houshold. | The Earl of Northumberland, Lord Constable of England for this present occasion. | Arms. |

His Highness the Duke of YORK.

| The *Sceptre*, with the *Dove*, born by the Duke of Albemarle. | *St. Edward's Crown*, born by the Duke of Ormond, Lord High-Steward for this present occasion. | The *Orb*, born by the Duke of Buckingham. | at |

| The *Paten*, born by the Bishop of Exeter in his Cope. | The *Regale*, or *Chalice*, born by the Bishop of London in his Cope. | Serjeants |

The

172   The Proceeding on the Day of

[margin note: This mistake is thus rectified in St Edward Walker's, then Garter King of Armes, his Manuscript, wch he left in ye Heralds Office.]

The *KING*
supported by the Bishops of
Bath and *Wells*,   and *Duresme*.

His Train born by the Lords
Mandevil, *Cavendish*, ~~*Ossory*~~ *Cranborne*, and *Percy*;
and assisted by the Lord *Mansfield*,
Master of the *Robes*.

The *Earl* of *Lauderdale*,
one of the *Gentlemen* of the *Bed-Chamber*:

Mr. *Seamour*,   Mr. *Ashburnham*,
both Grooms of the Bed-Chamber.

The *Captain* of the *Guard*.

The *Captain* of the *Pensioners*.

The *Yeomen* of *Guard*, in their
Coats.

{ The *Pensioners* with their *Pole-Axes* }

{ *Barons* of the *Cinque-Ports*, (their whole Number XVI.) habited in Doublets of Crimson Satin, Scarlet Hose, Scarlet Gowns, lined with Crimson Satin, black Velvet Caps, and black Velvet Shoes, carrying the *Canopy*. }

{ habited in Doublets of Crimson Satin, Scarlet Hose, Scarlet Gowns, lined with Crimson Satin, black Velvet Caps, and black Velvet Shoes, carrying the *Canopy*. }

{ with their *Pole-Axes*. }

When the *Proceeding* was entered the *Abbey-Church*, all, pass through the *Quire*, went up the Stairs toward the great *Thea* and, as they came to the top thereof, were disposed by the *Her* into two *Galleries*, built on either side the upper end of the *Quire*. the *North* side, the *Aldermen* of *London*, the *Judges*, and other the *Long-Robe*; as also the *Quire* of *Westminster*, with the *Gentle* and *Children* of the *King's Chapel*; and, on the *South* side, the *Knig* of the *Bath*, and *Gentlemen* of the *Privy-Chamber*.

Near the *Pulpit* stood the *Master* of the *Jewel-House*, and *Lord Maior* of *London*.

The *Nobility* were seated on Forms round about the inside the *Theater*: on the corner whereof, nearest to the *Altar*, adjoyn to the two uppermost *Pillars*, stood the *Provincial Kings*, *Hera* and *Pursuivants* at Arms, within Rails there placed.

Within the Rails, on either side the entrance of the *Theatre* from the *Quire*, stood the Serjeants at Arms (XVI. in number) with their Maces. And over the Door, at the *West*-end of the *Quire*, stood the Drums and Trumpets.

The *King*, being entered the *West*-door of the *Church* (within which a *Fald-stool*, and *Cushions* were laid ready for him to kneel at) was received with an *Anthem*, begun by the whole *Quire*, viz.

The first, fourth, fifth, and sixth *Verses* of the 122^d *Psalm*: Beginning thus;

> *I was glad when they said unto me, We will go into the House of the Lord*, &c.

He kneeled down, and used some short Ejaculations; which being finished, He thence proceeded up to the *Theatre* (erected close to the four high *Pillars*, standing between the *Quire* and the *Altar*) upon which the *Throne* of *Estate* was placed (being a Square raised five Degrees) on the *East*-side whereof were set a *Chair*, *Foot-stool*, and *Cushion*, covered with Cloth of Gold, whereon for a while He reposed Himself.

Immediately after, the *Bishop* of *London* (who was appointed to Officiate, in part, that Day, for the *Arch-Bishop* of *Canterbury*, whose age and weakness rendered him uncapable of performing his whole Duty at this *Coronation*) having the *Lord High Constable*, the *Earl Marshal*, the *Lord Great Chamberlain*, the *Lord High Chancellour*, and *Lord Chamberlain* of the *Houshold* before him, went first to the *South*, next to the *West*, and lastly, to the *North* side of the *Theatre*; and at every of the said three sides, acquainted the *People*, that he presented to them *King* CHARLES, the rightful Inheritour of the *Crown* of this *Realm*; and asked them, if they were willing to do their *Homage*, *Service*, and *Bounden Duty* to Him.

As this was doing, the *King* rose up, and stood by the aforesaid *Chair*, turning His Face still to that side of the *Stage*, where the said *Bishop* stood, when he spake to the *People*; who signified their willingness, by loud Shouts, and Acclamations.

The same Question was likewise put by the said *Bishop* to all the *Nobility* present.

Immediately after, this following *Anthem* was sung by the Gentlemen of the *King's Chapel*:

Bb   Let

Let thy Hand be strengthened, and thy right Hand be exalted, &c.

In which time, a large *Carpet* was spread by certain Officers of the removing *Wardrobe*, from the *Altar*, down below the *hault-Paces* thereof; and over that a *silk Carpet*, and *Cushion*, laid by the *Gentleman-Usher* of the *Black-Rod*, assisted by the *Yeoman* of the *Wardrobe*. Which being done, the *Bishop* of *London* went down from the *Theatre* towards the *Altar*; and, having made his Reverence, placed himself at the *North*-side thereof.

Then the *King* descended from His *Throne*, and proceeded towards the *Altar*, supported by the *Bishops* of *Duresme*, and *Bath* and *Wells*, with the *four Swords*; the *grand Officers*, the *Noble-men*, *Bishops*, who carried the *Regalia* before Him, and *Dean* of *Westminster* also attending. Being come to the Steps of the *Altar*, He kneeled down, and first offered a *Pall* of Cloth of Gold; next an *Ingot* of Gold of a pound weight, prepared by the Master of the great *Wardrobe*, and *Treasurer* of the *Houshold*, by virtue of their *Offices*. Immediately after, His *Majestie* retired to a *Chair of State*, set on the *South-side* of the *Altar*, a little below the Traverse of Crimson Taffaty.

After this, the *Bishops*, and *Noble-men*, who carried the *Regalia*, presented every particular to the *Bishop* of *London*, who placed them upon the *Altar*; and then retired to their Seats. And the *King* kneeled at a *Fald-stool* (set on the right side of his said *Chair of State*) whil'st the *Bishop* of *London* said the *Prayer*, beginning thus,

O God, which dost visit those, that are humble, &c.

Which *Prayer* ended, the *Bishop* of *Worcester* went up into the *Pulpit*, placed on the *North*-side of the *Altar*, opposite to the *King*, and began his S E R M O N; the Text being taken out of the 28th Chapter of the *Proverbs*, and the second *Verse*.

On the *King*'s right Hand stood the *Bishop* of *Duresme*, and beyond him the *Noble-men*, that carried the S W O R D S, who held them naked, and erect. The *Duke* of Y O R K sate a little behind Him on His left Hand; next to whom stood the *Bishop* of *Bath* and *Wells*, together with the *Lord Great-Chamberlain*.

His Majestie's Coronation. 175

The *Lord High-Chancellour*, and *Lord High-Treasurer*, sate on a Form behind the *Duke* of Y o r k; and behind them, in a Gallery, sate the *Dutchess* of Y o r k.

In the same Gallery also were placed

Baron Bateville, Ordinary *Ambassadour* from *Spain*.

Prince Maurice of *Nassau*, Extra-ordinary *Ambassadour* from the *Electour* of *Brandenburgh*.

Monsieur Weyman, the *Electour's Chancellour*, who was joyned in Commission with him.

The *Count Coningsmark*, Envoy from *Sweden*.

Monsieur Friesendorf, Resident of *Sweden*.

Monsieur Petcom, Resident of *Denmark*.

Monsieur Plessis Bellieure, Envoy from *Monsieur* the *Duke* of *Orleans*.

Signieur Giavarina, Resident of *Venice*.

Signieur Bernardi, Resident of *Genoa*.

Monsieur La-Motte,
  and } Envoys from the *Prince Electour*.
Monsieur Frays,

Monsieur Gormers, Deputy Extra-ordinary from *Hamburgh*.

An Envoy from the *Cardinal* of *Hess*.

The *Marquess de Montbrun*, with several other *Gentlemen-strangers*.

But *Don Francisco de Mello*, the *Ambassadour* of *Portugal*, was placed in the *Lord Chamberlain's* Box.

On the *North*-side of the *Altar* sate the *Bishop* of *London*, directly opposite to the *King* in the *Arch Bishop's* Chair, covered with Purple Velvet: the rest of the *Bishops* being placed on Forms behind him.

And higher, towards Saint *Edward's Chapel*, stood *Garter*, Principal King of Arms, with the *Officers* of the standing and moving *Ward-robe*, in Scarlet Gowns; the *Sergeant* of the *Vestry* with his gilt Verge, and other Vergers: as also some of the *Grooms* and *Pages* of the *Bed-Chamber*, who attended to do service, as occasion required.

Opposite to them, on the *South*-side of the *Altar*, stood the *Dean* and *Prebends* of *Westminster*.

Saint *Edward's* antient *Chair* (covered all over with Cloth of Gold) was placed upon the *North*-side of the *Altar*, a little lower then that belonging to the *Arch-Bishop*, but something nearer the middle of the *Isle*, and between the *King's* Chair of State, and the Pulpit.

Bb 2   Sermon

Sermon being ended, the *Bishop* of *London* arising from his Seat, drew near to the *Chair of State*, and asked of the *King* (who then uncovered His Head) whether He was willing to take the usual *Oath* of His *Progenitors*; *viz.* to confirm the *Laws* to the *People*, and namely the *Franchises* granted to the *Clergy* by Saint *Edward* the *Confessour*; to maintain the *Gospel* established in the *Kingdom*; to keep *Peace*; execute *Justice*, and grant the *Commons* their rightful *Customs*: unto every of which Questions His Majesty made particular Answers, That *He would*.

Then likewise did the *Bishop* of *Rochester* read the *Bishop's Petition* to the *King*; the *Prayer* whereof was, That He would preserve unto them, and the *Churches* committed to their charge, all *Canonical Privileges*; due *Law*, and *Justice*; as also protect, and defend *them*, and the *Churches*, under their Government: which His *Majesty* most graciously by a large Answer (which repeated the words of the *Petition*) granted, and promised to perform.

Afterwards the *King*, assisted by the *Bishops* of *Duresme*, and *Bath* and *Wells*, was led from His *Chair* up to the *Altar* (the *Sword* of *State* being born before Him, and the *Lord Great Chamberlain* attending) where He took an *Oath* to perform, and keep what He had promised.

Which *Oath* taken, the *King* was led, in like manner, back to His *Chair* of *State*; and immediately the *Bishop* of *London* begun the *Hymn*, *Come Holy Ghost, eternal God*, &c. the *Quires* singing the rest of it.

And a little before the ending thereof, the *Fald stool* was set again at the *King's* right Hand; whereat (as soon as the *Hymn* was finished) He kneeled) the *Bishop* of *London* standing before Him, and saying the following *Prayer*,

We beseech thee, O Lord, Holy Father, Almighty, and everlasting God, for this thy Servant CHARLES, *&c.*

This *Prayer* ended, the *Bishop* of *London* went to the *North-side* of the *Altar*, the *King* still kneeling; and forthwith the *Bishops* of *Peterborough*, and *Gloucester*, went, and kneeled on the upper haultpace of the *Altar*, where they began the *Letany*, the *Quires* singing the *Responses*; the *Dean* of *Westminster*, kneeling all the while on the *King's* left Hand.

After the *Letany* followed three *Prayers*, said by the *Bishop* of *London*

London at the North-side of the *Altar*; and, a little before the last of them was ended, the *Arch-Bishop* of *Canterbury* came out at the North-door of Saint EDWARD's *Chapel*, vested in an rich antient *Cope*.

The third *Prayer* being ended, the said *Arch Bishop* standing before the *Altar*, began the *Versicle*,

Lift up your Hearts.

Resp.

We lift them up to the Lord.

Arch-Bishop.

Let us give thanks unto the Lord our God.

Resp.

It is meet and right so to do.

Arch-Bishop.

It is very meet, and right, and our bounden Duty, that we should at all times, and in all places, give thanks unto thee, O Lord, Holy Father, &c.

Then the *King* arose from before the *Fald stool*, and went to the *Altar*, supported by the aforesaid *Bishops* of *Duresme*, and *Bath* and *Wells*: where He was disrobed by the *Lord Great-Chamberlain* of His *Royal Robes*, which were immediately carried thence into the Traverse erected in Saint *Edward's Chapel*.

Whilst this was in doing, the *Chair*, that was before placed at the entrance of the *Theatre* was removed, and set on the North-side of the *Altar*, betwixt it, and Saint *Edward's Chair*: whereunto the *King* being come, sate down, and was *anointed* by the said *Arch-Bishop*, (the *Dean* of *Westminster* holding the *Ampulla*, and pouring the Oyl out into the *Spoon*) first on the Palms of both His Hands, the *Arch-Bishop*, as he *anointed* Him, pronouncing the *Prayer*, which beginneth thus;

Let these Hands be anointed with Holy Oyl, as Kings and Prophets have been anointed, &c.

After

After which, the *Quire* sung this *Anthem*,

> Sadoc *the Priest*, and Nathan *the Prophet anointed* Solomon *King, and all the People rejoyced, and said,* God save the KING.

At the end of which *Anthem*, the *Arch-Bishop* said the *Prayer*, beginning thus;

> *Look down, Almighty God, with thy favourable Countenance upon this Glorious* KING, *&c.*

And then proceeded with His anointing on the *King*'s Breast, between His Shoulders, on both His Shoulders; the two bowings of His Arms, and on the Crown of His Head, in manner aforesaid.

Which being done, and the *Anointing* dryed up with fine Linen; and also the Loops of His Shirt closed up by the *Dean of Westminster*, the *Arch-Bishop* said the two *Prayers*, beginning thus;

> 1 *God, the Son of God,* Christ Jesus *our Lord, who is anointed of his Father with the Oyl of Gladness above his Fellows,* &c.
> 2 *God, which art the Glory of the Righteous, and the Mercy of Sinners,* &c.

During the time of this His *Unction*, a rich *Pall* of Cloth of Gold, was held over the *King*'s Head by the *Dukes of Buckingham*, and *Albe-marle*; and the *Earls of Berks* and *Sandwich*, as *Knights* of the most Noble Order of the *Garter*.

After these *Prayers*, the *Lord Great-Chamberlain* delivered the *Coif* to the *Arch-Bishop*, who put it on the *King*'s Head: and immediately after, the *Dean of Westminster* put the *Colobium Sindonis*, or *Surplice* upon the *King*; the *Arch-Bishop* saying the *Prayer*, beginning thus;

> *O God, the King of Kings, and Lord of Lords, by whom Kings do reign, and Law-givers do make good Laws, vouchsafe, we beseech thee, in thy favour, to bless this Kingly Ornament,* &c.

Then the *Dean of Westminster*, having likewise fetched the *Tishue-Hose* and *Sandals* from the *Altar*, arrayed the *King* therewith; as also with the *Super-tunica*, or *close Pall* of Cloth of Gold, and girded the same about Him.

After

After all this, the said *Dean* took the *Spurs* from off the *Altar*, and delivered them to the *Lord Great-Chamberlain*, who, having touched the *King's* Heels therewith, forthwith sent them back to the *Altar*.

Then the *Arch-Bishop* received the *Sword* of *State* in the Scabbard from the *Lord-Chamberlain* of the *Houshold*, and laid it upon the *Altar*, saying the *Prayer*, beginning thus,

Hear our Prayers, we beseech thee, O Lord, and vouchsafe, by thy right Hand of Majesty, to bless, and sanctifie this SWORD, &c.

This *Prayer* finished, the *Arch-Bishop*, and *Bishops* assisting, delivered the *Sword* back to the *King*, saying, *Accipe gladium per manus Episcoporum*.

Whereupon, the *Lord Great-Chamberlain* girt it about the *King*, and the *Arch-Bishop* said,

Receive this Kingly Sword, which is hallowed for the defence of the Holy Church, &c.

After this, the *Dean of Westminster* took the * *Armil*, made of Cloth of Tishue, and put it about the *King's* Neck, tying it to the bowings of His Arms; the *Arch-Bishop* standing before the *King*, with the *Bishop* of *London* on His right Hand, and saying,

Receive the Armil of Sincerity, and Wisdom, &c.

<small>* Armillæ sunt in modum Stolæ, & ab utraque scapula usque ad Compages Brachiorum erunt dependentes, in ipsis Compagibus laqueis sericeis connexæ.</small>

Next the *Mantle*, or open *Pall*, being made of Cloth of Gold, and lined with red Taffaty, was put upon Him by the said *Dean*; the *Arch-Bishop* likewise using the words of Signification, *viz*.

Receive this Pall, &c.

In the next place, the *Arch-Bishop* took Saint EDWARD's *Crown*, and blessed it, saying,

God, the Crown of the Faithful, &c.

In the mean time, Saint EDWARD's *Chair* was removed into the middle of the *Isle*, and set right over against the *Altar*, whither the *King* went, and sat down in it: and then the *Arch Bishop* brought *Saint* EDWARD's *Crown* from the *Altar*, and put it upon His Head.

Whereupon, all the *People*, with loud and repeated shouts, cryed, *God save the* KING; and, by a Signal then given, the great *Ordinance* from the *Tower* were also shot off.

At the ceasing of these Acclamations, the *Arch-Bishop* went on, saying,

God crown Thee with a Crown of Glory, and Righteousness, &c.

Adding thereunto the *Prayer*, beginning thus;

* At which words the King bowed His Head.

O God of Eternity, &c. *Bless this thy Servant, who* * *boweth His Head unto thy Majestie,* &c.

After which *Prayer*, the *Arch-Bishop* read the *Confortare*,

Be strong, and of a good Courage, and observe the Commandments of the Lord, to walk in his ways, &c.

In the mean while, the *Quires* sung this *Anthem*,

The King shall rejoyce in thy strength, O Lord. Exceeding glad shall He be of thy Salvation, &c.

Upon this, the *Dukes, Marquesses, Earls,* and *Viscounts* put on their *Coronets*; the *Barons* their *Caps*: And Mr. *Garter*, and the *Provincial Kings* put on their *Coronets*.

Then the *Master* of the *Jewel-House* delivered to the *Arch-Bishop* the *Ring*, who consecrated it, saying,

Bless, O Lord, and sanctifie this Ring, &c.

After which, he put it upon the fourth Finger of the *King*'s right Hand, and said,

Receive this Ring of Kingly Dignitie, and by it the Seal of Catholick Faith, &c.

And then used the *Prayer*, beginning thus;

O God,

O God, to whom belongeth all Power, and Dignity, give unto thy Servant CHARLES *the Fruit of His Dignity,* &c.

Which *Prayer* being finished, the *Linen Gloves* were delivered to the KING by the *Lord Great-Chamberlain*. Then the KING went to the *Altar*, ungirt His *Sword*, and offered it: which, being redeemed by the *Lord-Chamberlain* of the *Houshold*, was drawn out of the Scabbard, and carried naked by him all the following part of the Solemnity.

Then the *Arch-Bishop* took the *Scepter*, with the *Cross*, from off the *Altar*, and delivered it into the KING's right Hand, saying,

Receive this Scepter, the Sign of Kingly Power, the Rod of Kingdoms, the Rod of Virtue, &c.

Whilst this was pronouncing by the *Arch-Bishop*, Mr. *Henry Howard* (Brother to *Thomas* Duke of *Norfolk*) delivered, by virtue of his Tenure of the *Manour* of *Wirksop*, in the County of *Norfolk*, to the *King* a rich *Glove* for His right Hand; which having put on, He then received the *Scepter*. And after that the *Arch-Bishop* said the *Prayer*, beginning thus,

O Lord, the Fountain of all good things, &c. *Grant, we beseech thee, to this thy Servant* CHARLES, *that He may order aright the Dignity, which He hath obtained,* &c.

During which time, the said Mr. *Howard* performed the Service, *ratione tenuræ dicti Manerii de* Wirksop, of supporting the *King's* right *Arm*.

Next of all, the *Arch-Bishop* took the *Scepter* with the *Dove*, and gave it into the *King's* Hand also, saying,

Receive the Rod of Vertue, and Equity, learn to make much of the Godly, and to terrifie the Wicked, &c.

After which, the *King* kneeled, holding both the *Scepters* in His Hands, whilst the *Arch-Bishop* thus blessed Him,

The Lord bless Thee, and keep Thee; and as He hath made Thee King over his People, so he still prosper Thee in this World, and make Thee partaker of his Eternal Felicity in the World to come. Amen.

Then the KING arose, and set Himself again in Saint *Edward's Chair*, whil'st the *Arch-Bishop* and *Bishops* present, one after another, kneeled before Him, and were kissed by Him.

Whcih done, the KING returned to that *Chair*, placed on the *Theatre* behind His *Throne*, having then also the *four Swords* born naked before Him, (the *Arch-Bishops*, *Bishops*, and *Great Officers* attending) at whose arrival there, the *Arch Bishop* said this *Prayer*,

Grant, O Lord, that the Clergie and People, gathered together by thine Ordinance for this service of the KING, &c.

Then the *King* reposed Himself in the said *Chair*, whilst both the *Quires* sung *Te Deum*.

When *Te Deum* was ended, the *King* ascended His *Throne* placed in the midst of the *Theatre* (the *Swords*, and Great *Officers* standing on either side; as also the *Bishops*) the *Arch-Bishop* then saying,

Stand, and hold fast from henceforth that Place, whereof hitherto You have been Heir by the Succession of Your Fore-Fathers, &c.

After this, the *Bishops*, and *Nobility* did their Homage to the *King* in manner following.

And first the *Arch-Bishop* of *Canterbury* kneeled down before the *King's* Knees, and said,

I, WILLIAM Arch-Bishop *of* CANTERBURY, *shall be Faithful, and True, and Faith, and Truth bear unto You, Our Sovereign Lord, and Your Heirs, Kings of* ENGLAND, *and shall do, and truly acknowledg the Service of the Land, which I claim to hold of You, in right of the Church :* So help me God.

Which said, he kissed the *King's* left Cheek.
The like did all the other *Bishops*, that were present.
Then came up the *Duke* of YORK, with *Garter*, Principal *King* of *Arms*, before Him, and His Train born by two Gentle-men, who,

being

being arrived at the *Throne*, kneeled down before the *King*, put off His Coronet, and did His *Homage* in these words;

I, JAMES *Duke of* YORK, *become Your Liege-man, of Life and Limb, and of Earthly Worship: and Faith and Truth I shall bear unto You, to live and die against all manner of Folk :* So God me help. At which the *Drums* beat, *Trumpets* sounded, and all the *People* shouted.

The like did the *Dukes of Buckingham*, and *Albe-marle*, for themselves, and the rest of the *Dukes*.

So also did the *Marquesses of Worcester*, and *Dorchester*.

Next, the *Earl* of *Oxford* did *Homage* after the same manner for himself, and the rest of the *Earls*, who attended upon him to signifie their Consents.

After him, *Viscount Hereford* did the like for himself, and the rest of the *Viscounts*; and then the *Drums* beat, and *Trumpets* sounded again, and the *People* shouted.

Lastly, the *Baron Audley* in like manner did *Homage* for himself, and all the *Baronage*, who also accompanied him to the *Throne*, in testification of their Consents; which being finished, *Drums*, *Trumpets*, and *Shouts* followed.

Afterwards the *Duke* of YORK, and all the *Nobility* singly ascended the *Throne*, and touched the *King's Crown*, promising by that Ceremony to be ever ready to support it with all their power.

During the performing of this Solemn Ceremony, the *Lord High-Chancellour* went to the *South, West*, and *North*-sides of the *Stage*, and proclaimed to the *People* the *King's General Pardon*, being attended by Mr. *Garter* to the *South*-side, and by a *Gentle-man-Usher*, and two *Heralds* to the other two Sides.

And at these three Sides, at the same time, did the *Lord Cornwallis*, *Treasurer* of His *Majestie's Houshold*, fling abroad the *Medals*, both of Gold, and Silver, prepared for the Coronation, as a Princely Donation, or Largess, among the *People*. An *Ectype* of which is this.

The King being thus enthronized, the Gentlemen of His Chapel began this following Anthem,

> Beh'd, O Lord, our Defender, and look upon the Face of thine Anointed.

At the ending of which Anthem, the Trumpets sounded, and Drums beat again. In which time the Bishop of London went up to the High-Altar, and began the Communion; and immediately the King took off His Crown, and delivered it to the Lord High-Chamberlain to hold; the Scepter with the Cross to Mr. Henry Howard, and that with the Dove to the Duke of Albemarle.

The EPISTLE (taken out of the First Epistle of St. Peter, the second Chapter, and beginning at the eleventh Verse) was read by the Bishop of Chichester.

The GOSPEL (being part of the twenty second Chapter of St. Matthew, beginning at the fifteenth Verse) by the Bishop of Ely.

After which, the Nicene Creed was began by the Bishop of London, and sung by the Gentle-men of the Chapel.

All which time the King stood by His Throne.

But towards the end of the Creed He took again His Crown from the Lord Great-Chamberlain, and put it on His Head; as also the Scepter with the Cross from Mr. Howard, and that with the Dove from the Duke of Albemarle, and prepared for His Descent from His Throne towards the Altar, to receive the Communion.

And, as soon as singing of the Creed was fully ended, the King descended with the Crown on His Head, and Scepters in both Hands, (the Bishops of Duresm, and Bath and Wells, supporting Him) with the four Swords naked before, all the great Officers attending. In the time of which Proceeding the Quire sung,

> Let my Prayer come up into thy presence, as the Incense, and the lifting up of my Hand be as an Evening-Sacrifice.

Here the Arch-Bishop of Canterbury retired from the Ceremonies into Saint Edward's Chapel, and thence went home, leaving the remainder of his Duty to be performed by the Bishop of London.

At the King's approach to the Altar, the Bishop of Ely delivered unto Him Bread, and Wine, which He there offered, and then returned to the Fald stool, on the South side of the Altar, near His Chair of State; before which He kneeled down, and laid His Crown upon

the

the *Cushion* before Him, towards His right Hand; and the *Scepter* with the *Dove*, on His left; and gave again to Mr. *Howard* the *Scepter* with the *Cross*, who held it, kneeling on the *King*'s right Hand: the *Grand Officers*, and the *Noble-men*, with the four *Swords* naked, and erect, standing about Him.

Then the *Bishop* of *London* said this *Prayer*,

Bless, O Lord, we beseech thee, these thy Gifts, and sanctifie them unto this holy Use, &c.

At the end of which, the Lord *Cornwallis*, *Treasurer* of the *Houshold*, delivered another *Wedg* of *Gold* (which goeth under the name of the *Mark* of *Gold*) to the *Lord Great-Chamberlain*, who presenting it to the *King*, He offered it into the *Bason*, kneeling still at His *Fald-stool*, whil'st the *Bishop* of *London* said the following *Prayer*, beginning thus;

Almighty God, give Thee the Dew of Heaven, and the Fatness of the Earth, and abundance of Corn, and Wine, &c.

And next pronounced this Blessing,

Bless, O Lord, the virtuous carriage of this K I N G, *and accept the Work of His Hands,* &c.

Then the *Bishop* proceeded to the Consecration of the *Sacrament*: which being finished, he first of all received; next, the *Dean* of *Westminster*; then, the *Bishop* of *Bath* and *Wells*; and lastly, the *Bishop* of *Duresm*.

These four *Prelates* having communicated, and Preparation made for the *King*'s Receiving (who kneeled all this while before the *Fald-stool*) the *Bishop* of *London* gave the *King* the *Bread*, and the *Dean* of *Westminster* the *Cup*.

As soon as the *King* had received, this *Anthem* was begun by the upper *Quire*.

O hearken unto the voice of my Calling, my King, and my God, &c.

In the mean while, the King returned to His *Throne* upon the *Theatre*, with the *Crown* on His Head, and bearing the *Scepters* in His Hands.

When

When He came thither, He first put off His *Crown*, and delivered it to the *Lord Great-Chamberlain*: then the *Scepter* with the *Cross* to Mr. *Howard*; and that other with the *Dove* to the *Duke of Albemarle*.

After this the *Bishop* of *London* went on with the *Communion*; which being finished, the *King* (attended as before) descended from His *Throne* crowned, with both the *Scepters* in His Hand, (the rest of the *Regalia* being carried before Him; and thence proceeded into Saint *Edward's Chapel*, where He took off Saint *Edward's Crown*, and delivered it to the Bishop of *London*; who immediately laid it upon Saint *Edward's Altar*, all the rest of the *Regalia* being given into the hands of the *Dean* of *Westminster*, and laid there also. Then He retired into a Traverse, where He was disrobed of the Robes He was crowned in, which were delivered to the *Dean* of *Westminster* to lay up with the rest of *Regalia*) and invested with His Royal Robes of Purple Velvet, He came near to Saint *Edward's Altar*, where the *Bishop* of *London* standing ready with the *Imperial Crown* in his hands, set that upon His Head. All which being performed, He took the *Scepter* with the *Cross* in His right Hand, and the *Globe* in His left; and proceeded to *Westminster-Hall*, the same way that He came; and attended after the same manner, saving that the *Noble-men*, and *Bishops*, who brought the *Regalia* to the *Abbey Church*, went not now immediately before Him, as they did then, but were ranked in places according to their Degrees: all the *Noble-men* having their *Coronets*, and *Caps* on their Heads; and the *Kings* of *Arms* their *Coronets*.

The *Proceeding* being entred into *Westminster-Hall*, the *Nobility*, and others, who had Tables assigned them, went, and placed themselves thereat; but the *King*, (attended with the *Great Officers*) with-drew into the *Inner-Court* of *Wards*, for half an hour.

In the mean time, all the *Tables* in the Body of the *Hall* were served; viz. before the *King's Service* came up, and were placed in this manner.

1. On the right hand (viz. the *South-East* side of the *Hall*) were set two *Tables*, one beneath the other: at the upper end of the first (which had two *Side-Tables* to serve it) sate the *Bishops*; and below them the *Judges*, with the rest of the *Long-Robe*.

2. At the second *Table* (which had two *Side-board Tables* likewise to serve it) sate the *Masters* of the *Chancery* and the *Six Clerks*. At which likewise the *Barons* of the *Cinque-Ports* were then necessitated to sit (by reason of a Disturbance which some of the *King's* Footmen made in offering to take the *Canopy* from them) although the upper end of the first *Table* was appointed for them.

On

His Majestie's Coronation.

3.

On the other side of the *Hall* was placed likewise a long Table, which reached down near to the *Common-Pleas-Court*, whereat the *Nobility* dined.

And behind this, close to the Wall, at a shorter Table, sate the *Lord Maior*, *Aldermen*, *Recorder*, and twelve chief Citizens of *London*.

Lastly, within the *Court of Common-Pleas* was a Table set for the *Officers at Arms*, whereat they also dined. Each Table being furnished with three *Courses* answerable to that of the *King*'s, besides the *Banquet*.

At the upper end of the *Hall* (where, upon an ascent of Steps, a *Theatre* was raised for His *Majestie's* Royal Seat at this great Solemnity) a large Table being placed, the *Serjeant* of the *Ewry*, two *Serjeants* at *Arms* with their *Maces* going before him, bringing up the *Covering*, was spread by the *Gentlemen-Ushers*, and *Serjeant* of the *Ewry*.

This being done, the *Officers* of the *Pantry*, with two *Serjeants* at *Arms* also before them, brought up the *Salt* of *State*, and *Caddinet*.

A little before the *King* returned to Diner, two *Esquires* of the *Body*, took their Seats upon two little Foot-stools, on either side of the Foot of the *King's Chair*, (placed opposite to the middle of the Table) and there sate until the *King* came in to Diner; when rising, and performing their Duty in placing the *King's Robes* for His better conveniency of sitting, they sate down again at the *King's* Feet some part of Diner-time, until the *King* gave them leave to rise.

On the right Side of the *Throne* was erected a *Gallery* for the *Officers* at *Arms*. And opposite to that, on the other side, another for the *Musick*: and below, on the old Scaffolds, next the *Court of Common-Pleas*, stood the *King's Trumpeters*.

The Proceeding at carrying up of the First Course to the King's Table.

The two *Clerks Comptrollers*,
The two *Clerks* of the *Green-Cloth*,
And the *Cofferer* of His *Majestie's Houshold*.

All in Black Velvet Gowns, trimm'd with Black Silk, and Gold Lace, with Velvet Caps raised in the Head.

Six *Serjeants* at *Arms*, two and two.

| The *Earl-Marshal* on the left Hand. | The *Lord-High-Steward*. | The *Lord High-Constable* on the right Hand. |

All three mounted on Horse-back in their Robes, and with their Coronets on their Heads; having their Horses richly trapped.

Six *Serjeants* at *Arms*, two and two.

The *Comptroller* of the *Houshold*, The *Treasurer* of the *Houshold*, with their White Staves.

Earl of *Dorset*, Sewer.
Earl of *Chesterfield*, his Assistant.
The *Knights* of the *Bath*, carrying up the Service, two and two to a Dish, which was set upon the Table by the *Earl* of *Lincoln* Carver, assisted by the *Earl*-Sewers.

In the Rear came up the three Clerks of His *Majestie*'s Kitchin, all suted in Black, Fugar'd, Satin Gowns, and Velvet Caps, in fashion like those worn by the Clerks Comptrollers.

Diner being set on the Table, the *King* came forth from the *Inner-Court* of *Wards*, in His *Royal Robes*, with the *Crown* on His Head, and *Scepter* in His Hand, having the three *Swords* born naked before Him, and having wash'd, sate down to Diner, the *Bishop* of *London* saying Grace.

On the *King*'s right Hand, the *Noble-men*, that carried the three *Swords*, stood, holding them naked, and erected, all the Diner-while; at His left Hand stood the *Lord High-Chamberlain*, to whom the *King* had given the *Scepter* to hold. And at the Table's end, on the *King*'s left Hand, sate the *Duke* of Y o r k, in his Robes, and Coronet.

Soon after Diner was begun, the Lord *Allington*, by virtue of his tenure of the *Manor* of *Wymundeley*, in the County of *Hertford*, served the *King* of His first *Cup* (which was of *Silver Gilt*) and after the *King* had drank, he had the *Cup* for his *Fee*.

Next, *Thomas Leigh* Esquire was brought up to the Table with a Mess of *Pottage*, called *Dillegrout*, by reason of his tenure of the *Manour* of *Addington*, in the County of *Surrey*.

Afterwards, a little before the second Course was ready, Sir *Edward Dymock* Knight (being the *King*'s Champion, as being seized of the *Manor* of *Scrivelsby*, in the County of *Lincoln*) entred the *Hall* on a goodly White Courser, armed at all Points: and there having made a stand for some time, advanced in maner following;

First,

His Majestie's Coronation.

First, Two *Trumpets*.
Then the *Serjeant-Trumpeter* with his Mace.
After him two *Serjeants* at *Arms*, with their Maces.

{ Then one *Esquire* carrying his *Target*, having his *Arms* depicted thereon; and } { Another *Esquire* carrying the *Champion's Lance* upright. }

After them YORK-Herald at *Arms*.

The *Earl-Marshal*   The *Champion*.   The *Lord High-Constable*
on his left Hand.   on his right Hand.

Both likewise on Horseback.

Being come on some few steps, he made a stand: whereupon the said Herald proclaimed his *Challenge* in these following words;

IF any *Person* of what degree soever, high or low, shall deny, or gain-say Our Sovereign *Lord* King CHARLES the Second, *King of* England, Scotland, France, *and* Ireland, Defender of the Faith, *Son and next Heir to Our* Sovereign *Lord* CHARLES the First, *the last King deceased,* to be right Heir to the Imperial Crown of this *Realm of* England; or that He ought not to enjoy the same: *here is His* Champion, *who saith, that he lyeth, and is a false* Traytor, *being ready in person to Combate with him,* and in this Quarrel *will adventure his Life against him, on what day soever he shall be appointed.*

Whereupon the *Champion* threw down his *Gantlet*, which lying some small time, and no body taking it up, it was delivered unto him again by the same Herald. Then he advanced further forward, until he came to the middle of the *Hall*; where the Herald having reiterated the same Proclamation, the *Gantlet* was again thrown down, taken up, and returned unto him. And lastly, advancing to the Foot of the Steps to the *Throne of State*, the said *Herald* again proclaimed the same *Challenge*, whereupon the *Champion* threw down his *Gantlet* again, which no body taking up, it was delivered unto him.

This being done, the *Earl* of *Penbroke* and *Montgomery* (assisted, as before) presented on the Knee to the *King* a Gilt *Cup* with a Cover, full of Wine, who drank to the *Champion*; and, by the said *Earl* sent him the *Cup*, which having received, he, after three Reverences, drank it all off, went a little backward, and so departed out of the *Hall*, taking the said *Cup* for his Fee.

All which being performed, *Garter* Principal King of *Arms*, with the two Provincial Kings of *Arms*, having their Coronets on their Heads; and likewise all the *Heralds*, and *Pursuivants* at *Arms*, came down from the Gallery, and went to the lower end of the Tables, where they made their first obeysance to His *Majesty*. Then advancing up into the midst of the Hall, they did the like, and afterwards at the Foot of the Steps towards His *Majestie's Throne*, where *Garter* being ascended, proclaimed His *Majestie's* Stile in *Latine*, *French*, and *English*, according to antient usage, crying *Largess* thrice. Which done, they all retired backward into the midst of the *Hall*; and there, after crying *Largess* again thrice, he proclaimed the *King's* Style as before. And lastly, they went yet backwards to the end of the said *Noble-mens* Table, and did the same again; and from thence into the *Common-Pleas-Court*, to Diner.

Immediately after this, the second Course was brought up by the *Gentlemen-Pensioners*, with the former Solemnity; the last Dish being carried up by *Erasmus Smith* Esquire, who then presented the *King* with three *Maple Cups*, on the behalf of *Robert Barnham* Esq; in respect of his tenure of the *Manor* of *Nether-Bilsington* in the County of *Kent*, by performance of that service on the Day of the *King's Coronation*.

Lastly, the *Lord Maior* of *London* then presented the *King* with Wine in a *Golden Cup*, having a Cover; of which the *King* having drank, the said *Lord Maior* received it for his Fee.

By this time the day being far spent, the *King* (having Water brought Him by the Earl of *Penbroke*, and his Assistants) washed, and rose from Diner before the third Course was brought in; and, retiring into the *Inner-Court* of *Wards*, He there disrobed Himself: and from thence went privately to His *Barge*, which waited for Him at the *Parliament-Stairs*, and so to the *Privy-Stairs* at *White-Hall*, where He landed.

It is a thing very memorable, that, towards the end of *Diner*-time (although all the former part of the day, and also the preceding day, in which the *King* made His *Cavalcade* through *London*, were the onely fair days, that we enjoyed of many both before, and after) it began to *Thunder* and *Lighten* very smartly: which, however some sort of People were apt to interpret as *ominous*, and *ill-boding*, yet it will be no difficult matter to evidence from Antiquity, that Accidents of this nature, though happily they might astonish, and amaze the common Drove of men, were by the most Prudent, and Sagacious, look'd upon as a *prosperous*, and *happy presage*. And of this *Virgil* gives

us

us a very pertinent Example (in the eighth Book of his *Æneids*) where *Evander* having addressed himself in a Speech to *Æneas* for aid against the *Hetrurians*, and He being sollicitous how to answer his request, mark what Sign was immediately sent from Heaven.

> *Námque improviso vibratus ab Æthere fulgor*
> *Cum sonitu venit*, &c.

> For suddenly from Heav'n a brandish'd Flash
> With Thunder came, *&c.*

And presently after the *Poet* adds,

> *Obstupuêre animis alii, sed* Troius Heros
> *Agnovit sonitum, & Divæ promissa Parentis.*

> While others stood amaz'd, the *Hero* knew
> His Mother's Promise by the Sound that flew.

The same *Author*, in another place *, mentions the same thing as a Testimony of *Prayers* heard, and answered; as when Old *Anchises*, seeing the *lambent Flame* upon his Grand-Child *Iulus* his Head, lifted up his Hands to Heaven, and prayed to *Jove* for help, and direction, he was thus answered,   * Lib. 2.

> *Vix ea fatus erat Senior, subitóque fragore*
> *Intonuit lævum*, &c,

> Scarce had the grave Sire spoke, when suddenly
> It thundered prosperous, *&c.*

For so *Intonuit lævum* is interpreted by *Servius*, according to the Maxim of the Antient *Augurs*, who interpret *Thunder* from the *North*, that is (as they, contrary to the common *Astronomers*, accounted it) the left part of Heaven, for a prosperous *Omen*.

But, in reference to our present Purpose, we may proceed to a larger Interpretation, and conclude, that the Heavens, with Vollies of *Thunder*, and nimble Flashes of *Lightning*, seemed to give a *Plaudite*, and Acclamation, to this Grand and Sacred *Solemnity*; in like manner as we Mortals use to close our greater Triumphs with Fire-works, Bonfires, and the loud Report of our great Ordnance:

this

this Terrestrial Thunder being but the Imitator, and Counterfeit of the Heavenly Artillery.

And so I observe it expounded by *Claudian* in these Verses*,

*Claud. de Cons. Probini & Olybrii ver. 205.

> *Ut sceptrum gessere manu, membrisque rigentes*
> *Aptavere togas, Signum dat summus hiulcâ*
> *Nube Pater, gratámque facem per inane rotantes*
> *Prospera vibrati sonuerunt Omina Nimbi.*

> As soon as rob'd, and scepter'd, *Jove* aloud
> His Signal Favour thunders from a Cloud,
> Successful Lightning through Heav'n's Arches shines;
> Both at His Coronation happy Signs.

FINIS.

The Restoration year of festivities was completed by Charles II's cavalcade through the city of London to his coronation. John Ogilby, master of the revels, commemorated the occasion by expanding his brief 1661 commission – to embellish the four triumphal arches – into a large folio volume which included engravings by Hollar (the cavalcade, the coronation procession, Charles crowned in Westminster) and Loggan (the triumphal arches – unofficially designed by Sir Balthazar Gerbier). Such printed and engraved versions of Royal Festivities are exceedingly rare in England. Ogilby's text, completed by a censored version of Ashmole's description of the coronation itself, and first published early in 1662 by Thomas Roycroft, provides the most detailed account of the visual and literary sources for any English royal entry. The range of more than 130 sources amounts to a compendium of seventeenth-century English neoclassicism.

Ronald Knowles's introduction is divided into several sections corresponding to aspects of Ogilby's original text. The first section, *Multa dies variusque labor*, begins with the historical setting, moving from the national to the metropolitan to the personal. *Adventus Augusti* offers a reconstruction and appraisal of the Virgilian themes of the first arch in the light of contemporary panegyric. *Volvenda dies* discusses the way in which the advent of Charles was hailed as a Platonic Great Year or phoenix period, invoking a kind of messianic imperialism. *Neptuno Britannico* places Charles, as the British Neptune celebrated on the second arch, against the seventeenth-century controversy concerning dominion over the sea.

Ronald Knowles is a graduate of University College Swansea and studied at the Warburg Institute and Birbeck College, University of London. He is currently a Lecturer in English at the University of Reading and is writing on seventeenth-century political panegyric in England.

mRts

meðieval & Renaissance texts & stuðies
is the publishing program of the
Center for Medieval and Early Renaissance Studies
State University of New York at Binghamton.

mRts emphasizes books that are needed —
texts, translations, and major research tools.

mRts aims to publish the highest quality scholarship
in attractive and durable format at modest cost.